As I write this letter

greenfield books
ann arbor, michigan 1982

As I write this letter

An American Generation Remembers The Beatles

by Marc A. Catone

ISBN 0-87650-137-4
LC 81-86107

Published by greenfield books
a division of The Pierian Press, Inc.
P.O. Box 1808
Ann Arbor, Michigan 48106

Book design & layout
by Tom Schultheiss

The main title of this work
is based on lyrics from the song
P.S. I LOVE YOU
by John Lennon and
Paul McCartney.
These lyrics are
Copyright © 1962, 1963
by MPL Communications Ltd.
Assigned to and
Copyrighted © 1963 by
Beechwood Music Corporation
for the United States and Canada.
Used by Permission.
All Rights Reserved.

To
The Dreamweaver

Contents

List of Illustrations ix
Foreword, by Tom Schultheiss xi
Introduction xiii

1. *In February 1964, Everything Was In Color* 1
2. *"Sorry Girls, He's Married."* 13
3. *Those Lucky People* 33
4. *The Beatles And Me* 55
5. *The Biggest Beatle Fan Of All Time* 81
6. *No One Could Touch Them* 97
7. *We Were Never Let Down* 123
8. *I Still Can't Understand Them At All* 153
9. *A Discovery After The Fact* 161
10. *Just As Full Of Spirit* 179
11. *An Age Which Has Passed* 203

Epilogue 227

Illustrations

The art work included in this book has been made available free of charge courtesy of the individual artists credited below. Much of it was obtained through the kind cooperation of Bill King, editor of *Beatlefan* magazine.

Amy Bird   44

Lacey Callahan   139, 147

John Covert   xx, 30, 32, 143, 160, 172, 207, 217, 223, 224

April "Abbey" Geiger   27, 220

Marie Heerkens   117, 201, 213

Steve Leshin   94, 95, 176, 182, 183, 209

Susan K. Park   3, 5, 9, 17, 34, 49, 50, 54, 61, 64, 69, 73, 76, 87, 100, 112, 113, 115, 119, 120, 129, 131, 135, 136, 145, 162, 168, 180, 191, 192, 210

Judi Pettit   19, 186, 194

Susan Sedia   198

Tess Strofe   108

Jaime Sustaita   11, 21, 37, 71, 77, 105, 110, 122, 133, 189

All of the art offered for inclusion in this work, both by the artists above and by others, could simply not be included for a variety of reasons. The following individuals also kindly offered to donate their art work: Jane Collishaw, Christopher Cook, and Marty Reed.

Foreword

More than any other people, Americans as a nation have enjoyed a special relationship with The Beatles.

It all began in a cathartic, frenzied explosion of raw feeling, a tidal wave of sheer exuberance that helped to purge the open wound of a popular President not three months lost to us. It lasted, with almost unflagging intensity, for the better part of a decade, through an unparalleled period of international, societal, and individual unrest. It persists to this day.

This is not to diminish — at all — the impact of The Beatles in other countries, nor the fervor and devotion of fans in other parts of the world. For Americans, however, and especially for what was then the younger segment of our society during a troubled and uncertain time, one cannot speak of the 1960s and early 70s without also speaking of The Beatles.

Mixed inextricably into the mind-stew of at least one American generation are the unsettling memories of a distant war, a struggle for civil rights at home, racial strife, urban violence, protest marches, assassinations, political skulduggery, drug experimentation, sweeping changes in lifestyles, emergent feminism — and Beatles, Beatles, Beatles.

The American experience in the 60s and a particular

group of British musicians are bound together forever.

At the heart of our personal and social ferment, The Beatles and their music first helped enliven and then also to interpret an era seething with senselessness, a time straining against chaotic forces that seemed intent upon pulling apart the fabric of our lives.

And now, eighteen years from the beginning and over a decade after their dissolution as a band, The Beatles almost inescapably continue to fill the air waves and pages of our popular media. The war is over, the cries for struggle have grown distant and subdued, the divergent lifestyles have been absorbed into acceptability. The Beatles, their music, and their message, however, still retain a uniqueness, permanence and immediacy for so large a segment of Americans, on a daily basis, that it may be pronounced with certainty: the love affair continues. It not only continues, but has been renewed many times over by successive waves of American teenagers growing into maturity, as this volume will reveal.

Something happened to us as a people in early February of 1964, and the memory doesn't just linger on — it's occupied the guest room in our heads. For eighteen years, we have listened to the pundits, the critics, the journalists, biographers, chroniclers, interviewers, disc jockeys, insiders, friends and relatives tell us about The Beatles, and all the while we grappled uncertainly with the feeling that there was still a story to tell, a story as yet untold. It was a story less about The Beatles than about those who love The Beatles. And here it is.

Like The Beatles, this book has a special quality, and one which can never be duplicated. It is one of a kind. Time and events have decreed that nothing similar can ever be assembled again. It is a collection filled with hope, fond remembrances, humor, and love. It contains everything you might wish it to, and more. It will surprise and delight you with an eloquent, intelligent, evocative, funny, and always engaging running commentary on The Beatles, an endearing communal discourse made more remarkable because it is unrehearsed.

Did The Beatles affect your life? You've already answered the question by opening this book. You sure aren't reading this because you're indifferent, now are you? Whatever your reason for being here, you won't be disappointed.

Enjoy yourself. And remember I told you so.

Tom Schultheiss

Introduction

I am a Beatlemaniac. There are many others. Some of us "hide in the closet," confining our preoccupation to the privacy of our homes, others proclaim ourselves in the open, but we all acknowledge the same thing (at least to ourselves) . . . we are Beatlemaniacs.

Beatlemania is a joyful affliction. I first became exposed to it in 1964, when I was thirteen years old. Since I had no built-in prejudices or immunities, the early stages of the fever set in quickly without anything to prevent its movement, and spread, unshackled, to the very fiber of my soul. Beatlemania affects the spirit. Once it makes its way to your heart, there is no return; it blossoms and grows. It fills me with euphoria when I'm sad, hope when all I see about me is despair, and an appreciation of the value of peace among all peoples of the world when I'm lost in the everyday cycle of the material. Beatlemania makes me high.

There is one large insurmountable problem about Beatlemania . . . no cure. No cure! The symptoms can be alleviated, to a degree, with fantasy, wishing that things were different, and by placing polyvinyl discs on turntables . . . but there is no cure. There never will be a cure because the source of Beatlemania dissolved in 1970. No cure . . . never . . . yet I wouldn't want to give up this affliction for anything. I hope to always have it.

Fifteen years after they invaded North America, I sat and pondered the importance of The Fab Four from Liverpool. I knew that they were the single most pervasive influence on my life, but I wondered what others thought of them. There had been so many changes since 1964 . . . did others consider them as important as I did? I craved the knowledge that I was not alone in my beliefs. The Beatles were the most important influence on Western civilization during the second half of the twentieth century to me; I just had to know if there were other people in America who felt the same way . . . and if they didn't concur with my beliefs, what did they believe to have been important about The Beatles? I needed confirmation, to know if there was something that even I, an original Beatlemaniac, had missed during the whole Beatle experience. I also wanted to do something worthy of The Beatles, in tribute to them, to pay them back for all they had done for me. I wondered whether John Lennon, Paul McCartney, George Harrison and Ringo Starr realized how much of an impact they had on my generation and the world. Did they think that they were just a scruffy dance band who had made it big, or did they know why millions loved them?

It was from these ponderings that this book took root. In May 1979, I determined that the best way that I could find out the opinions of other people would be to place advertisements in various magazines and newspapers, inviting correspondents to write and tell me how they thought The Beatles had changed their lives and our society. I wanted to know if these people could still see any effects of The Beatles' era in existence today. I wanted to know if I was the only one left with posters on the walls, playing Beatle albums almost daily. I was confused about my own role in life and in that ambiguous word, "society." Here I was, rapidly approaching the end of my third decade on this planet, and I still didn't know what I wanted to be when I grew up. I attributed that feeling to The Beatles, because they had pointed out that the world was screwed up, with people saying one thing, doing another, and just going through a sham of an existence. As a teenager my mind was set: I would try my best to steer away from life as we knew it. I realized that it would be difficult to do in a world waiting to gobble me and the members of my generation up as soon as we became adults, but I vowed that if my only act of defiance was to remain a devotee of The Beatles, I would do it voluntarily, with no prompting or cajoling, but out of love for those four guys.

I received about 200 letters and inquiries from the various advertisements I placed in several newspapers, magazines, and other periodicals. My most successful ads (that is, the ones which drew the largest response) were those which ran in *Rolling Stone* magazine. Roughly 95% of the letters I received were in response to ads in that magazine, whereas ads in Beatle-oriented fanzines such as *Strawberry Fields Forever* and *The Write Thing* produced only one or two letters at most. My first ad appeared in *Rolling Stone* in June 1979, and my last ad in January 1980. All told, I spent about $425.00 in advertising. My first ads did not list my full name, nor did they really spell out what I was looking for. I didn't really know what I was looking for, so I described it as "research," and asked people how they felt The Beatles had affected their lives and society, and whether or not they saw any residual effects on their lives and society today. As the letters started pouring in, something started to happen within my head . . . I knew that I was not alone. There were others out there who had those posters on the walls and The Beatles' music constantly in the background of their lives. These letters were of great therapeutic value to me, and I saw in them the potential to help reassure other Beatlemaniacs as well.

Once a pattern of response was established, I became a bit bolder in my advertisements, this time dropping the "research" approach, fully proclaiming that "Author seeks your written opinions . . . ," and listing my full name and address. I realized through some of the responses I received that it would be more encouraging to a prospective respondent if they knew my name and address. Also, as the borders of my project became more defined for me, I developed a form letter to explain the nature of that project. Every single person who wrote to me received a response. I received many inquiries from those who didn't fully understand what I wanted and why I was doing this. Once I wrote back, either with a personal letter or form letter, people usually wrote back to me again. The majority of the letters I received were written by individuals who had no idea that their letter would be included in a book. This worked out quite well, as the letters were honest and uncharacterized by the caution one exercises when one knows their every word will be heavily scrutinized.

Once I had accepted a letter (I did not accept them all), each correspondent received a thorough explanation of the purpose of my book, and a legally prepared release form for signing, giving me the right to use and reprint, in part or in whole, their letters. It was very rare that I did not receive a signed release. The few problems I had were with those people who felt that they could not live with the terms of the release form. A provision exists in the release form that no payment should be expected now or in the future, and a few people objected to the fact that I could not pay them for their letters. I also decided that when the letter was reprinted, only the initials of the writer, along with their city and state of origin, would be used. A few people had problems with that. They wanted me to use their full names, or at least first names so the writer's sex might be conveyed. Although I would have liked to have done that, the possible violation of peoples' privacy was uppermost in my mind. The only reason that the contributors' names are not given in full is solely to protect their privacy and to prevent unsolicited intrusions into their lives. The vast majority of writers, I was sure, were unfamiliar with the often unwelcome consequences associated with public exposure of this type.

I began to notice that I was getting a disproportionate number of letters from people who were under 20 years of age. Therefore, my last couple of ads asked for people over 21 years of age to respond. Eventually, I received a well-balanced batch of letters to choose from. There are approximately 160 letters in this book. I used 80% of all letters received. The only ones that didn't make it were those which were too lengthy, crank letters (such as an obvious phony from "Elton John"), or letters for which the release form was never returned or for which impossible demands were made in return for permission.

My next challenge was to organize the letters in such a way that there would be an orderliness about them. I first toyed with the idea of grouping letters into chapters solely on the basis of the age of the writers. I was going to have letters from people who were original Beatlefans from 1964 in one chapter, second generation fans in another, and current day teenage fans in yet another. I soon realized that many of the letters had common themes, and soon scuttled the idea of "age" chapters for that of loosely organized thematic chapters. Many letters were perfect as written, others needed touching up for an occasional spelling or grammatical error. The biggest problem was the reorganization of the letter for the sake of continuity: introduction, body, and conclusion. I had tried to keep the writers as honest and uninhibited as possible, avoiding "instructions" and specific details in my advertisements. I didn't want a "staged" letter, written by someone for the express purpose of getting it into a book; I wanted a letter which contained the writers' unadulterated, honest opinions on The Beatles. Therefore, it proved a mighty task to reorganize some of the letters. Since many of the writers didn't know that I intended to reprint their letters, they naturally didn't pay strict attention to sentence structure, nonsequiturs, and misplaced paragraphs. I restructured these letters, but did not alter the writer's intent. In many cases, I preserved faulty grammar if to do so would be more in keeping with the writer's style of expression. I didn't want a bunch of letters that sounded like Marc A. Catone had written them all. I am proud to say that none of the writer's thoughts, arguments, or opinions have been discarded merely for the sake of grammatical perfection.

All of the letters published here were received during a finite period of time: June 1979 to June 1980. Up until now, many books have been written on the personalities, history, and music of The Beatles, but never before has there been a book written *by* Beatle fans *for* Beatle fans about how Beatle fans view The Beatles. This book purports to be just that: a collection of letters and essays by people who were influenced by The Beatles, individually expressing the importance of the band to them.

I am not a psychologist or a sociologist, and this book does not pretend to be a professional analysis based on precepts from those two fields. Apart from the sheer reading enjoyment offered to everyone in the pages which follow, however, it is hoped that people involved in those fields of study will find this work a useful tool. I have added my own narrative and thoughts, but not with the intention of detracting from any contributor's letter or essay. My thoughts merely provide a long letter from the author, binding and uniting all the chapters together. It is also hoped that this book will not only be of service to the devoted Beatlemaniac, but that it will increase the understanding of people who have never fully realized or accepted the fact that so many others can love The Beatles to the extent that they do. I am keenly aware that many of my peers never gave The Beatles a second thought . . . for you, this work may help in gaining a perception of why many people consider their consuming involvement with The Beatles to be the penultimate experience of their lives. There are a few negative opinions expressed in these letters, but whether the letter be a tribute or contain a rebuke, each offers a special insight into the reasons why its writer feels so strongly about the subject.

Acknowledgements

I am tempted to thank just about everyone I have ever known, but I will resist temptation (and writer's cramp) and acknowledge only those who have been instrumental in guiding my writing career, shaping this book, and accepting of my being a Beatlemaniac.

Donna Catone, for her patience and cooperation on this project since its inception.

Martha and Campbell Catone, my parents, for chaperoning a bus load of noisy kids to see The Beatles perform at Shea Stadium on Sunday, August 15, 1965.

Sara Russo, my sister, who was the first Beatlemaniac I ever knew.

Sid Mesibov, my uncle, who inspired me to aspire to a writing career.

Ruth Shaw Mesibov, my aunt, for all her advice and guidance given to me throughout my entire life.

Paul Esposito, my best friend, who, while working on his doctoral thesis, gave me the idea to advertise for correspondents.

Lorraine Esposito, for her friendship and affection, and the splendor of Mount Everest.

Steve Meltzer, for having the courage to tell me the news.

Steve Leshin, for all his cartoons, drawings, fantasies, and realities from Velvet Moose Enterprises, and for his commiserations as a fellow civil servant.

Susan K. Park, for her beautiful artwork and constant faith in me, both of which convinced me to finish this work.

The late Lillian Roxon, who took the time and trouble during her own busy writing career to start a correspondence with me (in my 21st year), and advise me of the do's and don't's of writing about Rock-and-Roll.

Tom Schultheiss, who has shown much faith in me (to the point where he is publishing this book!), and for his unabated enthusiasm and guidance in preparing this work.

The city of Danbury, Connecticut, place of my birth, where I first experienced Beatlemania.

All of the people whose letters and essays are contained in this book, for all the beautiful thoughts and love your words convey.

Groucho Marx and Lenny Bruce, two humorists who were polar opposites, but whose influence carried equal weight for me.

Allison Krause, Jeffrey Miller, Sandra Scheuer, and William Schroeder, all of whom I never met, but whose deaths I will never forget.

And to Yoko Ono Lennon, one of the two people to bring some sanity into an insane world, for her strength and courage to carry on, and for her conviction that there's nothing you can do that can't be done. **M. A. C.**

To ardent Beatle fans, most terms and "in-jokes" about The Beatles contained in the letters will be familiar. There are references to certain chronological events and musical achievements too numerous to list for those people who are not familiar with The Beatles' legend and music; however, a few points of reference are needed. Allusions to the "White Album," the "Red Album," and the "Blue Album" refer respectively to the following record albums: **The Beatles**, released in November 1968; **The Beatles 1962–1966**, released in April 1973; and **The Beatles 1967–1970**, released in April 1973. In some instances, the term "Beatlemania" refers to the title of the popular Broadway show of the same name.

And now we start . . . where else? . . . from the beginning . . . .

In February 1964, Everything Was In Color

How does one best describe the initial impact The Beatles had on one's life? One of the ways is to use a popular analogy which did not originate with this writer. The effect of The Beatles' arrival in the United States in February 1964 can be compared to the visual sensation the filmgoer experiences when watching "The Wizard of Oz." Everything is black-and-white in Kansas, but the moment Dorothy crosses into Oz, everything is in color. Prior to 1964, my world was drab and gray, and all of a sudden The Beatles came and brought color to the world.

Beatlemania began in Great Britain during 1963. Here, in the United States, Rock-and-Roll was reeling in a premature death. The army had rendered Elvis impotent, Chuck Berry was going to jail, Little Richard gave it all up for the ministry, and Buddy Holly was dead. A whitewashed version of R 'n' R dominated the Top Forty airwaves. The original rockers and black street singers were being replaced by people with names like Fabian, Avalon, Rydell, and Vinton — singers more in the mold of the crooners of earlier decades. America was ripe, but was America ready?

The Beatles, thanks to their talent, and an ad campaign by Capitol records (more the former than the latter), took the nation by storm.

I was a few months past my thirteenth birthday when I first heard about The Beatles. I wasn't the kind of kid who had his ear glued to a transistor radio. I had always liked the sounds, rhythms, and beat of Rock-and-Roll, but not having any older sibling, that type of music did not enter my home.

In early January 1964, I was watching "The Jack Paar Show" on a Friday night. Jack announced that he had an unusual film to show of an English Rock-and-Roll band and the hundreds of girls who fainted and screamed whenever they played. I was captivated by the sound of the music. I had never heard a song which sounded so beautiful, haunting, yet so fiercely upbeat. It was *She Loves You*, and that song remains my favorite Beatle song some 16 years later. Once I saw them on Jack Paar's program, I knew I had to see and hear them again. I soon discovered from my 8th grade classmates that The Beatles were coming to America to appear on "The Ed Sullivan Show."

Many of the letters I received addressed this initial appearance of The Beatles on "The Ed Sullivan Show." My memory of that occasion is very clear. I grew up in Danbury, Connecticut, which is about 65 miles away from New York City; therefore all newspapers, radio stations, and TV channels emanated from The Big Apple. The week of The Beatles' arrival was preceded by much hoopla in the NYC press, and when they finally landed at JFK airport on Friday, February 7, 1964, every arm of the media gave The Beatles priority over all other news. No matter what station you tuned in, The Beatles were there. You could see them on the "Six O'Clock News" as they strolled through Central Park or as they frantically got to their hotel just ahead of a screaming mob.

My first glimpse of them was at their premiere U.S. press conference upon arrival at the airport. It was then that I realized that these guys were totally different from any other teen idols. They gave witty answers to questions, and did not hide the fact that they smoked cigarettes. Annette and Frankie never did that! I was instantly able to associate their names with their faces. There was no long process of memorization. After looking at their names under a photo in the newspaper, I knew who was who and never forgot.

I was so excited by that Sunday night, when they were to make their initial appearance on "The Ed Sullivan Show," that I didn't seem to mind that Sunday was waning, and the next day I had to return to school. Eight o'clock couldn't arrive fast enough for me. The show was a gem. When it was over, I wanted more. It was a turning point for me as well as many of my correspondents.

❝ I am 28 years of age, which made me, in the year 1964, age 12 going on 13, just ready for something big to occur. And what occurred was The Beatles. Everything coalesced, myself with them. I wouldn't trade the memories of that time for a million dollars.

I'll never forget that first Ed Sullivan Show. I had been so nervous, sitting through the TV show, "My Favorite Martian." It seemed endless. Then, there was Sullivan, the opening credits, a commercial . . . . The Fab Four themselves. Tears running down my cheeks. I had no idea what was happening to me. This was out of bounds for me. I didn't like Rock at the time. It had only been the day before that I heard *She Loves You* and *I Want To Hold Your Hand* for the first time. I was intrigued by these wonderful sounds. It snuck up on me. The transistor radio those two songs played on had never seen the light of day, as it had been a gift from my parents two Xmas' before. Never played, it became my passport to these fantastic sounds.

I had seen their names in the paper on the 6th of February and wrote them on my blackboard "so I'd know who they were" I said to myself. So, for the first time in my life, I wrote "John Lennon," "Paul McCartney," "Ringo Starr," and "George Harrison." I gazed at them written, and placated, I erased them. I had no idea what I was to be magnetically pulled toward. Incredible!

And here I am, 15 years later, writing about them, which shows the power they still exert, even though they have 10 years parted. I can't imagine what my life would have been without them in it. I feel (though I know, of course, that I don't really know them) like they are my brothers. Somehow, I feel that close to them. I may have lost the "gee whiz," teeny bopper idolization of them, but I still have a feeling of caring about them and a deep, deep affection, if not always understanding, for them. Though it took me too long to understand where they were coming from for awhile, I find I now share the Peace & Love philosophy, as well as the rebelliousness they exhibited. They have profoundly influenced my life in a positive way.

They have also influenced society-at-large. When you consider that a bunch of clones can go on stage and pack them in as the show, "Beatle-mania," has (and in a poor way, one I disapprove of) that proves that The Beatles could still marshall people and their imaginations. It shows that since there are no Beatles, they will accept a cheap imitation if they can't get the real thing. The Beatles still wield a lot of power and they still have a musical impact on us. They expanded the simplicity of lyric and instrumentation in music. They expanded it for all to follow. The guitar became "The Instrument" to play. The Stones, Elton John, Peter Frampton, and Led Zeppelin owe them a debt. It became alright to wear one's hair as one wished, to shout Peace and not be made to feel like a freak. The Beatles mixed social statement with personal feelings in a rare mix. They helped stretch the musical and social mind; and that is permanent . . . its effects will always be known and felt. That's why so many want to have that again; to have The Beatles unite once again and bring it all together.

Alas, I feel that can never be. They are all too different now. I enjoy

George's and John's music (whenever John makes any). I loved *All Things Must Pass Away* and John's *Imagine*. Paul McCartney's solo music has never done much for me. *Band On The Run* was his brightest achievement to date, but otherwise his music is all blah stuff. I'm astounded at Paul's inane hogwash he calls music. My Heavens! Can this be the same person who composed *Yesterday, Michelle, Fixin' A Hole*, and *Sgt. Pepper's Lonely Hearts Club Band*? Now he writes such drivel, the standards he set in his hey-day beat him everytime. I keep hoping he'll come around, but I don't think it's likely.

Earlier, I referred to The Beatles as my "brothers." I was an only child, who was sick a lot; they really kept me going through many bad times. We both went through changes parallel to each other. They will always have a lot of my heart. They are very precious . . . I hope for the best for all four of them, and . . . I hope John comes out of retirement before too long; a voice like his is needed in today's world. **99**

C.C.
New York, New York

5

66 When I was a medical student at Johns Hopkins in Baltimore, the first night that The Beatles appeared on the Ed Sullivan show happened to co-incide with a "Beowulf Party" (decorations included a text of *Beowulf* taped to the walls). I and a friend were holding it in the basement of Hopkins' Medical Residence Hall. The party's ad had suggested, " 'Y dress crudely." My cohost wore a mop on his head, but I had let my hair grow long (for those days) and somewhat shaggy. Of course, that first Beatles TV appearance in the U.S.A. was historical. The party was also a success. However, I had my hair cut back to normal the next day. A day later, one of my pediatric patients asked me, "What happened to your Beatles' haircut?"

So, in a small way, I felt we had helped celebrate the first TV appearance of The Beatles in America. 99

A.O.
Columbia, Missouri

"You know how almost everybody remembers where they were when John Kennedy was shot? Well, I've found that lots of people remember that Ed Sullivan show in the same way."

66 When you sit down and think about it, it's difficult to pinpoint exact influences which The Beatles had on all of us because their influence was so wide-spread.

The first time The Beatles were on The Ed Sullivan show, I was 10 years old (I'm 27 now). I can vividly remember that night. You know how almost everybody remembers where they were when John Kennedy was shot? Well, I've found that lots of people remember that Ed Sullivan show in the same way. It's something we can all relate to; something we can all share. I was a raving Beatlemaniac with everything which went along: collecting Beatle cards, taking my Beatle looseleaf book to school, buying Beatle magazines, wearing a "John Lennon hat" (remember those?). I saw "A Hard Day's Night" 20 times the first week it was released. The same way with "Help."

The feeling I get when I see any of The Beatles on TV or in a magazine is that I'm seeing the face of somebody I know. It's hard for me to explain this. They made us think while we were singing along. Paul was my favorite Beatle, but I was always drawn to Lennon's head. I think they inspired a lot of kids to try for creative expression via music. After all, if 4 poor kids from a Liverpool slum could make it, why not me?

A Beatle reunion would be both positive and negative. I don't think that they could capture that magic again, but a reunion could help us remember what we once had. It seems that once they came on the scene *everything* changed; music, fashions, politics, religion. I'm glad I was a part of all that. I wonder if they ever think about their influence on us. Quite a responsibility!

Even as I got older and my musical tastes changed somewhat, I have to admit that the feeling I got when I listened to The Beatles as a crazy 11 year old kid has stayed with me all my life. I think that's a great gift that I was given. 99

R.R.
Philadelphia, Pennsylvania

❝ Can it really be fifteen years since I was requesting to hear *I Want To Hold Your Hand* more often than the radio station could play it in an hour? I was thirteen when I first saw The Beatles on The Ed Sullivan Show. I remember feeling the swell of excitement as The Beatles made their entrance onto my screen. When they began to play, I actually fell backwards, feet in the air, I was so lost and desperately in love. The next day I cut my hair, with bangs.

My husband began playing with his first band thirteen years ago. We have full time jobs, and children, but we work at Rock and Roll on weekends. We enjoy all aspects of this many faceted art form, and with a passion.

I recently got my first "Fan Letter" from an eleven year old girl and she said, "You are my idol of what I want to be when I grow up." I suppose that sums up The Beatles' influence on my life, and I hope I never out grow it. **❞**

K.D.
Mt. Vernon, Illinois

"I was thirteen when I first saw The Beatles on The Ed Sullivan Show. I remember feeling the swell of excitement as The Beatles made their entrance onto my screen. When they began to play, I actually fell backwards, feet in the air, I was so lost and desperately in love."

"During the height of Beatlemania, it was the general feeling of my parents, my friends' parents, and a large group of people that The Beatles would fade into oblivion."

❝ I was 13 years old when I saw The Beatles for the first time, February 9, 1964, on the Ed Sullivan show. What captivated me was not so much their hair or clothes, but rather the energy and the electric atmosphere they created. I still remember very clearly *All My Loving, She Loves You*, and *This Boy* sung by the Fab Four on our ancient black and white TV set.

During the height of Beatlemania, it was the general feeling of my parents, my friends' parents, and a large group of people that The Beatles would fade into oblivion. An article said The Beatles would ". . . soon go the way of hoola-hoops, raccoon coats, and whitewall tires . . . ." Any true Beatle fan knew The Beatles would be here for a long, long time.

I grew up with The Beatles. They were a big part of my life. They had a song for everything it seemed. I followed them in the newspapers and looked forward to their albums. With everything they did, they always seemed to stay one step ahead of everyone. One of my favorite albums, **Sgt. Pepper**, is a good example. It introduced printed lyrics as well as a whole new concept for album design.

One of the biggest influences on my life was the song, *Hey Jude*. I was just starting my junior year at high school when the song was released. I didn't relish the thought of going back to school, but *Hey Jude* helped lighten the load. I felt better everytime I heard the song. The Beatles touched me, as through their songs they seemed to say "It's all right, we understand." They were much more than a musical group. They were the voice and expression of an entire generation of young people who loved them. **❞**

L.O.
Eden, North Carolina

What was it about these four guys? Why was it that they attracted so much attention and instant conversion to their music? It was as if a contagious germ wafted its way throughout the under 21 populace of the world.

I became obsessed with them. I lived for just a word about them on the radio or TV, or a news report about them in the newspaper. I hung on every word. The Sullivan shows were the ultimate for any Beatle fan. Not once, not twice, but for three weeks in a row, The Beatles appeared on that show during February 1964. It was virtually impossible for anyone to be ignorant of The Beatles. You would have to be a hermit or someone totally out of touch with all mass communications not to know who they were.

But why did they catch on? Why did they become the most copied musical group in history? Why did The Beatles, as opposed to another group, The Beach Boys for example, exert so much influence on everyone in the mid-1960s?

There is no clear-cut, definitive answer to these questions. Certainly one can recognize the fact that their unconventional total disrespect for the older generation was part of it. They dressed in suits and ties, but they looked out of place in them. One knew that the ties and jackets were a facade. Underneath that conservative attire lurked four beings who were saying "O.K., we'll wear this stuff for all you promoters and Ed Sullivan producers, just to make you happy, but someday we'll rub your noses in it." The Beach Boys and others were popular on an extremely superficial level with the youth of America. Certainly, the surfing sound and harmonies were loved by all. Upon scratching the surface though, one found a fluffy, vapid and insubstantial musical style which appealed mostly to fans who would not, could not, and did not know how to stand up against misguided authoritarianism. Those who fell for The Beatles in 1964 recognized that their new found idols epitomized an affront to the established order. However, that is only part of it. The music, in and of itself, was also extremely influential as our next letter demonstrates:

❝February 2, 1964 was a day of music for me. I had just learned a tune by Al Hirt on the trumpet. I had been playing the trumpet for three years in the elementary school band. First chair, too! I was happy to have accomplished such a feat. I loved the trumpet, but many times my father had said to me, "Hey, why don't you learn to play the guitar," as he would pick out some boogie woogie for me. "The trumpet is a sissy instrument," he would say, but you could never convince me to drop the horn for the guitar.

February 9, 1964, 7:00 P.M., Central Time. The Beatles first appeared on the Ed Sullivan Show. I was twelve years old, running around the living room in my longjohns, shooting paper wads into a waste paper basket. Quite unexpecting! I had heard *I Want To Hold Your Hand* on WLS-AM (Chicago) a couple of times and I liked it, even though it was a far cry from what I was used to. When The Beatles came on the screen, I was hooked! By the time they had flashed "Sorry girls, he's married" across John Lennon's face, I had pitched my "sissy horn" and had my dad's Silvertone guitar in my lap . . . never looking back.

Monday, February 10, 1964. My friend and I were in his basement with guitar, amp, and his drum kit. A band was formed with another friend and we practiced everyday. We started playing at talent shows, ice cream socials, and private parties. We bought Beatle wigs, Beatle cards, Beatle mags, etc. Once we took "publicity pix" on top of my parents' garage, complete with drums and amps.

I was devoted. I bought a mag with the headline: WHO'S NUMBER ONE, THE BEATLES or THE ROLLING STONES? Well, I thought that was a ridiculous question . . . it caused me to have a dislike for the Stones. I did everything I could that The Beatles might do. When I read that George Harrison practiced bad table manners, so did I. My best friend didn't like The Fab Four and when I found that out, it put quite a dent in our perfect friendship. He's now a policeman, so you see there was a definite problem.

I was in mod fashion, and as they grew and their music became more expressive, I tried my hardest to keep up. I tried to speak in all the hippest British jargon . . . bird, daft, twit, nib, and all those groovy terms. In High School, I filled my study halls with learning Beatle trivia facts.

I always knew there was something about them I liked other than the obvious music, hair and girls, but I was too young and naive to know about politics, war, racism, and the like. I soon realized that The Beatles represented a whole way of life that was out of the norm for that day and age. Young people were getting fame, fortune, and POWER! We weren't too young to feel some sort of liberation. There were even Beatle cartoons for the tots!

I was getting better on the guitar and singing. I tried to enunciate my words like Paul, John, and especially, George, my favorite, just to feel the part. My hair was getting longer and my school's dress code was getting tougher. I was suspended from school a number of times due to my hair touching my collar.

Just when things were so set for me in understanding their music, along

10

George Harrison

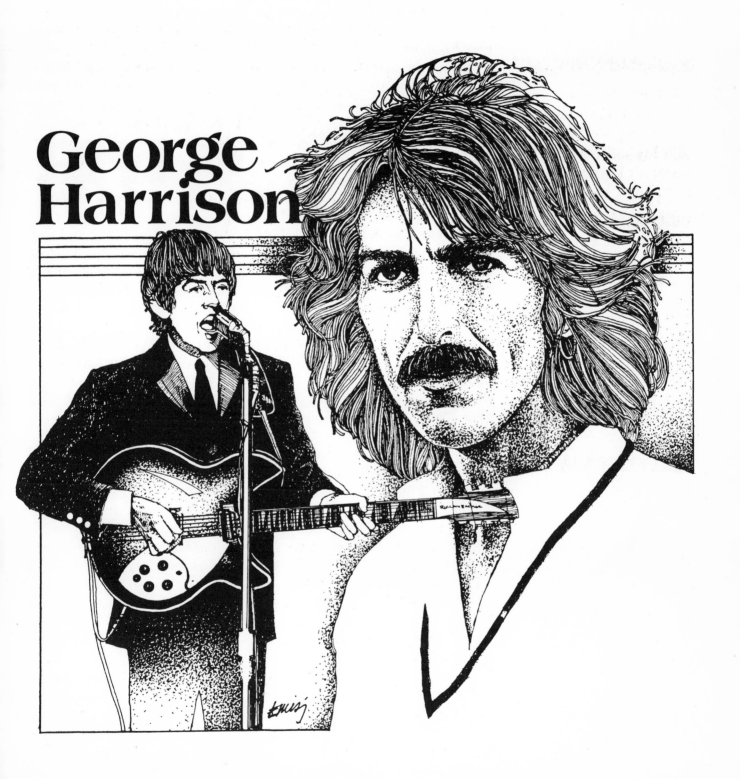

came **Revolver** and the timeless **Sgt. Pepper**. They had done it again! They changed the whole concept again, and I loved it. Another radical upheaval was "Marijuana." It started being around with so much Q.T. . . . and well . . . The Beatles did it. I made it out of High School, still playing in a successful local band, got married and became a father at age eighteen. The war in Vietnam was hot then and people all around were quite concerned with the draft, demonstrations, free love, drugs, and of course, Rock 'n' Roll.

I never got drafted, but I did get a divorce . . . and I also got busted. This was in 1970, a pretty bad time for me. The Beatles' music helped me through the slump. My problems didn't seem as bad to me when I compared myself to them and what they were going through. The best R & R band of all time had broken up, and it seemed to me that they would be pretty sad about it. I was sad, but I figured that they knew what they were doing. We all made it through those tough days.

I migrated from my hometown of South Bend, Indiana to Washington, D.C. in 1972 to play music in a bigger fashion. While in D.C., I started collecting Beatle stuff. My band wasn't doing too well, so I wrote to Paul McCartney to audition for his band, Wings. He didn't get my offer. I stayed with my band and got it off the ground as far as being a successful road band for three and a half years. We always played some Beatle songs just to keep the spirit alive.

I am now back in South Bend, still playing my music to earn my living. I also write and record songs, preparing for my future. Thanks to The Beatles! If it weren't for The Beatles, you and I could very well be fighting someone we don't know, in a rice paddy or worse. Everybody has benefited by The Beatles, mentally, physically, or financially. I have built my entire life from what they have taught me and would have to call them my "Four Fathers." I wish them all well! **"**

C.A.
Mishawaka, Indiana

"If it weren't for The Beatles, you and I could very well be fighting someone we don't know, in a rice paddy or worse."

2

"Sorry Girls, He's Married."

One of the most obvious effects The Beatles had was the hysteria they instilled in young girls; they provoked teenage females to the point of screaming, crying, and proclamations of undying love.

This was noticeable from its start in England, and it was the launching point for The Beatles' invasion of the United States. If young girls hadn't gathered for hours, even days, outside concert halls and movie theaters, The Beatles would have wound up being just another good Rock-and-Roll band in Liverpool, possibly popular England-wide, but they never would have made it to the United States.

There were obviously many male Beatle fans, but they weren't as vocal, and the emotions the band evoked were just not the same for males as for females. It was sometimes difficult to be a male Beatle fan in the early days of Beatlemania. Since the majority of fans seemed to be screaming girls, there was an ever so slight undertone of opinion that any boy who liked the Beatles so much had to be homosexual or have homosexual tendencies. Men didn't get excited over Rock-and-Roll stars, only women did. That was the prevailing attitude in the United States.

It is almost impossible to remember, but a scant 16 years ago our society was very male dominated, with a very heavy "macho" image that most males tried to live up to whether it suited them or not. America was still under the influence of the tough guy image. The Beatles' appearance on the scene was a jolt. I recall that my father's initial reaction was that out of The Beatles " . . . there wasn't a man among them . . . . " I didn't really understand what he meant by that. In 1964, I didn't even know what the word "homosexual" meant. I figured that he meant that they weren't rugged.

What an image, when you think about it! Four boys with their hair combed in bangs on their foreheads, bursting upon the basically "greasy" United States, with girls fainting whenever they saw them. Most older males couldn't comprehend this. The Beatles were largely responsible for breaking down long-established sex roles. They brought fashion and color to men's clothing, and through their music made more men pacifists than fighters. But in 1964, when they first arrived, guys who liked The Beatles were often the object of scorn and ridicule. It seemed to be an unwritten rule for males that it was O.K. to like their music, but just don't make any public displays about it.

Actually, I never felt like screaming or crying, I just sat there, mesmerized in front of the TV screen, movie screen, or in the field stands of Shea Stadium. The effect The Beatles had on me initially was to push my already blossoming sexual self-awareness further along. All the early songs were songs of being in love with, talking about, dreaming about, and being sometimes rejected by girls. I think that is the reason *She Loves You* and *I Want To Hold Your Hand* had such an impact on me. Although, at age 13, I had never experienced love, I felt glad for the guy in *She Loves You* who was being reminded that his girl still loved him. The words and that haunting melody still send shivers down my spine whenever I hear it. *I Want To Hold Your Hand* made me feel confident that someday I would have enough nerve to be with a girl and speak words of love to her. Of course, I didn't realize that these songs were doing this to me in such analytical terms back then . . . I just knew that the lyrics and music were producing a happy effect on me.

The moment I knew that John Lennon was married, yet was still able to have girls scream over him as if they didn't care that he was legally bound to another, I began to see him as the one out of the four with the most intrigue. I was excited by girls screaming, and often envisioned myself as a rock star with thousands of girls fainting and screaming over me. The fact that Lennon was married made him the favorite Beatle with many male fans. If you were being taunted for liking The Beatles by a male peer, it didn't seem to be so bad if you liked the one who was married, instead of cute Paul or loveable Ringo. Lennon's wittiness, and the fact that he didn't even take himself seriously, made him my instant favorite once I saw him at The Beatles' first press conference two days prior to their debut on the Sullivan show. And (as correspondent C.A. stated previously) once I saw the blurb run across the screen as Lennon sang — "Sorry girls, he's married" — I was a Lennon idolizer.

I wanted to grow up to be John Lennon. I imitated his accent, wore a facsimile of his famous cap, and when I made believe that I was playing the guitar in front of thousands of admiring fans I always played rhythm, and stood like Lennon. As a male Beatle fan, I tried to emulate all of The Beatles as best I could.

While I can articulate the effects The Beatles had on at least one young male fan, there is no way that I could possibly explain in these pages how The Beatles emotionally affected young women. Therefore, I will let several female correspondents speak for themselves.

"As an old childhood friend of mine said the other day, "It's kind of horrifying to think that 4 people who I never met could have affected my whole life in the way The Beatles did." We spent every minute of our day, working, playing, eating, learning, walking — concerned with the affairs of The Fabulous Four.

My whole concept of love derives from the emotions I felt as I watched them sing and saw their pictures in fan magazines, as well as the words they vibrated through our beings.

Don't get me wrong, I'm not a fanatic today. I felt myself torn apart with emotions as Paul McCartney was recently held captive in Tokyo, but I have never or could ever head a fan club of any sort. As a matter of fact, the friend I mentioned earlier confessed that she still has the hots for Paul McCartney (after 5 years of marriage and a baby in the oven). She admitted, "I still dream about Paul regularly. I'd leave [my husband] if he'd leave Linda within a snap."

I had mental flings with each of them. My memory paints a very vivid picture of me sitting in the schoolyard admitting to a very adolescent peer that, yes, I could even find redeeming value in Ringo. They each had an appeal to me at different times and I truly believed I could never be happy with any man if he weren't John, Paul, George or Ringo.

By sixth grade we all owned every album and played them solely, all day long. Going through puberty, we could recognize our first sexual stirrings. John or Paul's voice would whisper lovingly, *Do You Want To Know A Secret, Norwegian Wood, Here There and Everywhere*, and *Yesterday* — God, I'm getting horny just reminiscing.

My friend was "married" to Paul McCartney. I'm sure only a 6th grade female can fully comprehend what I mean by that, but we were flaky kids and we carried out a fantasy life — and sometimes it was more real than reality. We were going through one of life's major shocks — puberty — but we really believed we were married to The Beatles and we wrote notes back and forth to each other, made phone calls and carried on discussions with one another as if we were really Mrs. John Lennon or Mrs. George Harrison etc.

My friend had Paul, though. She was quite stubborn. She even wrote a 500 page novel portraying how she met him and the zany life they lived thereafter. She has since destroyed it. I think that was a horrible waste.

My nine year old brother was questioning my musical taste the other day:

"What kind of music do you like? Punk or Disco?"
"Neither."
"Beatles stuff?"
"Yes."
"Who would you say is your favorite group?"
"Beatles."

> **"My whole concept of love derives from the emotions I felt as I watched them sing and saw their pictures in fan magazines, as well as the words they vibrated through our beings."**

"But they broke up, who do you like now, Wings?"
"Nope. Still like The Beatles."
He glared at the Kiss album playing on the stereo and said,
"You know what? Me too."

It bugs me that my daughters will never fully understand The Beatles phenomenon. They changed so much and brought us so much joy. We grew up with them. They taught us about life and love, drugs, war, reality, and fantasy. We went through losing our minds over an Ed Sullivan appearance where you couldn't even hear the words they sang; to watching Paul shrink in "Help" and cover himself up in a gum wrapper; to dancing our first dance, slow and close, to *Hey Jude* on a moonlit summer eve; to spending our every waking moments tracking down the clues and the truth to "Is Paul really dead?"; to freaking out and going psychedelic — long hair and love beads, Mahareshi Mahesh Yogi. They dictated our styles, moods, lives. They shaped us. They made us.

I still enjoy their music (unless done by Muzak), but I have since picked up on the reality of having a husband and two daughters. I'd like those daughters of ours to get a sense of what The Beatles and the times they formed were like.

C.H.
Wappingers Falls, New York

P.S.: Didn't a whole generation feel this way,
or am I wrong? **"**

"It bugs me that my daughters will never fully understand The Beatles phenomenon. They changed so much and brought us so much joy. We grew up with them. They taught us about life and love, drugs, war, reality, and fantasy . . . . They dictated our styles, moods, lives. They shaped us. They made us. . . . P.S.: Didn't a whole generation feel this way, or am I wrong?"

❝I celebrated by 12th birthday in December of 1963. The Beatles either greeted my adolescence or pushed me into it. I have always loved the fact that I was 12 when Beatlemania hit. I was a teeny bopper type, just waiting to discover something new and exciting for my teenage years. Looking for that first "generation gap" and starting to listen to "pop" music, I had no great interest until John, Paul, George, and Ringo. What a fantastic experience!

I grew up with The Beatles. They started me off in the music world and carried me all the way to adulthood! Of course, once I reached adulthood, I wished I had been 18 or 19 and able to follow them around the world and partake of some of the pleasures of life with them. It wasn't until I got older and discovered what sex was all about that I switched allegiance from Ringo to Paul (the man has the most gorgeous thighs, lovely shoulders . . . the face — I could be here for hours).

I was talking to a friend whose Mum graduated from high school in 1952. We were discussing that our parents are still waiting for us to grow up and out of this "nonsense." During this talk I realized that her mom had no similar experience to compare with The Beatles . . . she had been too late for the Big Band Era and Frank Sinatra and too early for Elvis or Buddy Holly. It struck me as so sad that someone (a young teenager) should go through those awful years with no one to look up to and dream about.

I think of all the possible types of rebellion available to teenagers during Beatlemania, The Beatles were certainly a safer, wiser choice than many others. Even our parents almost liked them. Twelve years after, my Mom sits and shakes her head knowingly, as I recount dashing to the bank, then to a department store at 9:30 a.m. to await their 10 a.m. opening, with two toddlers in tow, to buy tickets to see Paul.

After 7 years of marriage, I contemplate divorce when my husband announces he has to go to the men's room in the middle of the concert. And me! . . . 25 feet away from Paul . . . and he insists I accompany him. He cannot and will not ever understand my feelings. I told him I'd meet him at the car, but gallant lad that he is, he does not want to leave me alone and unprotected in this crazy mob — alone — I've got Paul right up there, haven't I? He doesn't understand that even if I didn't know where the car was parked (which I do) I wouldn't care. I've waited twelve years, My God! to see Paul . . . and then he says, as we sit on the coliseum steps (it seems like miles away from Paul), "Doesn't the music sound better from back here?" Well, I can't believe I married this man . . . we can hear records at home . . . I want to see Paul and feel his presence and look at him forever. At the end, several people cast dirty looks my way as my voice jumps an octave and I try my damnedest to shatter glass with my screams. Maybe Paul will hear, maybe he'll comment later about some crazy girl out there, screaming her bloody head off. I hope. And I also resolve never to take my husband to another concert.

Last year I was ready to save whales in L.A. to see one or more Beatles, this year I checked out the airfare to Geneva ($834). I still hold onto the dream that someday it will happen. I am constantly trying to think of things to say that will so impress them, that we'll become instant friends. I hope I never grow up. Amen!**"**

B.C.
Louisville, Kentucky

"Look around you! Everyone has been influenced by them in one way or another. Hairstyles, clothing, musical tastes, sexual attitudes: all have been influenced by the lads from Liverpool. President Carter's hairstyle attests to the fact that if we did lose some battles, looks like we won the war!

I have been a maniacal Beatle fan since 1964. I was 9 years old when The Beatles arrived in the U.S. and I haven't been the same since. My life started then! I couldn't imagine life without them. I guess I'm not really a typical Beatle fan; I'm really much more into it than most people. For the past 15 years, I have followed them very closely and spent every extra cent on records, books, magazines, pictures, buttons, etc. My goal in life is to see one of them, which, believe it or not, I have never done. (Hard for me to believe too.) I'd also very much like to go to Liverpool someday, too.

John has always been my favorite, so he has influenced me most. My major interests in life seem to have been influenced by The Fabs, although it's hard to say which came first . . . The Beatles or my interests. Would I have been interested in the same things if The Beatles had never happened? I doubt it, but who's to say? At any rate, I was a music major for my 1st year in college, which was directly influenced by them, I believe. Their music is practically orgasmic to me. I've heard every song they ever did at least 500 times and I still get cold chills everytime I hear them! I can't begin to explain why this is the case — it just does that to me!

Nobody, before or since, has written music like Paul and John could. *I Am The Walrus* can drive me screaming into the streets! Eventually I dropped out of Murray State University and came to Louisville to attend the University of Louisville. I did not continue with music professionally due to disillusionment with MSU's program. What would be a logical new major in 1974 for a John Lennon fan? You guessed it . . . Political Science.

I finally graduated from U. of L. in 1978 with a B.A. in political science. I have worked on several political campaigns too. All of this, I suppose, can be attributed to John's influence. I do believe that if John told his fans to go out and blow up a nuclear plant, I'd run to the drugstore for dynamite. He continues to have that kind of influence over me. Strange, perhaps, but true. I'd like to drop acid once, but haven't yet. What John says about acid has really tempted me to do so.

John has also ruined my love life! I'm 24 years old now, and have been engaged twice. Both times I've broken it off. Both of my fiances have had trouble dealing with my Beatle preoccupation. They were somewhat jealous. Also, I've never found a man I thought is as great as John. Of course, I don't ever expect to have John, you understand, but I've decided that I'll stay single, because if I can't have John, I don't want any man. Nobody except John could make me happy.

Therefore, The Beatles seem to have influenced every facet of my life. I will love all of them for the rest of my life and will continue to be influenced by them. The fact that they are now apart is incidental to me."

A.L.
Louisville, Kentucky

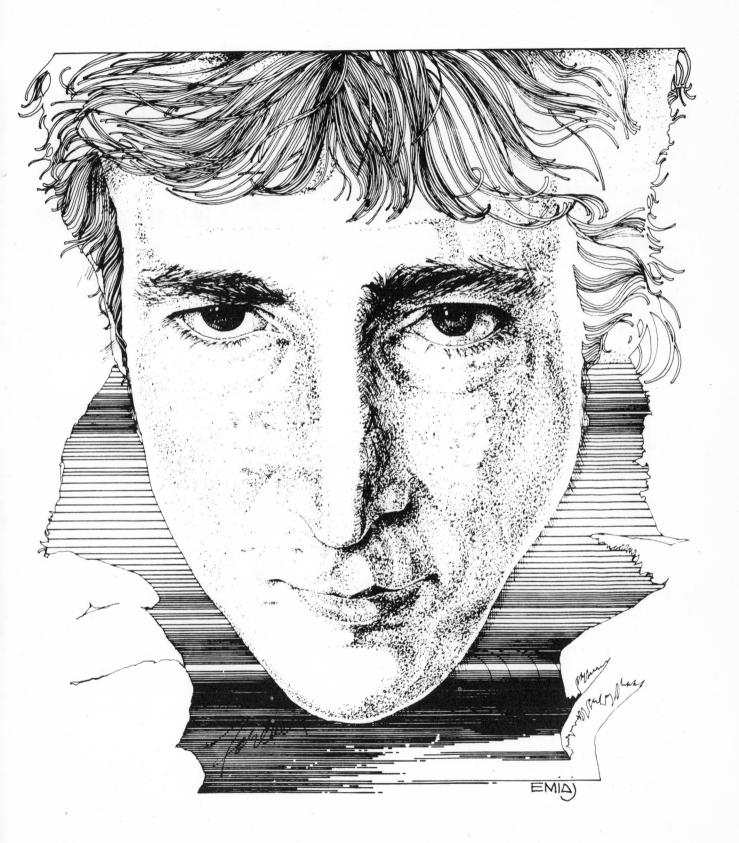

EMIA)

"I was born the year (1952) Rock-and-Roll was born. I can remember hearing Rock-and-Roll songs from an early age and music has continued to be important to me.

I agree with the theory that The Beatles' arrival to the American music scene brought us out of our post-Kennedy depression. A day does not pass without my thinking of a Beatles melody, phrase or lyric. I have cheered and wept through two Beatlefests. I am subscribing to 2 fanzines, own over 20 books on The Beatles and 63 assorted albums (including Japanese and Dutch imports and bootlegs). I constantly search for hard to find albums.

As I write this, the senior citizens nearby are playing *Let It Be*. Some of my most distinct memories are of first listening to new Beatles releases. My brother can tell his exact location upon hearing the news of Brian Epstein's death on a car radio. I did not have any money, as a child, to spend on records. My brothers and I saved up to buy **Sgt. Pepper** and we all listened to it for the first time together.

There has never been another group or artist to come close to their importance in my life. In my teen years I had huge posters of each Beatle on my walls and wore Nehru jackets. They took me (and I sincerely believe, the world) through the changes in political atmosphere, fashion, and naturally, music. There are two kinds of musicians today: those influenced by The Beatles and liars. I am pleased that their influence continues on kids today, helped by [the movie] "Sgt. Pepper" (I know a 7 yr. old who likes the original better than the movie soundtrack) and "Beatlemania" (I enjoyed a 3 hour car trip with a 12 year old by singing Beatle songs).

There's been much speculation and discussion regarding The Beatles' influence on society, especially our attitudes on drugs, different lifestyles, and politics. I was not immune. Would I get high today, would marijuana be as popular if not for them? Would our generation have been as politically active if not stirred up by them? Imagine the antiwar demonstrations without *Power To The People* and *Give Peace A Chance*? I know more about the family background of John, Paul, George, and Ringo than I do my own!

Whenever I am depressed there is nothing that can move my spirit as a Beatle song. The only one I have seen in concert is George. George's concert places among the best experiences of my life. It is my dream to see all in concert; it makes my heart race to think of a reunion. I have lived and loved, but no man has ever made me feel how I feel listening and watching The Beatles!"

J.P.
Schaumburg, Illinois

> "I did not have any money, as a child, to spend on records. My brothers and I saved up to buy Sgt. Pepper and we all listened to it for the first time together."

> "There are two kinds of musicians today: those influenced by The Beatles and liars."

❝I am 24 years old and probably have as much Beatlemania in me as I did when I first heard of them fifteen years ago. Maybe now it's a little more mature, but it's still there.

When I first learned of them, my sister and I (she was eleven yrs. old at the time) did the natural thing; we collected every album, picture, card, and magazine there was to buy. I was just beginning to learn what Rock-and-Roll was all about, so naturally they were my first big influence. We hated Elvis, The Stones, Dave Clark Five, etc., anyone who threatened "our boys." My dream at the time was to go to England. Last year my dream came true when I went to Europe for vacation. I looked up McCartney Music and went for a visit. I plan to go back next year and tour England. I want to go to Liverpool, especially if they build the monument for them.

As I grew up I liked other groups, but The Beatles were and still are No. 1! I still know every word to every song and play them regularly. We used to play Beatle records in a friend's basement and pantomime their songs. We had a set of drums and made our guitars from cigar boxes. At the time my favorite was Ringo, but in 1966, I switched to Paul and I'm still there. Now when I hear a Beatle song, it brings a feeling over me that's hard to describe. It's a warm feeling, and whoever I'm with can immediately relate an incident or what we were doing when that song was popular. Everytime it's one of their birthdays, kids' birthdays or anniversaries, I remember. What can I say? They are "my boys"!

Their initial impact on me was one of love, good music, and long hair. They helped an eight yr. old girl become aware of a new wave of music, new hair styles, puppy love, Beatle boots, *16 Magazine*, and what it was like to become a teenager. Their effect has left me with wonderful memories of growing up, things to tell my kids, good old Rock-and-Roll music, beautiful love ballads, and a reason to return to England. I sure as hell would not have wanted to grow up without them and I'm super-glad I will never forget them.

When Paul was asked how he wanted to be remembered, he replied, 'With a smile!'**❞**

L.B.
Speedway, Indiana

❝I'm 30 years old, and a schoolteacher who teaches Art to 6th, 7th, and 8th grade kids. I've had the same job for 9 years and I really feel that it is getting better all the time. Seems I've stumbled into a lucky vocation there; I've managed to combine my occupation and my hobby, and the kids keep me young.

I was in the 8th grade when The Beatles came to America and due to their influence, my Jr. High days were the most enjoyable of all of my school days, thus, I headed that direction when I decided to teach. I never even applied for High School positions.

I first saw The Beatles one night on The Jack Paar Show, with my mother, and by the time they had arrived to do The Ed Sullivan Show, I'd already purchased their records and was a devout Beatle fan. My Art teacher let us play the radio in class sometimes and they were introducing the **Meet The Beatles** album one day, so the entire class tuned in to debate whether it was any good or not. Guess which side I was on?

I developed 3 close friendships during that year . . . my 3 best girlfriends were also Beatlefans. I've found over the years that we migrate to each other for support the same way "Trekkies" band together or model train enthusiasts get in touch with each other. Jeany loved John, Karen had singled out George, Linda had a thing about Paul, and I found myself attracted to Ringo (I never called him Ringo though . . . he was always Richie to me) due to the fact that it seemed obvious to me from the very beginning that he was the peacemaker in the group . . . and that was my role, as my friends were somewhat volatile on occasion. I also have to admit that Pauly ran an extremely tight second for me then, and while I love them all still, Paul seems to be more the way I feel about myself now. He's contented with his family and friends and secure in the knowledge that he's doing a good job with his life. Richie seems to be floundering a bit in the "party animal" image that he's projecting lately.

Back to my schooldays. The four of us remained tight friends until our senior year when Karen and Jeany split away. August 13, 1966, we loaded into a tiny Ford Falcon and drove from Grand Rapids (where all of this history took place) to Olympia Stadium in Detroit, to sit in seats we bought (top price) mail order for $5.50, only 40 feet away from the stage to see our Beatles in concert. To this day, it's the only concert I've ever seen with any of them in it, and I can still close my eyes and visualize the absolute and total white blinding light from thousands of flashbulbs going off as they bounded onstage. It's something a person just never forgets.

Linda and I went on to the local Jr. College, then transferred to Western Michigan University. She was a piano and vocal music major, and I went into Art Education. We roomed together for 2 years, during which time the "Paul is Dead" hoax surfaced. Even at the age of 20, I remember being devastated by the special program on the radio that evening . . . Linda and I shared a bottle of wine and a few tears that night!

After college, Linda married her boyfriend of 4 years (who, she told me many times, had always seemed to her to have substituted for Paul . . . he was a musician too) and moved to Washington. Her marriage broke up after a few years, but she sings and plays in supper clubs in Michigan now and her new partner and she still include several Beatle numbers in their programs.

I, meanwhile, left Grand Rapids and got my teaching job. I'm still single and live alone (except for my Irish Setter and my Calico cat) in a little house in the country. There was a man in my life a few years ago, but I felt a great deal of intolerance in him, and believe it or not, his idea that I should rid myself of my Beatle collection and thus, my past youth (he had to be kidding) was truly part of the reason our relationship fell apart. Certainly there were a lot of reasons other than my Beatles hobby, but it was the first time that I sensed a definite hostility concerning their music and their obvious effect on my life. We spoke about the fact that their burst upon the scene had totally changed my personality. He could not begin to fathom that occurring and he refused to believe that it had actually happened. But then, he never had any heroes, no one he admired, respected, wanted to meet or be like, so how could he begin to understand? I asked only that he listen . . . . He wouldn't . . . and this carried over into many other facets of our relationship which I could never, after all, blame The Beatles for that!

I've never thrown any Beatle connected article or thing away. A corner of my library is dedicated to my books and scrapbooks. Due to my great love of The Beatles and thus England, I have a great interest in English literature and my three favorite authors are W. Somerset Maugham, Thomas Hardy, and Oscar Wilde. I have travelled to England twice. Both times I made my pilgrimage to Liverpool. I saw Penny Lane, John and Paul's Art Colleges, Ringo's pub, and I did something else I've been wanting to do since approximately 1964 and that was to *Ferry Cross The Mersey* (Gerry and The Pacemakers were my 2nd favorite group). I also visited the site of the Cavern Club and took in as many other sights as I could possibly digest.

I lead a normal respectable life. My pupils like me as a teacher (even though I only play Beatle albums during class). I get along well with my peers. My parents are proud of me . . . and I have a whole secret life that most of my friends know nothing about and which I allow to surface once every summer in Chicago when I go to Beatlefest. **"**

S.P.
Fennville, Michigan

"There was a man in my life a few years ago, but I felt a great deal of intolerance in him, and believe it or not, his idea that I should rid myself of my Beatle collection and thus, my past youth (he had to be kidding) was truly part of the reason our relationship fell apart."

❝ I was a seasoned radio listener at age 9 (the youngest of 4 kids) when The Beatles appeared on the scene. My two sisters and I bought **Meet The Beatles**; the first night we had it, we took turns singing the different parts and trying to improvise music as best we could (tissue-and-comb, harmonica, etc.).

Sally's favorite was Paul, mine George (Liz never really expressed a preference). The two of us bought bubblegum cards and fan magazines, saved newspaper articles, and top ten lists. We ended up with a sizeable collection. It somehow fell into Sally's possession; she decided some 7 years ago that it was of no further use to her, and without consulting me (I was in school in Paris at the time) SHE THREW IT AWAY !!! I have never forgiven her. I just try not to think about it.

I bought every album through **Magical Mystery Tour**, except for **Yesterday and Today** and **Beatles VI**. After **Magical Mystery Tour**, I didn't care much for a lot of their newer musical and lyrical stylings; songs like *Happiness Is A Warm Gun* left me cold, although *Julia, Blackbird*, and *Here Comes The Sun* are still beautiful. The only one I've kept up with since their split has been Paul. I have 7 of his albums; 2 solo, 5 with Wings. People call much of his work silly love songs, but I agree with Paul, what's wrong with that? My single favorite song is *Can't Buy Me Love*, followed closely by *She Loves You*. Both songs have such strong drive that it's hard to sit still even now when I hear them. **Sgt. Pepper**, the first total concept album, is pure genius. Naturally, a lot of nostalgia wells up upon hearing the old tunes (has it really been 16 years since *I Want To Hold Your Hand*?), but the musical quality and talent still comes through with impressive strength to grab me once again.

The most profound influence The Beatles had on my life manifested itself only a year ago, when I recalled the origin of a long-standing, but long suppressed desire to play the drums. I'd turned 10, back then, and was lying on my stomach, at the end of my bed, listening to Ringo singing *Boys*, keeping time with my hands on the edge of the mattress. I was really jazzed up by the music and thought, "That's what I'll do . . . I'll be a drummer!" That thought was almost immediately displaced by this one: "I can't be a drummer, I'm a girl." I couldn't think of a single female drummer (no big surprise, as there weren't any back then, or if there were, they were certainly not in the public eye), and I concluded that since there weren't any, it must not be allowed. So, I resigned myself to just keeping beat.

What brought it all back to the surface last year was the fact that I dated a drummer for awhile. I eventually got up the courage to ask him to teach me a couple of things, enough to acquire a slight understanding of how it's done. Why was courage needed? Because I fully expected a derisive laugh accompanied by a don't-trouble-your-pretty-head response. Ron, to his credit, didn't laugh at me, saying that he had had plenty of female students before. It was terrific encouragement! We broke up before he taught me anything, but not long after that I sought out a drum teacher and have now been taking lessons just over a year.

Just last week, I tried playing along with *Boys* for the first time, and by golly, it wasn't too bad!! In fact, it was really quite an exciting high. I'm quite aware that I have a long and winding road ahead of me, but I'm confident that someday I'll be able to make a living making music. I like Rock and Jazz and a large portion of my Rock roots stem from The Beatles. When I hear people comparing groups like the Bee Gees and the Knack to them, it makes me furious. The Beatles changed the course of Rock-and-Roll, those others have barely made a dent. **"**

A.O.
Reno, Nevada

It would take a professional to sort out how The Beatles paved the way for the women's liberation movement, but it does not take a lot to see that by their breaking down of the sex roles among America's youth, both boys and girls were freer to pursue things that had been closed to them in the past.

Our correspondent, A.O., from Reno, Nevada is truly representative of how women have now begun to perform tasks and pursue occupations which were once forbidden to them. In our next chapter, we will hear from people whose careers were directly influenced or enhanced by The Beatles, but before we do, we will now hear from a correspondent who shows that some 16 years later, female Beatlemania is not dead:

"The Beatles opened my eyes and my brain . . . . Nobody I had ever come into contact with had ever dreamt of the things they were doing and going through. They were an invaluable source of growth for me and helped open me up to a new world of ideas. I know I would be a different person today if they had not entered my life in the particular way they did."

❝ I was known as "Beatle-Woman" in college; I am a 24 yr. old Beatle-maniac, an original Beatlemaniac, ever since February 9, 1964, the first Ed Sullivan Show appearance. I collect the memorabilia, buy new stuff, magazines, etc., and still avidly follow gossip. I go to the conventions to find new stuff; I still care deeply.

I grew up on the white, upper middle class suburbs of the Midwest. I went to Catholic schools. The Beatles opened my eyes and my brain. I liked them in a faddish way when I was 8, 9, 10 years old and I read everything I could on them to find pictures. I began to read other things in the newspapers because of that. When The Beatles talked about religion, drugs, etc., I got interested because I wanted to know where they were coming from and what they were into. Nobody I had ever come into contact with had ever dreamt of the things they were doing and going through. They were an invaluable source of growth for me and helped open me up to a new world of ideas. I know I would be a different person today if they had not entered my life in the particular way they did.

I am "Beatle-Woman," so named by a Barry White enthusiast (don't ask me for my name for him), who defines everyone by their most obvious neurosis . . . he should talk! Beatle music so consistently wafted down hallways, that the music was more identified with me than my name. People in the building think I am weird. I say that I'm not fickle, and have "Taste," whatever that means. I realize Beatlemania is something we were all supposed to grow out of at age 12. When you are in your early 20's, female and have walls of Beatle pictures, there is bound to be a discussion of one's stunted growth and/or mental problems. I am proud to say that mine is a neurosis that has launched a thousand theories, not all of them complimentary. Everyone loves, or at least respects, The Beatles as a group. Everyone knows about Paul's eyes and John's wit, even if they wish they didn't. Arguing the finer nuances of **Revolver** lost its freshness by 1971. All of the group's music has been thoroughly picked apart, frontwards and backwards. They are now the standard by which every new Rock savior is measured. It's not easy being a Beatle fan in these disco days of Wild Runaways and Punk Cherries. Patti Smith cools, immersed up to her Rimbaud in words and riffs that surpass even Dylan's earthiest vision of himself as the missionary of the message. There seems to be more hype and fleeting flesh than any music around these days.

Being a Beatle fan can be a lonely experience. We have unsatisfiable tastes and very high standards that very few artists can break through. We are carrying a flameless torch. On another level, sexually, I have had trouble relating to men. I notice that the guys I find attractive are usually Anglo-Saxon types, who look suspiciously like The Beatles in some way. That is

"It's not easy being a Beatle fan in these days of Wild Runaways and Punk Cherries."

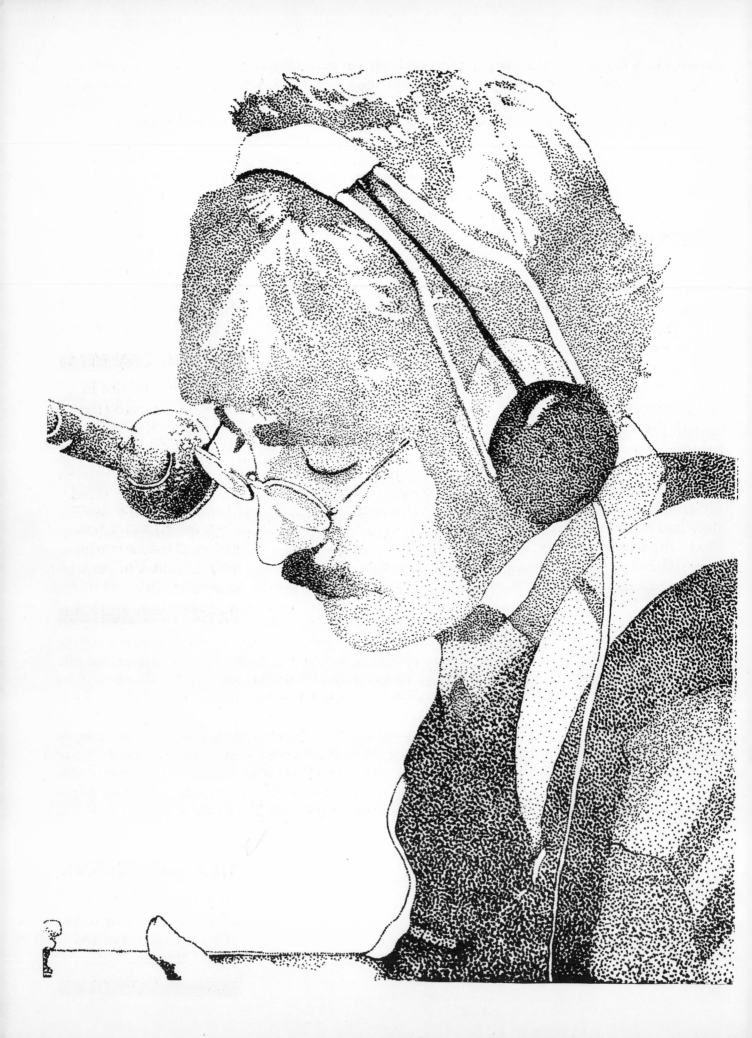

one outgrowth that definitely has been a drag. I held onto the fantasy that I could have a Beatle quite late into my teens, long after Paul got married. I always knew it was a fantasy, but still a strong one . . . it is probably the only detrimental part of terminal Beatlemania. I know of more severe than myself . . . MUCH WORSE! It is a problem that I'm learning to come to terms with.

I saw The Beatles in 1966, in Chicago (the ticket stub is in my wallet to this day). They were on for 20 minutes during which the amps broke down, and John wore sunglasses. I was one of those fans who yelled "Shut Up!" to everyone else. The other fans didn't and I never really heard anything except one verse of *Yesterday*. Recently, I heard the whole song quite well. The loneliness of Beatle-Woman became apparent when I showed up in Long Island, 4 hours early for a Wings concert, wearing a T-shirt glittering "Paul" across it. I escaped with everything, but my pride. Well, if Paul should appreciate his real fans, he's got to see them! I stood on my chair and made a fool of myself in the third row, singing *What Is Life* back to George Harrison . . . but he winked at me . . . . Hell! . . . . It was worth it.

I never thought whatever The Beatles thought; I always perceived them critically. I never took anything they said as truth or anything. John was and is my favorite. I respect him as an artist as I am an artist myself. John has said and done some real bullshit. Yoko has done some bullshit and ripped off other peoples' ideas. I could always suss out what I thought was just stupid talk and what was a great idea. That goes for all of The Beatles as well. The final lesson for me is that one has to be an individual and listen to oneself and not be influenced too much by one's limited environment.

I don't think any of the real fans expect a reunion. And in a way, so what? Let's look on the bright side. For those who just like one Beatle, especially George or Ringo, this is an ideal situation. You get him, pure, without the other three getting in the way. Finally, Ringo gets to sing (yes, I care). We get 4 albums a year, instead of one; each of them with a separate approach to offer. My pickiness dissipates rapidly when confronted with an ex-Beatle's album. They can get away with things that I will not accept from The Stones or Bowie.

I leave it to my amateur psychologist friends to diagnose the reasons for my inability to cope with change, reality, or accessible men. I keep attending Beatle conventions in search of solace and reassurance that this is a serious condition affecting quite a number of original Beatlemaniacs. My only conclusion is that everyone is a Beatlemaniac at heart, some of us need to be more conspicuous about it. Spending money on all memorabilia is the same as putting money out for fan club dues, except now it is a worthwhile investment. Whatever gets you through the night, if you can't have John Lennon. **"**

V.F.
New York, New York

> "I saw The Beatles in 1966, in Chicago (the ticket stub is in my wallet to this day). They were on for 20 minutes during which the amps broke down, and John wore sunglasses. I was one of those fans who yelled 'Shut Up!' to everyone else."

Romantic love still existing for The Beatles in women who were in love with them as teenagers? I never would have guessed that it would carry over into their adult lives, but obviously (as this chapter has demonstrated) it does exist. Our next chapter consists of letters by original Beatlemaniacs, of both sexes, whose careers have been affected by The Fab Four.

3

Those Lucky People

I taught myself to play the guitar. It was around 1965, and I was able to play the basic riff from *Day Tripper*. My progression never quite moved from that point to anything achieving mastery of the art, but I can play *Gloria* and *Smoke On The Water* with the best of them! I am told that my singing in the shower is up there with most of today's vocalists . . . in other words, my musical skills have yet to be realized, or maybe they are simply established as rotten. The truth is, I can't sing or play an instrument, but that never stopped me from wanting to be a Beatle.

I would practice singing and playing a fake guitar as a teenager, imagining that I was Lennon, Harrison, or McCartney. In my heart I knew that I would never be a Rock musician, but I always had my fantasies to sustain a desperate belief that someday people would flock around me in a concert hall. Unfortunate realities overcame me. I had grown accustomed to eating about three meals a day, wearing clothes, and having a roof over my head. Trying to be a Beatle would never earn me a living, and I became a petty bureaucrat working for the largest insurance company in the world. However, while my artistic skills failed me, other people did achieve success. They were influenced by The Beatles in the selection of a career or adjusting to a job. Oh, how I envy those lucky people, able to make a living at what they wanted to do, instead of being forced into a 9 to 5 just to make ends meet; a job which one never aspires to, but takes out of desperation. It must be glorious to enjoy what work you do; but to also like what you do and have The Beatles to thank for it is a double reward.

Herewith are a collection from those correspondents whose career or life's ambitions were altered or directly influenced by The Fab Four:

"If it weren't for
The Beatles entering my
life around the age of 8
or 9, I probably would
be a 9–5 secretary
somewhere . . . and bored
to death. Their influence
on me, musically, and
the doors they helped
open for others to follow,
defined my own career
in music."

❝My age is 25. If it weren't for The Beatles entering my life around the age of 8 or 9, I probably would be a 9-5 secretary somewhere . . . and bored to death. Their influence on me, musically, and the doors they helped open for others to follow, defined my own career in music.

It was after they played Chicago in 1965 that all the young men looked like Paul and seemed to have as much fun as these four.

For the past 4 years I've been a Rock Photographer, and I'm presently contributing to over 50 music publications. My only regret is not taking pictures at the Beatle concert . . . as they may never play together again. Photography in this field is very time consuming and can be hard work. 'Tis all!**❞**

L.M.
Chicago, Illinois

❝I didn't buy an album until I was age 15; up to that time I didn't buy singles either (I still don't) and didn't pay attention to music at all. That all changed with the release of **Sgt. Pepper, Revolver** and **Magical Mystery Tour**; they were my first indication that the limits of music didn't have to be defined by Top 40 radio. I moved from those albums to The Moody Blues and Frank Zappa as the known limits of pop music at the time; that was also the year I discovered Gershwin, which sent me into investigating jazz and classical music. Another influence I can trace directly to The Beatles' music of this period is that I acquired a sitar in 1971. I don't play it as consistently as I ought, but I have broadened my interests to include Indian and other non-Western music.

I wouldn't call The Beatles the most important change in my life; I reserve that place for a Ralph J. Gleason column in the first copy of *Rolling Stone* I ever bought; a marvelous essay entitled "An End to US and THEM." Still, The Beatles' experimental vein (post-**Revolver**) made me aware of the width of musical possibilities, going, in form and content, beyond (to quote Zappa) " . . . three chord songs about somebody's girlfriend . . . ." Even with the advantage of hindsight, I don't think anyone else in 1967 was doing what The Beatles and the Mothers of Invention were doing. They were experimenting, and, now as then, it's a trait not often found in a music business aiming down the well-beaten path in quest of the fast buck.

I'm now 28, currently a Music Director at a local radio station (a noncommercial National Public Radio station specializing in classical and jazz); I have a Bachelor and Masters Degree in speech. I'm white and a male, although I stopped taking race and sex seriously long ago. Last time I counted my record collection, there were over 650 discs.**❞**

P.D.
Carbondale, Illinois

"I'm now 28, currently
a Music Director at a
local radio station . . . .
I have a Bachelor and
Masters Degrees in
speech. I'm white and a
male, although I stopped
taking race and sex
seriously long ago. Last
time I counted my record
collection, there were
over 650 discs."

"The Beatles served as our parents when our real parents lost their credibility. They gave us morals (as evidenced by their early words against the war in Vietnam), clothes, drug styles . . . a sensibility. They gave us a feeling of what success could be without selling out.

I learned to write music at the same time that they came out. They showed me that anyone had the right to write songs. They were the first composers to give charity the rights to income from a composition (*Across The Universe*). They opened up young minds to the possibilities that something interesting could come from a foreign country. I have become an Anglomaniac, and have now been to England five times! The ultimate satisfaction I got in my job here, at a local sound service which specializes in a complete communications center, was assembling the audio system for the Beatlemania show on the west coast."

K.J.
San Francisco, California

"I'll probably never forget the first time I heard about The Beatles. I was already a teeny bopper AM radio freak. Their song (I forget which one I heard first) was incredible; here was a new sound that was completely different from songs before. I bought all their records, all of John's books, the magazines with their pictures, and anything else I could find. Unfortunately, I lived in a small town and never did get to see them perform live. But, oh how I listened and memorized . . . which brings me to present day.

I'm a singer and pianist. All my friends go to The Conservatory of Music in San Francisco. One day we were all going to jam at my house, but nobody could think of songs we all knew. (I'm into jazz, most of them are classical or Rock). My best friend, Michael, came over with the *Beatles Complete* music book, and we knew what the jam would be. We went half through the book that night and finished it in later sessions. Some songs became group "faves" and others were discarded (too hard, too easy, too untranslatable). Our "band" consisted of piano, drums, flute, recorder, harmonica, bass, guitar (sometimes 2), trumpet, and several part vocal harmony.

I now have the answer to my mother's question of the early 1960s. She wanted to know how kids, my age, were going to be able to sing the standards of a Rock era. Now, I know . . . we sing The Beatles very well, Mom, very well!"

A.S.
Oakland, California

66 When The Beatles first appeared on The Ed Sullivan Show, I was eight years old. From that point on they have been a major part of my life! As they started touring the U.S., I started beating on coffee cans and cardboard boxes, and eventually got my own drum set. I also learned the guitar and piano by ear, playing along with their records all through school. It was a fun hobby and a crazy dream of being in their shoes, but The Beatles got my undivided attention towards music.

Now, at 24, as a good drummer in an active Rhythm and Blues band, I feel great music in my life. The Beatles not only changed me, they mapped out the course of my career. This career is most certainly a long and winding road. I wish my band could have a Brian Epstein and a George Martin . . . if we did I have a suspicion that this story would have another chapter. Whatever happens happens! All I know is whenever I'm feeling blue and lonely, I go to my stereo and reach for any Beatles record. It cures me every time. Yeah, Yeah, Yeah!

M.K.
McGregor, Iowa

P.S.   When I was buying Beatles records, my father would ask me why and I would reply that I was investing in my future. He understood as he too was in a band when he was young. **99**

> "When I was buying Beatles records, my father would ask me why and I would reply that I was investing in my future. He understood as he too was in a band when he was young."

37

"The Beatles songs were the kind of songs which offered you a world of their own. I became totally absorbed with each and every song in body and mind. I would feel alive, centered, alert, sensual, and very real. You could forget everything and become part of the song."

❝ I first saw The Beatles on The Ed Sullivan Show when I was 9 years old. I loved them, watched them with my brother and sister, and they loved them too. I immediately bought their first record and listened to it all the time. Whenever our family traveled any distance to see relatives, my brother, sister, and I sang every Beatle song we knew in full harmony. It was one of the only times I can remember feeling close to both of my siblings, and being able to lead them in any kind of activity. I would always initiate these singing sessions. It always gave me a wonderful sense of strength and of enjoyment, and sentimentally enough, of love.

Whenever The Beatles put out a new record, I bought it, and began to play the piano and the guitar, on which I figured out a few of their songs. Their music blended into each year of my life in an important way. It helped me to build memories; the music enhanced my feelings about romantic attachments, friendships, and sometimes I even thought about and learned something of what they said in their lyrics. My girlfriends and I would have long discussions about each Beatle and why we liked one in particular. These debates lasted late into the night. I was in love with Paul McCartney, he was very real to me in my fantasies and in my music-oriented life. The Beatles came to play in Boston. A friend asked if I wanted to go see them, and this was before I knew who they were. I will regret this decision for the rest of my life.

I went to a school which offered a great variety of music to sing and play on different instruments. Most of the music was traditional gospel, classical, folk, etc. . . . when The Beatles came out, some of the kids picked up on it, and played it at music recitals. I remember a classmate playing *When I'm Sixty-Four* on his clarinet and I thought, "Hey!, just like on the record!" The Beatles songs were the kind of songs which offered you a world of their own. I became totally absorbed with each and every song in body and mind. I would feel alive, centered, alert, sensual, and very real. You could forget everything and become part of the song.

I am a songwriter and singer now, and I feel that The Beatles had a strong influence on my being this. I have only good memories of singing and of hearing their songs. The first time I formed my own musical group, we sang their songs. It was a way of getting together with friends and feeling close to people. Dancing became more exciting with The Beatles' earlier music. I went feet crazy over some of their earlier material. The Beatles allowed many people to put their musical, sexual, spiritual and lively selves and ener-

"I went feet crazy over some of their earlier material."

gy into listening, singing, dancing, and enjoying their music. It was like taking a 10 year course in Beatles music (Beatles: 101) by following their career. I learned how to concentrate (something I had difficulty with in school). Music was my religion. The Beatles developed a new concept of music and therefore my religious and spiritual life changed as new music forms were added to it.

Everyone liked The Beatles, even parents seemed to enjoy them, though the effects of The Beatles' hairstyles and clothing were to most parents' disliking. In a way, The Beatles helped to initiate a healthy confrontation between kids and their parents. Sexual and moral questions came up about The Beatles. I remember someone talking about their long hair . . . it was a big discovery, a fad, and it became a rebellious gesture against society.

The Beatles also created lives, images, characters, and life stories in their songs. **Sgt. Pepper** conjured up so many images, that I remember feeling as if I had walked into a new dimension of colors, feelings, and ideas after I had heard it. The Beatles made me feel that I was important. It was not that they were talking to me personally, they spoke to everyone, offered so much and created another dimension which I found completely satisfying, intriguing, and absorbing. They exercised my musical imagination. I began to think of myself as more of a full person, related to a larger scheme when I first encountered The Beatles. My friends, family, and I grew with them. I remember how I felt and what I was doing when each song came out. They played a very special and important part of my life, enhancing my sensations, and helping me to feel more alive and connected to this world."

L.W.
Arlington, Massachusetts

"The Beatles made me feel that I was important. It was not that they were talking to me personally, they spoke to everyone, offered so much and created another dimension which I found completely satisfying, intriguing, and absorbing."

"The Beatles helped me examine my values, explore new musical ground, discover my own personal creativity, and thus, myself."

❝I believe my life was influenced by The Beatles in a number of ways. In 1964, I was 14, living in the suburbs of New York City. I had a background in classical music, but appreciated Rock-and-Roll, thanks to an older brother. The music played on the radio in the early 60s was rather bland as I recall. As far as social activities, the high school dating game didn't interest me. When The Beatles arrived in N.Y., and appeared on The Ed Sullivan Show, a new light seemed to shine. I rushed out to buy their first album, which I played every day after school. I started to buy Beatle magazines and read them during "study hall" in school. I met my best friend that way. Beatlemania got me through the dull high school classes and gave my life a direction of sorts, as well as an identity with the thousands of other Beatle fans. Parents scoffed, but to us The Beatles were witty, talented, and loveable. The British fashions and long hair were a welcome change from the current fashions.

A curious outgrowth of all this was my attraction to the then obscure Rolling Stones, whose raunchy music and looks must have appealed to my budding sexuality. I managed to go to the Stones' first U.S. concert, and from then on Mick Jagger replaced Paul McCartney as my dream (what a contrast!). By then The Beatles were more or less acceptable and I needed a more shocking idol. I later met the Stones through a fan club. By now my friend and I were devout followers of many British groups. We attended many concerts, bought records, and developed an appreciation for Blues and Soul (later on, Jazz, Folk, Bluegrass, Indian, African, Latin, etc.). We started exploring Greenwich Village. Our attitudes developed into what was later to be labelled "Hippie." We went to anti-War marches . . . not because it was the thing to do, but because we genuinely believed in it. We attended Woodstock, our hair grew, but for me . . . no sex or drugs until I attended college in Buffalo, and became acquainted with radical types, most of whom quit school to join communes or travel. I did graduate, despite LSD induced goallessness, and headed for Europe. When two high school students persuaded me to move with them to New Mexico, I was ready for new landscapes. I got a job there on an alternative newspaper for a year. I eventually moved to Colorado where I met my future husband (still scorning convention, we lived together for 2 years).

The 70s have been comparatively tame, as reflected in the lousy Rock scene, with the blessed exception of the genuine musicians, who are still here to remind us what it's all about. The Beatles helped me examine my values, explore new musical ground, discover my own personal creativity, and thus, myself. Sound typical? It was good to be growing up then. I hope my 2 year old son's adolescence will have such a positive focal point as The Beatles gave mine.❞

J.G.
Mesa, Arizona

66 'What Have The Beatles Meant To Me?' Sounds like my high school term papers! In fact I wrote on that very subject more than once. I approached it then with near missionary zeal. I still do I'm afraid.

I was 13 when The Beatles first grabbed the attention of all my peers. I was curious to find out what everybody else was talking about, so I borrowed a radio and I heard *I Want To Hold Your Hand* for the first time. I was impressed and talked my gullible mother into buying me the single and was thrilled to find out I got a bonus B-side of *I Saw Her Standing There*. But what clinched it for me was the novel look of the four faces on that picture sleeve. I have to admit it . . . they were the most beautiful hunks of mature manhood my naive little eyes had ever focused on. When you look back now, you can see they were just boys, green around the ears, pretending to be so sophisticated and worldly. The best part of it all is that we grew up with them. Once we committed outselves to Beatlefandom as a way of life, we followed every move they made, and we matured as they matured, and we followed where they led.

People ask me now, "Aren't you trying to relive your childhood?" But I say no, because I didn't just like what I was, I like what IS as well! Everything the four have produced and accomplished, shown us, and given us has become a part of my life. So, I'm with them today as I was with them in 1964. They've influenced my life so completely that it might be easier to answer how they have not affected me. At least the list would be shorter!

My singular goal as a teenager was to finish school so I could take off for a summer in England. I had seen The Beatles three times in concert, but that was still too remote for me. It had to be more personal. In 1969, I spent three weeks lingering on the sidewalks in front of the Abbey Road studios in London as The Beatles came and went in the process of making their last LP. Since then I've been back to England 7 additional times. It's like a second home, and I usually manage to see one of The Beatles on each trip.

I not only wanted to be as close in touch with The Beatles themselves as possible, but also as close as I could with all their fans all over the world. Beatle fans have always been close-knit with a network of friendships that have lasted a decade or more. I started my first Beatles fan club in the good old days when they were still together. But aside from that advantage, the fan club scene is much more active and exciting today. I'm still running a club 13 years later and it's now one of the biggest ones in the world. What amazes me is that I have members as young as 10 years old. Hard to think that they were only just born when The Beatles were breaking up! The youngsters are as vocal and active in fandom as we ever were, but I'm not ready to give up my place to them yet! As one of the original hardcore fans, I just hope I can continue to share my experiences and love for The Beatles with them. 99

Beatles Rule
B.F.
St. Paul, Minnesota

"When you look back now, you can see they were just boys, green around the ears, pretending to be sophisticated and worldly. The best part of it all is that we grew up with them."

41

"I was born in November, 1951 to a lower, middle class, but upwardly mobile set of very young (22 and 19) parents. I was the first child, the first grandchild, the only niece (no nephews either) in a white, Jewish family. All this led to an extraordinary amount of individual attention lavished upon me for the first five and a half years of my life, until my sister came along. In many ways I was encouraged to a wide variety of interests many of which weren't standard for girl children. My parents were liberated with respect to education and ability. However, I grew up rather bright, well read, and precocious, and as a result had few friends my own age. This being the case, my tastes were unusually heavily influenced by my parents, hence, I went for books rather than TV, school before play, and my pop standards/show tunes, and even a smattering of classical before Rock-and-Roll. The only contact I had with Rock was through my grandfather, who owned a line of juke-boxes and would give me records. I hardly ever played Rock-and-Roll because I didn't like it. I had heard of Elvis, Fabian, Fats Domino, Chubby Checker, etc., but they failed to make much of an impression on me.

In January, 1964, I was 12 years old, in the seventh grade, top student in the special progress class, with one very close friend, one fairly close one, and very few "casual" friends because they were hard for me to make or keep. I was the last chosen to a team, the first to have my term paper completed, the one with the longest list of optional books read; the darling of parents and teachers, and an anathema to other kids my age. I could sing every song in a dozen hit shows, but had never heard of WABC, WMCA, or WINS, which were the local Rock stations.

On February 5, 1964, I was visiting my fairly close friend, who started talking about some strange entity called The Beatles. I had never heard of them. She was quite amazed at that revelation and showed me a picture she had clipped from the newspaper. I suppose it says something, that now, over 16 years later, I can still see this photo in my mind's eye — from left to right were John, Ringo, Paul and George walking down a street. John's carrying an overcoat in his right hand, Paul, a record or magazine in his right hand, and Ringo and George have their hands in their pockets. I thought Paul was cute, and resolved to learn where the aforementioned radio stations could be located on the radio dial. I went home and began the search, and suddenly heard a song I knew had to be by these Beatles, although one hour earlier, I had not even heard of them. It was *Please Please Me*. There was no gradual indoctrination into it; I saw the picture, heard the song, and fell in love. The Beatles collectively, and John and Paul, in particular, became my gods, my idols, my food for thought, the stuff my dreams were made of, the subject of innumerable short stories (all of which had the same ending — boy meets girl and girl definitely gets!), and most importantly, the source material for my wildest fantasies . . . the ones I shared with my closest friend. These were very private ones which were to become increasingly erotic as the early teen years moved onward. As was my wont, I read about them voraciously . . . every book, newspaper article I could get my hands on. I saved all the clippings, learned all the words to their songs, knew every fact about them, had complete sets of bubblegum cards. None of this served to make me popular, but it did give me a certain air of authority, and I found myself in the frequent position of arbitrating disputes and being the person to go to with questions about The Beatles. My inner world, the polar opposite of the outer one, became increasingly enriched with colorful new people, places, ideas, and actions. I began to truly enjoy the time I spent with myself, instead of wondering what was wrong with me. I never became the beloved of the world, but I was slowly coming to grips with my individuality and learning to like myself. By the time The Beatles and I came to a parting of the ways in 1969 (John's actions had totally bewildered and confused this still rather naive 18 year old) I had a full and rich private life which I made no excuses or apologies for. I had the capacity to totally turn off the rest of the world without ever touching drugs, and only rarely, liquor.

My interest in The Beatles led me to become more aware of some practical matters such as clothing, hairdo, make-up. I turned my interests towards my abilities and began to do small things like interviewing Bruce Morrow (WABC disc jockey, "Cousin Brucie") for the school paper, and I became a correspondent for *Datebook* magazine. Nothing big, but satisfying to me. I have continued to live my life, pleasing myself and always keeping part of my mind and heart reserved for my fantasies (which the new wave of analysts tell us is very healthy, so I've been right all along!). The Beatles' music still influences my choice of music and I prefer listening to mid-60s music above all others. A great deal of my discretionary income goes to collect records, photos, books, etc. My conversations are sprinkled with quotes from songs and movie-lines.

The "parting of the ways" mentioned earlier, lasted from 1969-1979. During those years I married and divorced, found myself a career which I enjoy and am good at, graduated with honors from a local college, set up my own home, and generally carried on with my life. I always enjoyed hearing The Beatles music on the radio, but never got around to putting any of the old records on. I gave away or threw out a considerable portion of the memorabilia I had collected, and yes, I do often kick myself when I see how much these are now worth. In 1979 I rediscovered them, and became an ardent fan again. When "A Hard Day's Night" is on TV on a Saturday night, the date gets postponed.

Certainly, in my mind, the very least The Beatles did was to make a certain type of behavior acceptable and respectable to the under 30 culture of that time. All those 18--30 year olds are now 28--40 now, and coming to power in the establishment. It's not too outrageous to consider the effect of grass, hash, cocaine, meditation, LSD, grooving, flower power, make love not war, hippiedom on the corporate structure in the next 10--15 years when former and current Beatle fans become chairpersons of the boards! Society is looser, less moral, but also less hypocritical about it, and more accepting of doing one's own thing than in 1964. Did The Beatles do this? I doubt it, as it is difficult to distinguish between their changes on society from societal changes which were taking place anyway. The changes were reflected in their

"It's not too outrageous to consider the effect of grass, hash, cocaine, meditation, LSD, grooving, flower power, make love not war, hippiedom on the corporate structure in the next 10—15 years when former and current Beatle fans become chairpersons of the boards!"

changing music, and they are certainly inextricably bound up in these changes. Only time can tell. The attitudes and opinions affected by them undoubtedly influence many young people (those under 13 in 1967--1969) and helped shape their attitudes. Those 13 year olds, who are now under 23, are a different breed than my age group. They are much more cynical, harder, and burned out at a younger age, and I think the relationship between their tender years and The Beatles activities is one that should be deeply explored. Many of these children heard the word, and the word was "drugs," failing to realize that this scene was only part of a much larger search for self on the part of four young men, who couldn't have lived much of a normal life during some very important years. The early 20s is a time for full realization of who one is and what one's place is in the world, and look how The Beatles spent those years! No wonder they took off on their search. Far too many people didn't realize it for what it was. **"**

S.F.
Brooklyn, New York

❝I'm 23, female, and a free-lance writer. I have been a Beatle fan since 1968, when I was 12. The Beatles were important on my thinking for sure, John especially. They were my idols at a critical period in my life and throughout my adolescence.

I didn't become a Beatle fan because of their music. In the beginning it was really an attraction to their personalities, again, particularly John's. I was persuaded to read Hunter Davies' book and something clicked as I was reading the bits about John. My appreciation of their music came later on. They were fantasy objects for me and the fantasies they inspired were crucial in building up the confidence I needed to try my hand at writing fiction. Writing fiction and fantasizing go hand in hand. I came to appreciate my imagination and to actively develop it. Creating characteristics about people and their situations is probably my favorite pastime these days, which began with those early adolescent Beatle fantasies. The Beatles were my most important role models, and since they were creative people, I was encouraged to pursue a creative career.

I was swept up in the whole peace/hippie movement at an age when most of the kids around me were not. The Beatles had a lot to do with that. I've always felt somehow cheated since I was too young to be much of a hippie. I still get fired up over certain causes and have a yearning to go out and crusade. My politics aren't as radical as they used to be, but I'm always willing to help someone out in defending his or her rights.

After writing, Rock music is my biggest love. The Beatles were the first band I got into and from them I went on to the Stones, the Who, etc., etc., most of the big 60s bands. I really enjoy writing about Rock personalities, and have just finished the second draft of a book on the Stones. I doubt that I would be quite so passionate about Rock music and musicians if not for my early passion for The Beatles. John Lennon's influence goes so deep that I don't think it would be possible to weed out all of the different effects he has had on me.❞

D.F.
Ardsley-on-Hudson, New York

" It must have been early 1964 when I first heard The Beatles sing *I Want To Hold Your Hand*. I was 13 years old, living with my family consisting of two brothers, two sisters, older than me. The radio, record player, and all the teenage fads at that time, were not new to me. I resented the idea that my older sisters could go out at night and dance and whatever they did at that time, while I had to stay close to home. I did notice that my sisters were very influenced with Top 40, 45 rpm records, dances, etc., and that they related all this to the way they felt about boys. Songs like *It's My Party And I'll Cry If I Want To* (I mean I never cried at a party), *Cathy's Clown, Donna*; anytime Ricky Nelson sang a song on the tube, everything anyone was doing had to stop, and there were my sisters drooling in front of the television. Anyway, I realized at the time, that if you were young, cute, had a guitar, and could sing, girls would stop, look, and listen.

Down the street from our house was a family similar to ours, in as much as there were two boys and two girls. One of the girls, Nancy, was my age, and I was very infatuated with her, and her older sister, Carolyn. Both were very foxy, and I was always trying to find a way to impress them. The week that I heard *I Want To Hold Your Hand*, I was spending a lot of time at the two girls' house. One day, Carolyn came in with a 45 rpm record from a new group called The Beatles. The girls were really knocked out by this music, and when they wanted to turn me on to this song I acted as though I was into The Beatles for a long time; of course I had never heard of the group before! I got to know the song very fast and very well. One day, soon after, I was alone in the girls' living room singing along with the record when they both walked in on me. I was very embarrassed. They complimented me on my singing, to make me feel better, but I realized then that my voice blended with the record. That's when I bought the 1st album by The Beatles, learned all the lyrics, melodies, the haircut, *16 Magazine* . . . I wanted to be a Beatle.

That same year, I asked my folks for a guitar for Christmas. No luck, so eventually I saved enough Blue Chip stamps to redeem an acoustic guitar. I learned chords with an instruction book, and sheet music of Beatle songs. The next year my folks finally realized that I was musically inclined, they bought me an electric guitar. By that time, 1966, I was in high school where I met many other young men, like myself, who were influenced by The Beatles. All through high school I was in Rock bands which were influenced by The Beatles. Of course the country and the world saw a lot of bands then, with some touch of Beatle influence, but it was evolving. I knew the only way I was going to be in the running was to write my own songs. I was right. That's what made The Beatles . . . they were different. What you sang and wrote about was the key.

Band after band, the battle of the bands . . . I looked for something different. In 1968, for me it was "Chicago Transit Authority." Back then they sounded like The Beatles with horns and good vocals. I used to go to the Fillmore West in San Francisco whenever those guys played. We would talk to them on their break and it was the best thing that ever happened to me, or so I thought. The summer of 1968 found me riding through the hills of Oakland . . . *Hey Jude* comes on the radio for the first time. What a song! So simple that it's complicated. 1968 was a good year for me, I was introduced to my first recording studio. I was a bass player at the time. I was always stealing licks from Paul McCartney. My first recording was in 1969 when a band called "Fire" was making a 45 record and their bass player was sick. I got the job. This is something for me to remember because soon after, Fire changed names to Tower Of Power.

1970, I was out of high school and went to Junior College. I also took piano lessons. In 1971, I got out of bands and started to sing in steak houses with guitar and vocals. In 1972, I began to drive great distances, like to L.A. and Denver, playing music in bars or wherever I fit in. Everytime I had a bad night with original songs, Beatle songs came in handy. I knew them all . . . it got me a lot of attention. Paul McCartney's solo album made me feel good about what I was doing. You see, all the musicians I grew up with were still in bands, or not doing music at all. Paul left The Beatles and did his own thing. That really influenced me!

In the winter of 1972–1973, I was driving through Lake Tahoe, Nevada looking for a place to play. Someone mentioned a Mexican restaurant that had live music. I walked into this place with the intentions of being really humble. I was carrying my guitar, and you get a lot of looks with one of those things. Well, before I could even find a place to sit, I realized that the band was playing a song I had written. I turned around to look at the band, and there was an old high school friend, Steve, singing away! We spent the rest of that winter writing songs and playing at Tahoe.

Those boys I met in Tahoe left when the snow melted in 1973. They went East, but I went West to Santa Cruz. I got in a few more bands, and in 1974, the boys came to Santa Cruz to look me up. They had a girl singer with them and a piano player, all together 7 people in the band. I gave them a place to stay and got them some gigs. They were fighting a lot and it didn't look too promising, but they were good! Well, they broke up one night right before my eyes, and immediately started talking about a new band. They wanted me to play bass, like in the old days. We called the band Fly-By-Night, and at the time I had no idea we would make albums, play concerts with every big pop star in the business, including recording with George Harrison, Leon Russell, and Tom Scott.

We rehearsed everyday from 10 a.m. to 5 p.m., until we felt we could deal with any situation. While this was going on Dino Airali was producing his first album with Phoebe Snow in New York. Dino was looking for a new artist to record, that's when he found Larry Hosford, a songwriter. Dino gave Larry some money to record, and Larry called Fly-By-Night to back him in the studio. We did his first album in Nashville in 1974/1975, and travelled all over the country, trying to sell the record.

We started the second record, the one with George Harrison, in November, 1975 in Los Angeles, at Capitol Records, Studio A, the same studio The Beatles knew so well. Larry Hosford with Jim Norris on drums and myself

> "We called the band Fly-By-Night, and at the time I had no idea we would make albums, play concerts with every big pop star in the business, including recording with George Harrison, Leon Russell, and Tom Scott."

on bass were in that studio for a week, preparing the basic tracks for the L.A. musicians to show up and put their music on top of this stuff. Everyday at 4:00 p.m., we would go to the studio, sometimes Dino would be late as he had just become the president of Dark Horse records, Harrison's company. He was a very busy man and would come in and always tell his stories of Harrison, who he saw everyday.

Dino came in one day and mentioned he had invited Leon Russell down to the studio. Since Shelter Records was owned by Leon, it was only right to see how your fellow artists were doing. Leon was to come on Thursday or Friday with some friends, but who? I had met Leon a year before this, at his home in Tulsa, Oklahoma, spent some time with him, one on one, so I knew what to expect from him. He's always been fun, never a bad word, and made a point to make me feel good. So, on Thursday evening, on the way to the studio, a few of us guys stopped at a cafe to grab a bite, somewhere around Hollywood and Vine. We ran into two young ladies, I mean cute and young. Someone invited them to the recording session. At 8 p.m., the engineer and I and the two girls were in the dark engineer room looking into the studio where Dino and Larry and about five other singers were recording. When it's dark in the engineer's room, and light in the studio, people in the studio can't see the people in the engineer's control room. They were working on *Direct Me*, when in the control room, leaning against the entrance door, someone was trying to come through the door, so I turned around to let them in. It was George Harrison! My first impression was a smile, and then I said "George, we heard you were coming!" We spoke about the song, he mentioned the bass intro to the song. I thanked him because that was me playing bass on that track. He didn't stay long, just long enough to leave a message for Dino. He said he would be back tomorrow night with Tom Scott.

The two young ladies had never heard of George Harrison before. They heard of The Beatles, but were too young to have been influenced by them. The next night we started vocals on some tracks and finished others. When we got back from dinner, Leon was already there writing chords down to the song while the tape was rolling and never missing a note. George and Tom Scott arrived soon after. It was not easy to get close to George as there were ten other people in the room. We all sat around listening to the tape, I remember Tom Scott mentioning he never played country music before. I explained that we all came from a Rock/Pop background and that we were trying to be different with our music. He played great. George pulled out his slide guitar. Slide is the one thing I identify George with. We all had a great night. By the time we got really rolling, George, Leon, Larry, and myself were all drunk. We went in the studio and were jamming on different tunes. Larry wanted George and Leon to sing on a cut called *Wishin I Could*. Both of them were pretty intoxicated by that time, which was great cause the song takes place in a bar, and some of the jokes those guys were pulling would stop the session.

A lot of good things happened that night, most of them very personal,

"They were working on *Direct Me*, when in the control room, leaning against the entrance door, someone was trying to come through the door, so I turned around to let them in. It was George Harrison! My first impression was a smile, and then I said "George, we heard you were coming!"

and not meant for public discussion. During the next years, I came in contact with people who worked with The Beatles and I have heard some amazing stories about those guys. My manager remembers the day he took John and Yoko house hunting in L.A.; I have a friend who snuck into a Wings' party, by sleeping in the basement of a mansion in Beverly Hills, and he hung out with Paul most of the night.

The Beatles have touched a lot of people in my life, not all for a positive direction. Music is something every person needs! Most people wish they had some musical talent. The Beatles made people wonder if they had any of this talent, and went head first to try and pursue a career . . . it's easy to get in, but real hard to get out of. I was one of the fortunate to start early. My intentions have changed since the early days of impressing girls. Leon Russell, George Harrison, Tom Scott, Jesse Colin Young, Jose Feliciano, Jim Messina, Willie Nelson, Neil Young, and many more have all helped me direct my intentions toward a real meaning for wanting to perform. If it weren't for The Beatles, I doubt if I would have even been in music at all . . . I really doubt it! **"**

D.S.
Castro Valley, California

We have just seen how influential The Beatles were to those who chose music and writing as their careers, but would anyone ever have guessed that a particular Beatles' song would have such an impact on a person that it provided the physical setting for an occupation? Read on . . . .

"For the most part of my life, I have been a Beatles fan. I am a first generation Beatles fan. I was a part of Beatlemania when it was young and fresh, and took this country and shook all of its youth who felt it. Every phase of their lives, I followed John, Paul, George, and Ringo. I laughed with them and shed many tears for them. At the age of twenty-nine, I'm still theirs. As I spend time to look back on it all now; nothing has placed a mark on my life, as much as their song, *Strawberry Fields Forever*. For Strawberry Field IS real! Thanks to The Beatles, I became a part of their song. I would love to share my story with John Lennon, if given the chance, because I'll not be able to tell everything on paper.

October, 1971 took me to Liverpool's Lime Street Station. No one greeted me as I got off the train. Standing on the platform, feeling scared and lonely, a young lad took notice of me, and offered to carry my luggage to the main part of the station. He welcomed me to Liverpool and hoped I would have a pleasant stay. I was feeling better already. Sitting on my case and resting my back against the wall behind me, I wondered if John ever stood here. I smiled at the thought as I started to daydream about what brought me to this place called Liverpool and Strawberry Field. It was the previous year which first brought me to England. After The Beatles stopped touring it was decided among their fans that if The Beatles won't come to us, we'll go to them! Once you knew where to go when you got there, you had it made, but your timing and their timing had to be just right. You had to be at the right place at the right time. Then you hoped they would be in the right mood for meeting you. If you've been through it, you know what I'm talking about. Well, by the time I made it to England, The Beatles had broken up, but by then the fans had a place to meet . . . APPLE. Outside Apple I stood eight hours a day, five days a week for four weeks! It paid off, I got to meet Ringo and George. I thank them for being so kind.

For Beatle fans, a trip to Liverpool was a must. I was lucky enough to be able to spend an evening at the original Cavern Club. What a night to remember! A band played, but at midnight they played all Beatle records. During this same visit to Liverpool, I ventured over to Beaconsfield Road, and stood outside the gates of Strawberry Field, looking in. It looked so peaceful, with only a faint sound of a child's voice. Then I wondered what it was that John had to write a song about this place. Suddenly the daydreaming was broken by the voice of an older woman asking for me by name. I stood as she introduced herself as the matron at Strawberry Field, and said that the mini-bus was waiting outside the station to take me home. We passed through the city center onto Allerton's Penny Lane area, then onto Woolton, to my new home for one year. Sheltered from the high Victorian wall in front, and hidden from its many trees, Strawberry Field looked like a house in a ghost story. In 1973, its walls were pulled down at the age of 103. Its earliest records date back to 1870. but it didn't become a children's home for the Salvation Army until 1934. John Lennon knew it when it was a home for girls only. Story has it that John was always "larking about" and making trouble for himself at the home. I really can't say what as I wouldn't want it to get back to John and have it not be at all true. My friend, who lives there, was a child in the home herself at one time. She's the same age as John, and also a Beatle fan. So put two and two together and that's how Strawberry Field knew I was a Beatle fan. My friend took me to her room the first night I was there. We had just got the children to bed and wanted to talk. I walked in and it was wall to wall Beatles. I just had to tell her. We became the best of friends. I now own the Beatle pictures she once hung on her bedroom walls.

You've probably been thinking that I went to work at Strawberry Field just because of The Beatles. Not true. After my first visit to England, I fell in love with the country so much, I felt that I had to return to live there for one year. With a special love for children . . . what better way, but to have a live-in job in a children's home? After a great deal of research, I came across a list of homes in England. Some that I wrote to never gave me a reply. Others said that they weren't taking overseas workers, and one disappointment led to another. One day, feeling sorry for myself, I was listening to the radio and the song, *Strawberry Fields Forever* came over the air. That's it! I thought, why not?!? Why not write to them? So what that I'm a Beatle fan and what people would think! God, it is in your hands. I wrote and two weeks later, I got a reply saying the job was mine. It wasn't easy, the red tape I went through with the British government was unreal, but I won't go into that.

My job at Strawberry Field was everything from filling up the coal heaters, to cooking, and mending the children's clothes, to washing their faces and drying a tear, to walking to Penny Lane and then getting the bus back with twelve children; everyone knew where we were from. Sunday mornings dressed in our Sunday best, off to the 'army. One mini-bus wasn't enough, so two trips were made to Walton. I remember the prayers, the songs, the joy and the blessings they brought to my life. God bless the Salvation Army for they do your work well. Oh . . . Christmas! . . . the best part of it all. It was the first time in my life that I didn't wonder if I was getting anything for Christmas! On the eve all 42 children and nine staff members sat on the front stair case and sang Christmas hymns to the Salvation Army Band. Our voices rang throughout that great house . . . and I thought about my family back home. And I thought about The Beatles and wished them well . . . now I knew why John Lennon sang his song and I thanked him. That night at the foot of each child's bed, we hung stockings filled with goodies. Three times during the night, I was awoken by a child's cry saying "Father Christmas has been!" Christmas morning . . . what a joy to see so many children open up gifts . . . all at once! I can't tell you the excitement of it all!

The children that come into Strawberry Field are abused and in some cases, emotionally disturbed. Ages are 3–15, both boys and girls. It is their home until a foster home is found or they are able to return to their parents. In many cases, they stay until they are old enough to go out into the world at the young age of fifteen. The old house was pulled down in 1973. The new house stands on the same grounds. Where the old house once stood is a

"My job at Strawberry Field was everything from filling up the coal heaters, to cooking, and mending the children's clothes, to washing their faces and drying a tear, to walking to Penny Lane and then getting the bus back with twelve children; everyone knew where we were from."

play area. I joined in with the children and other staff members as we watched our house go up. I am one of two people in the world who has a brick from the old house.

Towards the end of 1972, I left Strawberry Field. I left behind many new friends, times spent at The Beatles fan club, sunny walks to Penny Lane for fish and chips, and fans asking what tree John sat in. I left a city I dearly loved more than my own in the States. With tearful eyes I said goodbye to the matron, where it all began . . . at Lime Street Station. As the train pulled away, I hung my head and cried in fear that I would never return to Liverpool and Strawberry Field. Even today, when I leave on that same train from the 'pool, I cry heavier tears. In 1974, a guiding hand must have been with me, as I returned to Strawberry Field to work for six months. This time in the new house. I learned upon the opening of the new house, John Lennon made a donation.

I will always be grateful to The Beatles and that one special song, for I feel if it wasn't for The Beatles I would never have ventured to England in the first place, and never would have met the many people who have touched my life in such a wonderful way. To them I say thank you . . . to them I try to build a statue to be placed in Liverpool. It's true, "All You Need Is Love" and "Strawberry Fields Forever."

M.W.
Saginaw, Michigan

> "In 1974, a guiding hand must have been with me, as I returned to Strawberry Field to work for six months. This time in the new house. I learned upon the opening of the new house, John Lennon made a donation."

P.S. In September, 1979, I made my fifth visit to Liverpool. I spent a few hours at Strawberry Field and the staff told me of the many problems they are having with Beatle fans. The effect on the children upset me. From what the staff told me, I wrote a poem:

When you go round where "nothing is real"
That place called Strawberry Field,
Don't ask the taxi to take you to the door,
And what's more don't ask the children
If you can see more.
It's their home, it's their house,
You wouldn't like it done if it was yours.
Lunches aren't allowed,
Especially on the grounds,
That's where the children play,
Please don't take that away.
So stay at the gate,
And don't stand there so late,
For then the children can't come out to play.
PRIVATE is this land.
Please understand. **"**

4

The Beatles and Me

One of the surprises to come out of my letter gathering project was the sometimes absolute honesty displayed by those discussing very personal, and in some cases, painful memories. Respondents went into great detail about their individual personalities in order to demonstrate how The Beatles were a part of their lives. At times I felt as if I were prying or opening up someone else's mail. The integrity of the letter writers was overwhelming. I almost felt guilty that I knew so much about people's inner thoughts, but was unable to reveal anything to my correspondents about my own personal life.

It is not that I assume everyone is waiting with bated breath to hear me tell all, but rather with a sense of responsibility and dedication to the hundreds of people who wrote to me, that before entering some chapters talking about peoples' personal lives, I talk about The Beatles and me.

Every individual encounters obstacles and problems as they grow up. The teenage years are one hassle after another in dealing both with those who surround your life, and also with yourself. I can now look back with a certain degree of perspective from the comfortable age of 30, and see where I went wrong and right. Five years ago that would have been impossible, as I was not yet far enough removed from the

1960s, but that era, like it or not, is long gone.

The past and one's childhood always appear to be the good old days in retrospect, but I am not so far removed from that time that I cannot see it was not all peaches and cream. It wasn't. I always felt different from other people my age. I think that part of that feeling had to do with where I lived, and the nationalities and religions which made up my community. I grew up with a lot of Roman Catholics of Italian, Polish, and Irish background in Danbury, Connecticut. The town was basically a manufacturing town (Danbury had once been known as "The Hat City" because of the many hat factories). However, I had a problem right away in relating with other children my own age as my father was an Italian "non-practicing" Roman Catholic, and my mother was an Eastern European "non-practicing" Jew, and most of the kids I hung around with were parochial school students who went to church every week. I never knew what to consider myself. I became comfortable in not being able to identify with any particular group, but I still felt excluded from social groupings to an extent as I had no real bond, other than neighborhood proximity, to the people I played and attended school with. I had no use for religion or saying that I was Italian or Jewish. I still don't. I was so used to being whatever I perceived myself as being that when, at the age of 10, my parents decided that I and my 8 year old sister should have religious instruction, I rebelled against the idea. For about three or four years, I attended Jewish religious instruction. It wouldn't have mattered if the instruction had been catechism class, because I was already set and spoiled in my ways of not believing in organized religion. I knew my parents did not believe in it, so I saw through it myself.

I had a rather fatalistic view of life at an early age. It seemed that one was born, went to school, went into the army, got married and had a job, had kids, retired and then died, with no other activities happening in between. It wasn't until I started to have sexual stirrings at about age 12 or so, that I realized that there might be some pleasantries in later life, but I was pretty content in just being a kid with no responsibilities. I had a pessimistic view of being an adult. I can fully remember my parents struggling to get by and not being able to enjoy themselves. Although there were many families which were far worse off economically, those times shaped my thinking about growing up. Adulthood wasn't something I aspired to, it seemed so complex. A lot of kids would say that they couldn't wait until they were 21, so they could do what they pleased . . . not me, I dreaded it. It also seemed to be so stupid to expect that all male children should have to go into the army, navy, etc. I can remember seeing the futility of fighting wars and dying in them long before Vietnam was a household word.

What, you are probably asking, does this have to do with The Beatles? By early 1964, at age 13½, I was ripe for something to enter my life and give me hope. The Beatles did that. They were the closest thing to religion that I have ever experienced. They gave my life a purpose, and seemed to give me clues about life that until that time had not revealed themselves to me. Their utter contempt for the societal structure imposed upon us all gave me courage to question authority.

However, The Beatles were very private to me. I managed to still be a very shy, introspective, introverted individual who waddled inside of an overweight frame during high school. I had difficulty in making friends. It was strange to be able to get along well with others, and have friends at school, but not have those friends spill over into my after school life. I now realize that I deliberately isolated myself from others, I didn't want to get involved as it seemed that to do so would be giving up some personal freedom. However, I had The Beatles, who proved to be my best friends of all. Around 1966, during my sophomore year of high school, I began to come out of my shell a bit. I partied a little more, and began to attend certain social functions with people my own age, but I still did not have enough confidence or courage to act on my own, mostly becoming familiar with people that I met through my sister, who was only a year and a half younger than me.

As I stated in an earlier chapter, I wanted to be a Beatle, John Lennon in particular. All of the early Beatle songs about being in love affected me. I wanted to experience love. I also was becoming increasingly biologically ready for some sort of physical affection. We all tend to remember our "first love." Those first memories are endearing and can last a lifetime, but if there are also some bad times mixed in with the good, that seems to predominate. I had such a girlfriend. We "Went Together" or "Went Steady" for about a year and a half. Of course, at the time I imagined myself in love with her, not able to recognize that it was more of a sexual awakening than a love relationship. However, to my 15--16 year old mind, I was totally and faithfully in love forever. We would get married someday . . . etc. . . . the whole number. We finally split up during Memorial Day weekend of 1967, and I was profoundly saddened. Although I had seen it coming for awhile, it was still a shock. The aftershock played a role in my future relationships with women, making me more insecure and shy than when I was a pre-teen. However, the factors which were among the reasons we split up were a common phenomenon occurring at the time.

Kids who had been friends for years were suddenly dividing into distinct groups. By late 1966 and early 1967, The Beatles had become more than the loveable mop-topped quartet that played on "The Ed Sullivan Show" three years before. They had become spokesmen for an increasingly militant generation. I had been an early and outspoken critic of the war in Vietnam. Once I heard *We Can Work It Out* and its chorus telling us that life was too precious to waste by fighting all the time, I knew that war was wrong. However, some kids couldn't or wouldn't understand the new philosophical and musical directions The Beatles were taking, and this caused a rift between people who had been friends. It's a split which probably deserves the attention of a trained psychologist or sociologist to determine what type of people became "hippies" as opposed to those who remained "straight." My girlfriend was very "straight" and her friends were as well, whereas I, listening to The Beatles and becoming involved in denouncing the Vietnam War, went in the opposite direction. It was not the only reason for our breaking up, but it played more than a minor role. However, The Beatles saw me through this crisis in a way which neither they nor any other musical group has been able to do since.

We broke up on Memorial Day in 1967, but she still asked me to meet her at the War Memorial Building on Thursday night, June 1st. I suppose I still had some hopes of working it out when I agreed to meet her. Our secret meeting place was behind the War Memorial Building in Rogers Park, a large city park close to where I lived. So, there I went, after dinner, to meet her, wondering what I had to gain, as seeing her would probably make me wish that she could be mine again. I waited and waited until finally I realized that I had been taken . . . I had been stood up. I felt like a fool, and dejectedly began my trek through the park towards home. I became aware of how totally alone I was . . . and not just in the sense of no longer having my girlfriend, but literally . . . I was alone! There was not another human being in this vast city park except for me. There were no people playing tennis on the courts, no baseball games underway, and it was June 1st! I couldn't understand it; for some inexplicable reason, I was the only one there. I looked off in the distance and could see the traffic moving along on South Street, but I couldn't hear it. There were no racing motors, no honking horns. As I looked up towards the sky, a strange sensation went through my body. It was sunset and I had never seen a sunset like the one which was unfolding before my eyes. The clouds were assorted wisps and bunches of the ones we used to call "Johnny-Appleseed" clouds. All the clouds were gathered in the eastern sky and the sun was now a huge fireball sending its rays filtering throughout the entire area. The pure orange light shone on the clusters in a way which I never thought possible. I felt . . . no . . . I knew that this display was for me . . . someone . . . some higher power was trying to tell me something or preparing me for something about to happen. I knew what had just occurred would never happen again, and all of a sudden the traffic noises hit my ears and people began to arrive at the tennis courts and the ball fields. I felt that my whole life was about to change . . . radically change, and it would never be the same again.

And the next day was Friday, June 2, 1967. The date may not seem to be significant, unless you are a Beatle freak and know that on that date The Beatles' album, **Sgt. Pepper's Lonely Hearts Club Band**, was first available in record stores in the United States. I had been hearing the songs from that album on the radio for the past week and knew that the album was coming out. So, after school, I purchased **Sgt. Pepper**; it was the first stereo recording I had ever bought. I was anxious to hear the one song which the radio would not play. Apparently, the BBC had banned its playing on the grounds that the song contained references to the taking of drugs. It was *A Day In The Life*.

It was the last black band on the second side of the record. I placed the phonograph needle at the beginning of the track and sat with my right ear to the right speaker and the lyrics, printed on the back of the album jacket, directly in front of my eyes. The left speaker was not far from my left ear as the song began. The melody was unlike any heard previously. John Lennon's voice sifted slowly through piano and acoustic guitar, yet was sharp and crystal clear. It sounded as if Lennon was singing in a large empty room. The words were sad and spoke of death, but the second verse went by and told me that it would love to turn me on. Lennon's voice faded in and out of an echo, blending in with an orchestra that was getting louder and louder and more complex as it continued in an accelerated climb up the musical scale. There was a dull rising hum going on throughout it all, and I went deeper and deeper into a trance as the music quaked higher and higher in successive crescendos. I was totally immersed, when, without warning, the music went down the scale in one great swoop, bringing me completely down with it.

I felt as if I had just woken up from a deep sleep. As I was coming to, the lyrics of the song, now being sung by Paul McCartney, were saying just that. The libretto spoke of someone waking up and getting out of bed. This was followed by Lennon humming in a vowel sound to the music . . . again I was lulled into another trance, except this time my senses were sharp and more perceptive than before. The sound of Lennon's voice stayed with me, then all of a sudden I heard IT. IT reached a point . . . a crack in Lennon's voice before the next verse began. IT was not of this earth. IT was so indefinite and intangible. Then, suddenly, I realized that there were so many more things of importance in this world than this one sour juvenile romance of mine. All my feelings against war and those who perpetuated it coalesced into a groundswell of determination that I would not be a part of it, never!

I have often wondered what that "IT" was. I have concluded that it was some universal sound which summoned up feelings of brotherhood for my fellow man. Perhaps, IT was infinity. I'll never know, but that one moment on a late spring afternoon in 1967 changed me just as The Beatles' arrival in 1964 had done three years before.

Sgt. Pepper became a turning point for many people, if not for a whole generation. As they say, there are a million stories out there. What follows are a few which my correspondents sent to me, and which I'd like to share with you. Read on . . . .

66I was a miserable teenager. I had the usual amounts of growing pains which teenagers do, but I was awkward, shy, and lonely. As I got older, I seemed to be more and more confused about everything. By the time I was fifteen, I had a growing drug problem to go along with the growing pains.

The release from my sorry state of mind was The Beatles. When I look back on those years, the few moments of happiness came from listening to The Beatles. They were my dearest and best friends. Every word of every song is engraved in my memory. When they broke up I was, of course, crushed. Ten years later I still miss them even more than when they were together. Modern music certainly misses them. Nobody has come close to doing the things they did with their music. I'll probably yearn for them ten years from now.

I feel lucky to have been young then and to have them as the major good memories of my teenage years. As Paul said, I believe in yesterday.**99**

T.A.
Denver, Colorado

"When I look back at those years, the few moments of happiness came from listening to The Beatles. They were my dearest and best friends. Every word of every song is engraved in my memory."

> **"It would be inaccurate to say that they changed my life, yet it is completely accurate for me to say that during an unsettled time of turmoil and extreme turbulence in my life, a time of growth and change, The Beatles were among the more important factors in my life."**

❝ I'm not quite sure that it would be totally accurate to say that The Beatles radically changed my life in specific ways. If any musician has managed to have that kind of extreme, direct impact on my life, it would be Dylan. It is not my purpose to diminish the importance of The Beatles as entertainment value, intellectual value, and creative stimulus in my life. It would be inaccurate to say that they changed my life, yet it is completely accurate for me to say that during an unsettled time of turmoil and extreme turbulence in my life, a time of growth and change, The Beatles were among the more important factors in my life.

I don't think there were very many teenagers, addicted to Rock-and-Roll, during the sixties, who did not find The Beatles to be an extraordinarily exciting phenomenon. I remember clearly the electric excitement which accompanied the sudden meteoric rise of The Beatles and their following dominance of the world of Pop and Rock music. Most of my peers were overcome by Beatlemania and became undying, diehard fans. Initially, I found them exciting and interesting, but I could not really be described as a Beatlemaniac. The fanatical stage of my interest in The Beatles developed during the second phase of their success; their turn from the early good times Rock-and-Roll to more intellectually and philosophically interesting music, with its reflections of the youth culture, drug culture, Eastern religion, and all the good, bad, beautiful, and ugly of the intense youth consciousness of the time. *Nowhere Man* was one of the first Beatles' songs to begin to make a true believer out of me. That song can still be offered as one of the best examples of the way their music attracted me at that time. The discussions of alienation in the media and among intellectuals were merely a puzzling flow of apparently irrelevant words in the rural environment in which I grew up. For me the alienation was a real and painful element of my life, perhaps the dominant element at that time; alienated from society, role models, my peers, and my total environment, songs like *Nowhere Man* were sources of great solace for me. It was incredible to me that great artists could express the way I felt so brilliantly . . . that great artists could appear and tell the way I lived as it was. The alienation in my life continued to deepen, and in 1970, I found myself in a mental hospital, suffering from serious depression and paranoia. Although I have made three additional trips to that hospital since then, my feelings of alienation have tended to decrease and now, at age 30, after years of intellectual attacks, I have mounted on my problems with my life situation. I find myself somewhat more at peace with the way things have gone for me and are shaping for me. I still feel deeply. . . very deeply . . . about how sensitively and brilliantly The Beatles managed to express the way I felt during my late teenage years. Their music did not at all contribute to irrational tendencies in my thinking, which threatened my health at times, but rather, the truth . . . and it was literal truth . . . in their songs provided comfort for me when I needed it most and inspiration to keep on trucking.

The Beatles, with their complex, interesting, and pertinent lyrics gave me support for my early development as an intellectual. The conventional view of Rock-and-Roll during the sixties was that it was nothing more than the music of the party. Not that there was anything wrong with that, but the view was that Rock provided no dimensions beyond that. Dylan and The Beatles helped change that, consistently producing music of obvious intellectual merit and interest. Their records combined entertainment with intellectual potential. My early interest in creativity in writing was provided by The Beatles with John Lennon's obvious gifts as a creative artist providing inspiration for me. All aspects of their total style, and certainly their sound and lyrics, showed clear evidence of the creative spark, and gave much fuel for my own interest in this area. Songs like *Eleanor Rigby, Penny Lane, Here Comes The Sun, Paperback Writer,* and *Strawberry Fields Forever* were so creatively energetic that they contributed much toward the various early sources of inspiration for my own creative development. Their emphasis on love, their love songs, most certainly *Hey Jude,* have always been near my awareness in various romantic encounters. **99**

J.L.
Perryton, Texas

" When I think of how I could have turned out . . . Suzy Cheerleader . . . not knowing how to think . . . . My mother was an early rocker, one of our family heirlooms is a choker she wore when she saw Buddy Holly . . . she got me out of bed on a Sunday in February, 1964, when I was 7 years old . . . . She said just to watch the TV because it would be important, and there were The Beatles. The next thing I knew, I was saving up my allowances and playing their albums over and over again. To this day, I know almost every lyric by heart.

I was an only child; they were like 4 older brothers. I knew their middle names and their favorite color. I sent Paul birthday cakes and the rest birthday cards; they were part of my everyday life. As I got older, I followed whatever they did and studied Yoga for 6 weeks on my own when I was in 6th grade, thanks to George. John started me on writing poetry. My entire philosophy of life was conceived because of them, just by being different and new. They gave me the courage to be different and to think for myself. Later, they got stoned . . . I got stoned . . . then acid, then I mellowed out with them. I think we all grew up together; they're like family; I have every album ever made and I think of those albums as personal letters. In my worst times of depression or unhappiness, one album of theirs can give me enough strength to pull it together again.

What can I say? If I were ever to meet them, all I would want to say is "Thanks for helping me to make my life what it was and what it will be." They'll always be the best no matter who or what comes along. **"**

Peace,
C.M.
St. Paul, Minnesota

"I have been a Beatles' fan since 1964, the year I graduated from high school. Before The Beatles, I was a Rock-and-Roller with leanings toward juvenile delinquency, but also inclined to protest the bomb and the threat of war. I had heard of Beatlemania in January of 1964, but still hadn't heard any of their records. I never suspected that I would be a victim. It was blissful insanity. At last, my generation had a quartet of idols.

The night of my high school baccalaureate ceremony, a Sunday, I sat in front of our television wearing my cap and gown, but refusing to go until I saw the Fab Four on Ed Sullivan. My parents were ready to kill me, but I wept and wailed and I even threatened to not go at all. Shortly after that, my mother became a Beatles fan herself.

Rock concerts were rare in '64, but I made plans to see The Beatles in Kansas City, September 17, 1964 at Municipal Stadium. It cost $8.50 to sit on the field. . . considered by many of my friends to be sheer lunacy to pay such a price to see some crazy long hairs. I was in Row 13, middle section, and wow! . . . I'll never forget it.

While my contemporaries went off to college or an unheard of place called Vietnam or got married, I got heavy into the music scene. I was a groupie, then a hippie, always into new experiences. My friends were musicians, and we were really devoted to knowing what our idols, like The Beatles, were up to.

Before The Beatles, I figured that I would get out of high school, go to college (or hopefully get married), and settle down. Dull! Today, at age 33, I have never been married. I've had numerous jobs, but have had some success as I own a home. The inside of my house is dominated by antiques, and a very large record collection, a smell of incense, and tapestries on the walls. I don't look my age, but I do act it. I have friends of all ages, but enjoy living alone with my dog and eleven cats. The important thing is I'm happy (a little weird by most peoples' standards), very happy.

The Beatles were a big turning point in my life. God only knows what would have happened to me if I'd never heard *I Want To Hold Your Hand* or *She Loves You* or if I had never felt their magic and love. I have boxes of Beatles paraphernalia and at one time, all of their 45's and albums."

K.K.
Marysville, Kansas

"... I made plans to see The Beatles in Kansas City, September 17, 1964 at Municipal Stadium. It cost $8.50 to sit on the field ... considered by many of my friends to be sheer lunacy to pay such a price to see some crazy long hairs. I was in Row 13, middle section, and wow! ... I'll never forget it."

65

66 22 February, 1975. I am in Grants Super Discount Department Store, (now defunct for obvious reasons) in the record section, looking through the albums. Inexplicably, my hand is drawn to the section labeled Beatles; perhaps because of its proximity to Cassidy, David, perhaps the name rang a little bell in my troubled, adolescent mind, perhaps it could have been fate. Who knows. I could have been drawn to the Bee Gees (God forbid). It only matters that I bought **Sgt. Pepper's Lonely Hearts Club Band**, heavily subsidized by my grandmother. (Sure, she's hip.)

I take it home and tear open the cellophane with my pudgy fingers, and remove the sleeve. The little cut-out sheet falls out. I pick it up, confused . . . this is not kosher. The Partridge Family never enclosed this sort of thing. I set it aside for further inspection and remove the clean, scratch-free disc, (there is an apple on the label!) and place it on my turntable, turn on my compact stereo, and panting slightly, devote the whole of my concentration to my modest speakers. The sounds that emerge are foreign and strange. At first I am embarrassed. You jerk, I chastise myself, you have put it on the wrong speed! Maybe you have to play hip records at a faster speed?

You can see my confusion. These guys were different, much different than anything I had ever seen or heard since I sprang from the womb. After an initial period of adjustment, I found that I liked them. It seemed to me that The Beatles created their own world through absurd images and ideas, and it was one to which I could relate . . . fanatically . . . . My fanaticism further increased as I realized that none of my classmates were extremely fond of The Beatles. The girls all liked the Carpenters. The guys all liked Led Zeppelin. And me? Well, I liked The Beatles. I became known as "The Girl Who Likes The Beatles." People would point at my Beatles T-shirt, stare at my "I LOVE THE BEATLES" button, and whisper, "There is the girl who likes The Beatles . . . heretic!"

Weaker souls would have bowed under to this peer pressure, and run right out to get the latest fab poster of Karen and Richard. Not me. Now, this is not to imply that I am particularly strong, in fact, I may be the only person in my graduating class who can boast a record of .0010 of a second in the flexed arm hang. Nevertheless, I revelled in my fellow students' view of me as a creature strange and different. It certainly helped the formation of my identity. I knew that I wasn't like the majority of my fellow students, and this started my self-evaluation process much earlier. If I wasn't like them, who was I like?

My floundering attempts at finding the answer to this perplexing little mother of a question, were influenced by my sixties fetish. First there were my mini-skirts when everyone else's were modestly below the knee. In addition there were my purples, pinks, psychedelic patterns, and love beads. Next there were the hippies. I had a mad, overwhelming desire to be a hippie. I read exhaustively of hippie literature, researched communes, and decided that this was definitely the life for me. I was laid back and mellow . . . and I flashed peace signs a lot. All things must pass, and eventually I realized that I could get the hots for guys not wearing dirty, patched jeans, long,

"... I bought Sgt. Pepper's Lonely Hearts Club Band, heavily subsidized by my grandmother. (Sure, she's hip.) ... I take it home and tear open the cellophane with my pudgy fingers, and remove the sleeve. The little cut-out sheet falls out. I pick it up, confused ... this is not kosher. The Partridge Family never enclosed this sort of thing."

dirty ponytails, and honest scruffy beards. I cleaned myself up, became preppier, and laid off the peace signs. All this was just casting about for the answer, varying my appearance, instead of my actual character.

Although the changes were not as obvious, The Beatles affected my character. Primarily, they broadened my musical world beyond *Tiger Beat* magazine. Through them, I discovered an abiding interest and love of art and avant garde Rock, especially Roxy Music and Eno. They also gave me strict standards, ones that turn me away from AM radio because I consistently find something lacking. Sure, modern groups may have the beat or the lyrics or the personality, but do they have all three? I hate to be a snob, but The Beatles . . . I am more aware of trends too, and was listening to New Wave music several years before everyone else. In fact, I find New Wave artists such as Nick Lowe, Elvis Costello, and Ian Drury more like The Beatles in their ability to synthesize beat lyrics, and personality, than say, the Bee Gees.

Another thing that developed directly due to my interest in The Beatles was my sense of humor. Perhaps I flatter myself, but I consider myself to have a sense of humor. I have no illusions, all credit for this is due to The Beatles. Although the Partridge Family undeniably had a certain gentle, self-deprecating humor, The Beatles were funny. After a brief and tentative stab at Henny Youngmanesque humor, I discovered my natural style. The Beatles showed me zaniness, and how much irreverence can be. Most important of all, The Beatles brought out my skill as a writer.

My writing skills have their roots in a long, involved almost "War and Peace" style story which my sister and I made up about The Beatles. We would add installments each night before we went to sleep; I would have the roles of all The Beatles, their wives, and children, while my sister was Paul's mother. This went on for months when we finally tired of it. I then got the idea of writing a story. I had a dream. The story would be about a musical group who were trying to make it big, and who were worried because they seemed so much like The Beatles. I started writing and almost five years later, I am still writing it. And I love it. I love writing and I know that all I want to do is write. My life has purposes. And in a very real way this has influenced my life. I can enjoy myself a lot more in college, knowing why I am there, what I am setting bravely off to accomplish, and where I want my life to go. I really think I'm much happier than my Mechanical Engineer friends, who seem to have no outlet for their creativity.

I think that The Beatles acted as a catalyst for me. They started my whole process of self-discovery, weeding out and deciding what I wanted to do. Although they still influence me in their modest way (whenever I listen to a Beatles' album everything I've ever thought or felt about them is reaffirmed) I think their job is done. They helped me to grow up, to "find my space," to learn how to go with the flow. **"**

K.E.
Durham, New Hampshire

> "I think that The Beatles acted as a catalyst for me. They started my whole process of self-discovery, weeding out and deciding what I wanted to do. Although they still influence me in their modest way (whenever I listen to a Beatles' album everything I've ever thought or felt about them is reaffirmed) I think their job is done. They helped me to grow up, and to 'find my space,' to learn how to go with the flow."

"I grew up in Okmulgee, Oklahoma. Okmulgee is a city with 17,000 people and I think that I was the only person in my hometown who was moved, even in the slightest way, by The Beatles. My best friend told me that he didn't like them, and I thought he was insane. I had a particular attraction to John Lennon. I think the first thing which drew my attention to him was that his name contained the same amount of letters as mine. There were times when I would imitate him, and for a few minutes, I would become John Lennon while playing my make-believe guitar, singing *I Should Have Known Better.*

In school, I can remember no talk about The Beatles or their albums. The only things which The Beatles brought to my school were strict dress codes, particularly in hair styles. I never did pay any attention to the dress code and wore my hair as long as I could, until my Dad said it had to go. In fact, he made me go back to the barber shop because he didn't like the way the barber cut it. To this day, Dad teases me about my hair and beard, but now he can't do anything about it. I don't remember anyone, especially girls, talking about who their favorite Beatle or song was. I think the whole Beatle thing passed by everyone, but me. The Beatles were always on my mind. I would write "The Beatles" all over my school notebook, and I always bought their new records when I could scrape up enough money.

I listened and learned from everything they did, even though I had trouble with some of the things done, such as John's escapades with Yoko in the late Sixties, but I felt everything they did was important, and was for a good reason, or they would not do it. The Beatles DIDN'T MAKE MISTAKES as far as I was concerned. I would try to talk to my classmates about them, but would get a "what-is-he-talking-about" look. I HAD to be the only local fan of The Beatles in Okmulgee, Oklahoma. The local radio station played their songs, but I think they stopped playing them during the John Lennon–Jesus Christ hoopla. There wasn't a big Beatle records burning or "Stamp Out The Beatles" protest, which surprises me now that I think of it. Could it be that no one knew about it except me?

I was 15 years old when The Beatles broke up and I felt a deep personal loss. I felt that the whole point of buying albums was useless. The teachers of millions of young people had decided to close down the school before everyone was ready for graduation. And what was worse was that none of my friends seemed to be too upset about it. One friend was hoping for some more John Lennon–George Harrison songs. He got this idea when John and

"I was 15 years old when The Beatles broke up and I felt a deep personal loss. I felt that the whole point of buying albums was useless. The teachers of millions of young people had decided to close down the school before everyone was ready for graduation."

68

George wrote a song, *Cry For A Shadow*, in their early years. He thought that since there was one Lennon--Harrison song, then why shouldn't there be more now? And Klaus Voorman could play bass. Voorman on bass? That seemed obscene to me. No one could replace any member of The Beatles. I still have hopes that they might get together some day and play again, but I doubt that will ever happen. Their lives are much too complicated now. Can you imagine the arrangements that would have to be made for a Beatles re-union? It would be crazy.

I am so glad that they were around while I was growing up. I place them right along side my parents when it comes to my up-bringing. The Beatles, Mom, and Dad were and are very important people in my life. I hope to meet John Lennon someday, and tell him just how important he has been to my life. The Beatles are a part of my family and I will always love them. Honesty is what The Beatles taught. **"**

D.L.
Tulsa, Oklahoma

"I am so glad that they were around while I was growing up. I place them right along side my parents when it comes to my up-bringing. The Beatles, Mom, and Dad were and are very important people in my life . . . . The Beatles are a part of my family and I will always love them."

"Honesty is what The Beatles taught."

"They were definitely a factor in the development of my system of values. Their songs were more than just melodies or lyrics, they were messages that ran deeper, and carried more meaning than I was aware of . . . I think that the main thing I learned from The Beatles effect on me was to love myself."

"I am 26 years old, a college dropout, married, no kids, anti-disco, and 70's survivor. I have traveled the United States extensively, and am currently the vice president and marketing director of an international marketing corporation, which I also happen to be a co-founder of. I'm non-political, like money, but drive a beat up 1971 VW and drink only domestic bottled H2O. I am a former drug-dependent, an affliction I picked up in the mid 70s, and have been chemically free for over 3 years. I don't smoke and belong to a local sports and health club where I work out 3 times weekly. I practice Yoga (Hatha) to release business tensions. I could label myself as being diverse, but the fact of the matter is that years of drug related confusion caused me to seek many outside cures, when in reality, all answers I found were from within.

The Beatles had an effect on me right from the start, 5th grade, I believe. I loved them, my parents hated them . . . they were a catalyst for a rebellious nature which was bottled up inside of me. They gave me my first cause . . . to let my hair grow, which is something I fought for years. They set off internal reactions which made me want to question authority and to defy it, if I didn't agree. They taught me that love was more than an act, but was a trust spawned from a common ground. They were spiritual spacemen, who dared to seek something higher than the drug/sex/money myth of happiness. They were definitely a factor in the development of my system of values. Their songs were more than just melodies or lyrics, they were messages that ran deeper, and carried more meaning than I was aware of . . . I think that the main thing I learned from The Beatles effect on me was to love myself. It is evident to me that as individuals, they did love and believe in themselves, simply by the fact that they are still alive today! **"**

S.M.
Minneapolis, Minnesota

66 The Beatles brought happiness into my life on February 26, 1977, when I married my wife after meeting her through correspondence from a Beatle fan club magazine.

We first met on October 1, 1976 and married four months later. We had a baby girl one year later on February 7, 1978. She is 18 months old now and as healthy as ever. I'm from Nutley, New Jersey and my wife was born in Montreal, Quebec. We are now living in Montreal and I'm working, and we are a very happy family.

To this day we are still Beatle fans. I receive a monthly book from England and I subscribe to *Strawberry Fields Forever* magazine. On occasion I'll buy a few records and other items I might like to have.

We thank John, Paul, George, and Ringo for our happiness in life; without them we would never have met. 99

N. & G.A.
Montreal, Quebec, Canada

**“ I’m 21 and that would make me 6 when The Beatles started their height of popularity. I have an older brother, four years older, who raised me on The Beatles. Since a guy raised me on them, I never got the orgasmic effect that The Beatles had on their other female admirers. Perhaps age 6 was too young, and by the time I cared what a man was, The Beatles no longer had screaming fans. The point is, I was raised on their music (my brother is a musician) and their individual lives (I’m a people fanatic).

I was very aware of the impact The Beatles had on society even though I was quite young. Who could ignore it though? Beatle boots, hair styles, comics, clothes, albums, etc.; at first I liked The Beatles because, like religion, you’re exposed to it and that’s the way it is. Eventually you decide for yourself whether you want it or not. I chose to want it.

There are several big events in my life which all had something to do with The Beatles and have made them the only group I will defend to the end. Some of these events are meaningless to others, but I look back at them as some of the only things that I remember at that certain time period:

Chicago 1964 — My mother, brother, and I drive by McCormick Place seeing “The Beatles” written on the marquee. I enthusiastically state that I want to see them. My brother immediately replies, “That would be supid, you wouldn’t hear a thing with all those screaming girls. Besides, you’re too young.” I didn’t think I was too young.

Chicago 1966 — Mom told my brother that he had better not destroy his Beatle albums during the “more popular than Jesus” crisis because “ . . . those albums will be valuable one day.”

Europe and Chicago 1967 — Our tour guide was a Dutchman, who sat me on his knee in the bus, on the front seat, and sang *When I’m 64* to me. When I hit the states, I immediately bought the album.

My brother calls me into his room to point out on the song, *Sgt. Pepper*, that while McCartney is shouting “1,2,3,4,” Lennon weirdly whines “5” during Paul’s “4.” Thus begins my exploration into all the things that made The Beatles so refreshingly different from everyone else.

Pennsylvania 1968 — I was the only girl my age who just had to see the “Help” reruns on TV. The only girl who could sing all the songs and quote the funny lines and laugh prematurely before every funny scene. The only kid who wanted a sunken bed like John Lennon’s. The only girl my age who thought the media competition between The Beatles and The Dave Clark 5 (and at that time The Monkees) was so ridiculous because there was no comparison. Couldn’t everyone see that?

Findley Lake, NY, 1975 — Senior year of high school. For chorus I got to arrange a song for us to perform. I chose *When I’m 64*. I wrote on The Beatles for my final in music appreciation class. I didn’t turn on the teacher to The Beatles, but I got an “A.” Perhaps I really failed. I was in a talent/ beauty contest. I arranged a medley of songs on piano, sang *Yesterday* and recited *In My Life* (my favorite song). The judges didn’t place me, but after I performed my talent to the audiences, a reporter from Erie, covering the contest, unknowingly told my boyfriend that I was the sure winner; the

“. . . at first I liked The Beatles because, like religion, you’re exposed to it and that’s the way it is. Eventually you decide for yourself whether you want it or not. I chose to want it.”

town thought the same. Perhaps, I really did win?

Tiffin Ohio--Heidelberg College, 1975 — My freshman year I got a particular boyfriend initially because he was so impressed a "girl" was such a devoted and knowledgeable fan of The Beatles.

Heidelberg College, 1977 — I was on the student activities board, in charge of concert and dance. I sponsored a Beatles Week, incorporating a lecture, dance, trivia contest, movies, and a name that tune. I did all the research.

College, 1978 — A male friend of mine sent me a rose because "I heard of a Beatles Weekend on the radio and immediately thought of you."

One last embarrassing note. In 1976 I pledged a little sister sorority to a fraternity in college. Every night of pledging activities, I kept a newspaper clipping of The Beatles pictured in front of a banner which said, "Help!" I kept the clipping in my bra for safekeeping. Because of this, my sorority nickname was "Stuffer."

The Beatles music is eternal and uncomparable (yes, even the Knack, who are undeservedly packaged as a reincarnation of The Beatles, will never get my vote). Their lives are so interesting and their personalities so individualistic and challenging (even though Ringo does bore me at times). I follow their solo careers, although I only buy McCartney albums. His albums bore me at times because most of his lyrics are meaningless and incohesive, but to me it is better than Krishna, Yoko, and Richard Perry produced pop songs with a singer who should remain an actor, or is it the other way around?

My musical training keeps my ear to the record player. I'm a DJ and that keeps me informed. 100% of The Beatlefans are genius just like the group. Even if Arthur Fiedler were still living, he would not be playing classical Knack. **"**

L.O.
Clymer, New York

73

"I was born in August of 1956. I almost died within 2 hours; I was rushed back for bronchial pneumonia, turning blue.

At 8½ years of age in 1964 meant dolls dresses for me. It was a time in my life that I was aware of things which some 8 year olds weren't. I was a prodigy in art. Being an artist, I was sensitive. I spent most of my time in hospitals because of childhood sicknesses. I watched TV a lot and realized that all those dumb ads on the screen were nothing. I was in a clinic when I saw The Beatles on the news. I was impressed, so I asked a nurse who they were. She simply replied, "The Beatles." It sounded so nice and sincere. "But are they girls?" I said pointing to the TV. "Oh no, they're lads, boys you know, can't you tell?" I was embarrassed at first, but I learned a lot about them from that nurse. I have never told my Dad and Mom this, but I was told at the time that " . . . the young boys with long hair were making parents mad because they steal their daughters' hearts . . . . "

I couldn't say that they stole my heart, but they made me feel happy. I almost saw The Ed Sullivan show in February, 1964, but I got a nose hemorrage on that day and ended back in the hospital. I stayed for two years. I missed the Shea Stadium concerts too. I guess I lost track in those two years. I still got bits of Beatle things and gossip from those who were faithful and believed these lads had what people really wanted. I started drawing pictures of them in my clinic bed. I've lost them since. I still have some drawings of them. I struggled to keep my faith in these guys and there were those who tried to oppress me and wipe out my beliefs. My father was one who didn't have faith in me or in anybody's feelings, but his own. This caused me a lot of pain in my life.

I've got a small collection of Beatle things I've been holding onto. I stole Beatle artifacts from local libraries, newsstands, etc. trying to catch up with my Beatle history. I even tried writing to them care of The Beatles Fan Club. No reply. In school, I couldn't think straight, I couldn't relate too often to people, except for one close friend, who was a faithkeeper too, but only with Tom Jones. Even when I ran away from home in 1966, I went to a woman's house and she had Beatle albums and a daughter who loved them. We exchanged ideas and feelings. I was eventually found, but was enlightened with new feelings that The Beatles were my own, and no one could change my mind, not even my Dad.

I kept running away because my Dad ripped up my Beatle albums and other prized Beatle items . . . even drawings I did. This kept up for a long time until he gave up and I won to a point that now I have my own mini museum. I have created 3 scrap books in The Beatles honor. In the front window of my museum are two Beatle cartoons.

I still get looks when I tell people that I love The Beatles. They've helped me realize that if the world is against you, you must prove the world wrong, and by them doing so in songs, I am able to do it in art.**"**

P.P.
New York, New York

❝ The Beatles are greatly revered by me. I was born in February of 1958. When The Beatles came to America, my parents bought a Beatles album, and I loved them.

My brother and I were pantomimists to their songs for my parents. I remember that I wore a suit and brought a guitar to kindergarten and pantomimed to two songs, *I Want To Hold Your Hand* was one of them. The class loved me for it, and they clapped (cheered) like I was really one of The Beatles.

I listened to the album all the time. I had a sack full of bubblegum cards and would look at them while listening to their music. My granddaddy (I called him "Pa Pa") was a barber. He didn't like them or their long hair. He called me a Beatle for wearing "bangs" cut straight across the top of my eyebrows.

I love them now even more so. They were unique, sincere, fun-loving, friendly, and a sharply dressed group. I started guitar lessons and bought two guitars because of them. They have so many songs of joy, sorrow, love and the other emotions of life. They were never too uppity to feel sadness in their songs once in awhile. I get emotional with their earlier songs. I once psyched myself up for a softball game by listening to their music. It cleared my mind and helped me concentrate.

I wish they hadn't got into trouble by saying they were more popular than Jesus Christ . . . I think that's what messed them up. But as for me, here I sit in Schofield Barracks, in the service, stationed in Hawaii. I am still a Beatle fan. I'll stand up for them. I wish they would get back together. **❞**

K.N.
Americus, Georgia

> **"I remember that I wore a suit and brought a guitar to kindergarten and pantomimed to two songs, *I Want To Hold Your Hand* was one of them. The class loved me for it, and they clapped (cheered) like I was really one of The Beatles."**

> **"Their songs always made me happy. It's funny, but you never forget the words . . . . It seemed like their songs were a message to everyone. They were far above the norm and if they had stayed together, they would have taken us far into distant lands."**

❝ I was a little girl when The Beatles were really popular. I'm 24 now, but I saw them here, in Cleveland, when I was 7 years old. Their songs always made me happy. It's funny, but you never forget the words. As for how they changed my life . . . I think that if it wasn't for them, I wouldn't be as interested in music as much as I am. The Beatles were very versatile and I know they showed me to be that way. It seemed like their songs were a message to everyone. They were far above the norm and if they had stayed together, they would have taken us far into distant lands. Maybe I am romanticizing, but for all my life, I will love them and hope my future children do also.

I did some acid once, and was getting pretty freaked out until my girlfriend put on **Rubber Soul** and it really calmed me down. I had been getting a bit hysterical. I was then able to expand my mind and just groove, but you don't need drugs to enjoy The Beatles, they're a natural high! **❞**

D.G.
Cleveland, Ohio

"I am a fairly good artist. To me, one of the biggest ego boosters was when I saw John Lennon in Philadelphia in 1975, when I was 18 years old. I gave him some hand-painted T-shirts and my hero said he liked them. I had handed them to him in a box and he said, "Is it illegal?" I (very paranoid) cut him off and said, "Yes, but did you like them?" and he said, "Of course I liked them . . . of course I liked the T-shirts."

The influences The Beatles had on me were from each one individually. I was a fanatic when I was a teenager and collected over 8,000 bubblegum cards, dolls, records, and posters (I once had 50 posters on my walls and ceiling). I was pretty much a loner as I grew up. Their music was inspiring and uplifting. John Lennon helped me through a tremendous amount of anxiety. I went through terrible pain one year in my life, e.g., deaths in my family, nearly getting killed in a car accident, losing my job; you name it . . . it was my year for growing pains. I would play his "scream" records, *Cold Turkey, Instant Karma*, and *Mother* . . . they served the purpose of screaming for me.

I learned the most important lesson in my life through George. I had been studying different religions, and I started studying his Krsna religion. I did huge paintings (on large 6 foot pieces of satin) just to send to him as presents. He never acknowledged them of course, but the religion itself had me really led astray and a bit brainwashed and confused. He is *Not Guilty*. Anyway, it helped me two ways . . . I learned how powerful a mind is (John Lennon supposedly said once that talent is just knowing you can do something) and that I could achieve as near perfection in my artwork as I could by simply accepting nothing else. George Harrison helped me, unknowingly, to get deeper into my own religion. Music which says something and makes you think and take a look at your own values is my favorite kind of music. Also, Beatle music which is light can keep you positive and light as well.

When I was 19 my father died. We hadn't been getting along well for awhile, until the last year of his life. When I was young and played my Beatle music for hours or watched Beatle movies over and over, my father could not understand it at all. He stormed at my door one night, thinking that I must be doing something . . . on drugs . . . to be locked up in my room for hours. We had not been getting along well and one day I put on John Lennon's *The Luck Of The Irish*. Well, rather than a will-you-turn-down-that-noise, he was really deeply moved by it. He was shaving and stopped in the middle of the shave, his eyes slightly teared, shaking his head . . . "What a shame . . . what a shame" and talking to me about it. This memory is important to me . . . we talked and there was no generation gap, we were on the same frequency. **"**

M.W.
Edgewater Park, New Jersey

"The Beatles brought us so much; they got our minds working to understand things like the evils of war and big business, and the worse of them all . . . government."

❝The Beatles had the biggest influence of anything in my life, and the effect still maintains its presence. I was seven years old when I first heard The Beatles, and it had an effect on me that I still don't understand.

The tremendous influence of The Beatles has greatly confused my psyche. I have no idea what my personality is since my old one has been lost for awhile. At this moment in time, I am trying to decide which personality I wish to portray. My choices are, being the foolish joker like Ringo, quiet and godly like George, cute and thriving on love like Paul or mysterious and rebellious like John. And like Lennon, I am not understood by my peers. Not being sure of which personality to portray, I realize that The Beatles still have a major influence over my mind and senses. And there is nothing I can do to stop it . . . not that I necessarily want to stop it.

The Beatles brought us so much; they got our minds working to understand things like the evils of war and big business, and the worse of them all . . . government. The Beatles are truly the Princes of Rock and Roll, the most influential people the world has ever known. They taught us and they led us. We followed them with meaning and love. They told us that *All You Need Is Love*, and when it was over and we accomplished most of what we tried to do, they told us to *Let It Be*. But the end will never really come because The Beatles were like a dream. And as long as we still dream we're waiting for them to be in our dreams tonight.

I see a lot of bumper stickers and T-shirts with the saying, "On the eighth day God created ———" (whatever Rock group someone wants to add in). What is funny to me is that those kids don't realize that after the eighth day, God didn't realize he created so many groups, so on the ninth day he gave them a leader, and created The Beatles.❞

R.S.
Smithtown, New York

❝I was born in 1955 and was given the **Meet The Beatles** album when I was eight or nine years old. From then until 1969–1970 I bought each of their albums (or received them as gifts) as they were released in the U.S.A. I never saw them live, nor did I belong to any fan clubs. I didn't really want to get into their personal lives; their music told me everything I wanted to know about them.

I have no way of measuring their influence on my life because of the time span and considering how old I was when I started listening to them. All I know is that their music was like a key which fit into my head. I would listen to their music and nothing else mattered. I guess I could say if there hadn't been any Beatles, my life would have been different. There was never and never will be a group like The Beatles again. When things broke up in 1969–1970, well I felt that it was just time for a change for them. I was about 15 and was going through changes too. I wasn't outraged or even sad . . . it was just time.

I have followed each of them as individuals. With the four of them, they can do no wrong musically. I have all of Paul McCartney's albums. I guess he was easier to identify with than George Harrison. Harrison, the mystic, fit in well with my dabblings in eastern religions. John Lennon sparked my political awareness, and Ringo . . . he's just Ringo.

The music of The Beatles will never be outdated for me. I've been listening to them for 17 years and treasure all my old and battered albums. The feelings I get from each of their albums tells me the story of how I was feeling and what was happening during that time. It's like slipping into the past and being in a time capsule of my life. Each album and song has personal meanings for me and I will always love their music. When someone asks me who my favorite group is . . . I still say The Beatles (followed by Jethro Tull and Steely Dan), and I must say the song that is my all time favorite and conveys a lot of 60's feeling is *Hey Jude*.

The only regret I have about The Beatles is that they were so different, so good, that now every group that comes along is compared to them. That makes me mad as hell . . . it's actually an insult. There will never be anyone who can come close to being what they were, at that time in history.

I don't see them getting back together. The time has past, they have all changed, they have their own lives, and all I can say is that what John, Paul, George, and Ringo gave to the world is good enough for me, I'M SATISFIED!**❞**

V.S.
Fort Lauderdale, Florida

> "All I know is that their music was like a key which fit into my head. I would listen to their music and nothing else mattered . . . . The feelings I get from each of their albums tells me the story of how I was feeling and what was happening during that time. It's like slipping into the past and being in a time capsule of my life."

I believe in extrasensory perception. I also believe that my skills are not very well developed in ESP. The Beatles brought out what little ability I have. I can't readily identify the suit and number of a card when someone holds it backside forward in front of my eyes, nor can I perform astral projection (supposedly my sister can, but that's another story), but The Beatles bestowed upon me one power, and that was to be able to know when I was about to hear one of their songs on the radio before it was even announced or had started to play. Now this may seem not to be a very remarkable feat. Obviously, at the height of Beatlemania, anybody's guess that within the next few minutes their local Top Forty station was going to play a Beatle cut was a pretty good bet. However, what I'm talking about is the ability to wake up one morning and have a feeling in one's bones that you would hear a brand new Beatle song played on the radio that day.

This happened to me many times. Admittedly, a few of those times, I had been aware that a new Beatles single was imminent, but the vast majority of those instances were when I just had a feeling that I would hear a new song by them without any prior knowledge that The Beatles were about to release a new record. It is a bit scary to think about it today, but I accepted it all as part of The Beatles magic back then. I would just wake up one morning, on a Saturday or during summer vacation, and just know that when I turned on the WMCA Good Guys or WABC, I would hear a new Beatle song within minutes. It was uncanny, but all of a sudden there it was. "For the first time . . . a WMCA exclusive . . . The Beatles' *Eight Days A Week*" or *Day Tripper*, or *Hello Goodbye*, etc.

The power waned when The Beatles were no more. I guess that was appropriate. If the power was only good for predicting Beatles' songs and The Beatles were no more . . . what was the point?

To many, The Beatles transcended music . . . they were more than just a Rock-and-Roll band. In the chapters to come there will be letters from those who are still fanatics and those who feel that The Beatles changed our culture for the better and forever more.

5

The Biggest
Beatle Fan Of All Time

The bulk of the letters sent to me did not fall into any one category. The next three chapters contain correspondence which are classified, but actually many could have been included in categories previously explored, as well as overlapping within the confines of the next three groupings. All tell why the writers feel that The Beatles are important.

I always thought that I had to be the biggest Beatle fan of all time. I was amazed to find out that many of the people who wrote in also considered themselves to be the greatest Beatlemaniacs of all time. Many times, the opening lines of a letter would read . . . "I saw your ad, and just had to write because I have got to be the biggest Beatle fan of all time. . ." Obviously, not everyone could be the biggest fan. This had quite an effect on me and altered my way of thinking to an extent. If I am not the most fanatical Beatle fan of all time, and all these other people are claiming the throne, how does one determine the extent of Beatlemania?

I finally concluded that there is no accurate way to measure this phenomenon. Everyone was justified in feeling that they had to be "the biggest" fan. However, I was wrong to assume that just because The Beatles may have affected someone, but not the same exact way they affected me, that my experience was somehow superior to others. The fact that

The Beatles touched so many different individuals resulted in the same number of different effects, and each are equally valid. Each experience is so personal, that naturally one assumes that they are unique. Actually, it is this similarity that binds Beatle fans together. Each feels independent, but all feel things that need no explanation among them.

For many Beatlemaniacs, collecting memorabilia and other nostalgic artifacts is their main objective. I have never been able to get excited about a swatch of bedsheet from The Plaza Hotel or a leaf that fell from a tree and happened to graze Ringo Starr's shoulder as he walked down Abbey Road . . . but to many this is their life's pursuit. People pay enormously ridiculous sums of money for these things, but obviously they wouldn't do it unless they felt a need for it. I can understand the need. The need is to feel closer to the individual Beatles . . . to feel as if one has touched something that was part of The Beatles' lives.

Some fans do this by getting very involved in the domestic lives of The Beatles. They know all the favorite colors, wives' names, children's names, and each family member's birthday. Many make gifts and mail them on special occasions. I don't even know how many children Paul McCartney has, I can't remember what George Harrison's son's name is, and whether or not Ringo and Maureen Starr are finally divorced. The only person's life that I know that well is John Lennon's, but even so, domestic data on the individual Beatles and their families does not arouse my curiosity.

My fanaticism consists of collecting records. That has always seemed to be the one way to be the closest to The Beatles. Although they transcended the role of being musicians, music is what made them. What better way to feel The Beatles and try to understand what they were all about than to collect their records?

When The Beatles split in April of 1970, it took a while for me to realize that there would no longer be any more Beatle albums. It wasn't that I was extremely slow or stupid, it just took a while for the idea, an unpalatable one, to sink in my brain. Once the realization held firm, I became quite despondent. Heartbroken is a better description. What was I to do? I no longer had my Beatles. I went through a very intense period, during the summer of 1970, searching for Rock-and-Roll's roots. I began buying old Chuck Berry and Little Richard records, trying to discover the flame which ignited The Beatles into song. My successful search, via Rock's early masters, led me back to my frustration of no longer having any new Beatles' records. If only, I thought, there was some new material by them, never before released . . . or even better . . . live concerts of The Beatles! There had never been a live recording of them released (up to then), and I yearned to hear how they had sounded in person. My memories of seeing them twice at Shea Stadium could not sustain my desires. This pursuit of new material by The Beatles led me into my particular form of Beatlemania . . . collecting bootleg recordings.

Bootleg records are records which are made without authorization from the artists and the artist's representative. The artist receives no royalties. Much of this material, particularly by The Beatles, is culled from live concerts, radio concerts, and studio outtakes never released by the artist. (The legalities and illegalities of such recordings by The Beatles are discussed at length in the book *You Can't Do That*, by Charles Reinhart.) The majority of bootleg recordings are usually of poor sound quality, as much of the material, never intended for commercial release, was recorded under less than outstanding circumstances. However, to a fanatic and afficianado of The Beatles, these recordings are like Heaven, regardless of the sound . . . because it is THEM, in a rough state, still making enjoyable music. So, I don't care if my very first bootleg of The Beatles at The Hollywood Bowl sounds as if it were recorded inside a tin can, or that the concert at The Star Club in Hamburg was recorded using a hand-held microphone on an ancient reel-to-reel tape recorder . . . I still enjoy listening! The gems among the lemons, such as **The Beatles At Budakon, Live In Houston**, and **Pop Goes The Beatles**, their weekly show on the BBC, make it all worthwhile.

Recently, my concentrations have been drawn to The Beatles' various studio albums as they were released in their native England. The English versions are not only far superior due to a finer quality of polyvinyl used, but also because such albums as **Help, Rubber Soul**, and **Revolver** consist of different songs than their American counterparts. Albums from Japan are even better than the English recordings, as both the craftsmanship and polyvinyl used is very high in quality.

That part of being a Beatlemaniac, my penchant for collecting bootleg recordings, is but one part of being a fanatic . . . as the following letters reveal . . . .

"I have been a fan since 1963 and own every recording made by The Beatles as a group or as individuals. I recently spent $100.00 for the rare album, **The Beatles vs. The Four Seasons** (even though I already have all the songs on several different albums and singles), $50.00 for a Capitol EP, and $20.00 for the picture cover to *Love Me Do*.

My entire life has been centered around them. I have lived, ate, and slept Beatles for 16 years . . . and I still never tire of hearing *I Want To Hold Your Hand* or *She Loves You*. I have Beatle dolls, plastic models, neon signs, 1-inch by 1-inch pieces of bedsheets which they slept on, lunchboxes, games, puzzles, wigs, etc. I pride myself on having almost every item available, missing only several singles and albums and memorabilia, all of which I am still searching for today. As you can see, I'm hooked.

The amazing thing is that not everyone is like me. I do not know one person who shares this interest as me, not even to half the degree. I know lots of people who think The Beatles were good, but who also think they're gone, it's over and disco is here to stay. They think that I'm nuts to be so nuts. My wife is one of these people. She loves to listen to the records, but is amazed by the loyalty and money and time which I spend to keep the myth going. I had reached the point, several years ago, where I thought that I might be the only one left . . . that all the 1964 Beatlemaniacs had left the fold. I seriously envisioned myself as the only person collecting all this junk, to one day show my kids and tell them about the greatest four human beings ever. But then . . . light! I started receiving several lists from companies springing up all over the United States, selling Beatle items at premium prices. Ahh, there was someone else who shared my enthusiasm . . . and it was going to cost me! $500.00 for a mint Butcher cover . . . outrageous, isn't it? In most cases you don't even get the record!!!

How do I tell all my friends that the joke is really on them? How do I tell them that 75% of today's lifestyles are a direct result of The Beatles? Stop and think of all the changes which have taken place since 1964. We are a different race . . . a different society. And where did you first read about these changes? By reading about the then current happenings of The Beatles. What are they wearing, how long is their hair, how do they play their style of music, how do they feel about war/politics, what do they think about religion, who do they like as entertainers, what do they do with drugs? These were all questions which the world was asking. And when they found the answers, they followed. People, who once thought the length of The Beatles' hair was so outrageously long, now sport hair longer than the original mop. The Beatles placed a new meaning on the word "hip." B.B. (Before Beatles) only beatniks were hip, but A.B. (you guessed it) everyone could be hip and still be a member of the establishment. The Beatles wanted to meditate, and we went with them; they wanted Nehru suits, and so did we. Unfortunately, The Beatles got satisfaction from drugs, and many of us died. It is evident that they were not gods, nor did they want to be, but everything they did was so magnified . . . so scrutinized, that their lives, no matter how personal, became ours. And we followed.

Today, the effects of The Beatles still remain . . . oh, you might have to look harder to find them, but the remnants of the 60's are still with us, some good and others bad. Although the acquisition of a new cat or dog by a former Beatle does not make front page news anymore, there are still a lot of fans who care, and still follow. I really think that many people might be closet-Beatlemaniacs, afraid to show their inner selves. It almost seems that there is a movement to dethrone the Fab Four, both musically and theoretically. *Rolling Stone* magazine hates every new release by them as individuals. I think *Rolling Stone* has several bad reviews pre-written, awaiting the next new record by Ringo, John, Paul or George. And that's irritating. How can you turn your back on those who have given you so much? How can you write off the most powerful force of a decade which this world has ever known? I don't know . . . I refuse to . . . and by the sounds and cries for The Beatles to reunite, I don't think that the public has either. No single force has been able to change so many different aspects of our lives as they did. Elvis did so musically, JFK politically, and Peter Max artistically. But The Beatles changed it all. They created a total package for us to live by.

They have given me so much, that I can never repay them fully. They have made me what I am today, and what so many of us are . . . a product of the 60's . . . a product of The Beatles. I only wish that more people would recognize this. **"**

G.C.
St. Louis, Missouri

"I think *Rolling Stone* has several bad reviews pre-written, awaiting the next new record by Ringo, John, Paul or George. And that's irritating. How can you turn your back on those who have given you so much? How can you write off the most powerful force of a decade which this world has ever known?"

"I was born in 1956, so I sort of missed the 1960's, but I can remember watching The Beatles on TV at Shea Stadium, and seeing the cartoon show, but I really didn't know who they were. I also remember my parents talking about what John said about The Beatles and Christ (my own opinion on this is they weren't mad because he said it, they were mad because he was right!).

I was born in England. My parents and I came to the U.S. in 1963. My parents took it the same way as other parents in England, they just passed it off. It wasn't until 1974 that I really started paying attention to music. The music of the 1970's turned me off. Many books which I read described that when The Beatles broke up, it was an era of music over, no guiding light, no lighthouse in the fog. The Fab Four as individuals helped some, but it wasn't the same. I believed this very much, so I bought a couple of books and Beatle records, and it went from there. I quickly got a case of Beatlemania and loved it. I bought all their albums, books, magazines, posters, saw "Beatlemania" three times, Beatlefests, and listened only to radio stations which played their songs. One day in October, KNET in Los Angeles played all the Beatle songs from A to Z, non stop. It was great. And then on February 7th, they celebrated the anniversary of The Beatles arrival in the United States. Every time there is a rumor about The Beatles getting back together, KNET will give full details. I keep hoping that the rumors will turn into truth.

The Beatles have given me something to believe in, and someone to look up to. I wouldn't care if the reunion concert was at the South Pole and the tickets were $100.00 or more, I'd be there one way or another. Let's all hope there is one more concert in the future. Can you imagine all those Beatle fans from past, present, and future, all in one place at the same time . . . WOW! . . . the largest city in the U.S. A concert like this would just cement their legend in history although it's already there."

P.T.
West Covina, California

"I am 23 years old and an avid Rock fan. I was only 7 years old when The Beatles came to the U.S. in 1964, and I paid no real attention to them. **Sgt. Pepper** turned me on to them and from that time on there was no turning back for me. My nickname is Eleanor Rigby. I can listen to their music all day, and sometimes do. I have never met any of The Beatles, but have soaked up so much on them that I feel as if I do. I subscribe to a Beatles Fanzine and am going to Beatlefest in Chicago this August.

I feel that they had quite an effect on society at large, especially in terms of making it more open and positive. Rock-and-Roll as a youth medium had died for a few years until The Beatles brought it back to life. They brought a positive feeling in a time of fear and confusion. The positiveness they brought, died in the 70's and I join George Harrison in hoping the 80's will bring it back.

'All You Need Is Love.' "

E.O.
Charleston, West Virginia

❝Well I'm only 23, but I've been a fan since the "dark ages" of the 1960's. My bedroom walls and door are covered with Beatle pictures. I've been going to Beatlefests since 1976. I have all their albums. I even got John Lennon's autograph and a picture of his Christmas tree in the mail because I made a present for his son, Sean. I was so damned thrilled. I even got to meet Allan Williams, The Beatles' first manager. He signed my program booklet. I have it in a drawer with the rest of my Beatle books, mags, paperbacks, etc. . . . I even managed to "borrow" 38 Playbills from the Shubert Theatre in Philadelphia, where "Beatlemania" played. I did have some help in "borrowing."

I think their influence can be seen by the thousands of people coming back each year to all the Beatlefests, the thousands who still remember them, and those who still buy and play their records. If that's not being influential, I don't know what the hell is! Groups like Herman's Hermits, the Dave Clark Five, the Monkees, etc., would never have gotten started if someone like The Beatles didn't come along and say, "See, it's alright to wear your hair this way, and wear this kind of clothing and play loud and the whole bit." I even think that the way some of us look today was influenced by The Beatles. Today's best musicians have learned from the very best . . . listening to their Beatle albums until the records were worn thin.

I wear my hair combed down in front to look like The Beatles. I brushed it all across my forehead and shook my head like Ringo would have in one of their concerts, put on the album **Live At The Hollywood Bowl** and all that screaming was just great. Long live The Beatles. Fab Four 4-Ever. Beatlemania lives!❞

A.P.
Marcus Hook, Pennsylvania

> "I wear my hair combed down in front to look like The Beatles. I brushed it across my forehead and shook my head like Ringo would have in one of their concerts, put on the album Live At The Hollywood Bowl and all the screaming was just great. Long live The Beatles. Fab Four 4-Ever. Beatlemania lives!"

❝I was only six when The Beatles became popular and have vague memories of how my sister used to get excited when she heard them. And she cried when she saw them on the Ed Sullivan Show. I also remember her getting a chance to see them for free at DC Coliseum, but my Mom told her no. She was so upset.

I remember most of those early days from my sister. I took a liking to them in 1968 and 1969. My sister was doing away with all her memorabilia and threw it away. I could almost kill her now. At the end of 1969 I took an extreme liking to an album, **Beatlemania Born Again.** I went Beatle crazy. Anything and everything I could get my hands on. I tried to find some of my sister's stuff that she may have overlooked. I did. I found things in the paper, books, articles, and most importantly, albums. I had flipped and my friends knew I had. The Beatles were almost just a memory to my age group, but they had yet to physically break up.

I got an album a week, until my collection was complete. My allowance went right to the record store. I became a Beatle hermit. I would stay in my room for hours on end, trying to learn all their songs . . . every hum, yeah, grunt, moan, and whisper. I took my albums everywhere. I even helped our local radio station put together a Beatle weekend. They used some of my records.

My bedroom was wall-to-wall John, George, Ringo, and Paul. I ordered back issues of magazines just to get literature on them. The years from 1969 to 1975 were totally devoted to The Beatles. I am still a maniac about them, still buying books and albums and you name it, I'll buy it.

The grandest occasion occurred when I saw "Wings Over America." McCartney was/is my favorite Beatle. One quarter of The Beatles is better than nothing. My friends still ride me about loving The Beatles so much. I've finally obtained all their music on reel-to-reel so I can listen to them for hours non-stop. This has a tendency to drive some folks crazy, but not me. Even my two year old daughter can sing the first stanza of *Hey Jude* and *Michelle*.

The Beatles had a very strong impact on my life, and as one fan, I'd love nothing better than to see them get back together. ❞

S.S.
Silver Springs, Maryland

❝ The Beatles changed my life, for better, forever. Watching them on Ed Sullivan was my initiation as a teenager. They were an impossibly beautiful, unattainable dream. They helped me explore my feelings in the safety of my own home listening to their records. I love them. Even if they have no way of knowing I love them, they have eased the world's pain a little.

This past summer I went to London and the experience abounded with sounds and sights which showed me how truly special they will always be. In all my daily dealings with people, The Beatles' influence stays with me. The kaleidoscoping, telescoping appeal of their music is even more powerful than before. The songs can comfort, soothe, cajole, caress, and tickle. They are my friends though we've never met. They would know somehow. I have been touched beyond measure. Beatlemaniacs are unique. They reduce life's troubles by "spinning round with the sounds." And if you can't understand it, I grieve for your misfortune.

The Beatles were the voice of the 1960's. They were alternately blamed and credited for every social change. In that very turbulent time, we grew up together. Today their music is everywhere . . . in supermarkets, as commercial themes, movie themes, etc. They were the musical backdrop that is now mainstream. The reason so many clamor for a reunion is that since their breakup nothing has filled the void.

Their image on my memory is clear. They are with me every day. They were magic. They still have the power to touch me. ❞

J.P.
Montgomery, Alabama

> "The Beatles changed my life, for better, forever. . . . . They helped me explore my feelings in the safety of my own home listening to their records. I love them. Even if they have no way of knowing I love them, they have eased the world's pain a little."

❝ The Beatles had a very strong influence in my life. They still do today, especially Paul McCartney. I can recall going to the local music store in my home town of Kansas City, Mo., to buy *I Want To Hold Your Hand*. From then on it was magic. There was a certain feeling then that is still within me today.

I have read almost every book out and collected much memorabilia. I guess you could say I'm a fanatic. When Paul McCartney came to San Francisco in 1976, I travelled there and had the most marvelous time in my life. Some of my photos are quite nice. That was McCartney's first visit to the Cow Palace since he played there with The Beatles.

I have over 250 photos of Paul and The Beatles (with and without Wings). Most of them I took. I sit at my art table everyday to do my art and look above at my wall . . . photos surround me. I love it.

It's apparent that The Beatles had quite an effect on society. Over a decade later their music is continuing. As for me, I'm still in a fantasy. I know . . . a feeling within me . . . that I will never lose. If there was ever to be a reunion, I would travel anywhere for the experience. ❞

S.C.
Florence, Oregon

" My outlook on popular music took a turn when I discovered The Beatles. I was about 9 then; I'm 21 now. I've been buying their albums and singles and memorabilia ever since. Between Capitol, Apple, and Parlophone, they have a small fortune which used to belong to me (not counting all of the bootleg company people).

Actually I was too young to understand the initial impact that they made at the time, but now I can see where all of the pieces fit. I got as excited about The Beatles in the early 70's as the public did when they first surfaced in the 60's. This only proves their music is immortal. I know of people who are 15 or younger now and they dig The Beatles as much or, if it is possible, more than I do.

Had it not been for The Beatles, I wouldn't have met the guy I'm now seeing. He's a Beatle freak too and our first discussion revolved around **Sgt. Pepper's Lonely Hearts Club Band**. Since then I've been one of the happiest people in the world. The Beatles and the word, "genius," are synonomous. I can't see how the 60's and early 70's could have been so powerful without them. They controlled the minds of the youth at that time. Believe it or not . . . they still do. A day doesn't go by in which I don't think about them or play one of their albums.

I probably would have never done acid had I not read and realized how much John Lennon enjoyed it. I'm not saying that I did it just because he did, but I figured it was good enough for him hundreds of times; it would be good for me too. And it was. I can't believe he has done it so much because it was so intense for me, but I can relate to so much of their music after experiencing it. I've finally seen Strawberry Fields and felt as if I could have been a walrus too had I wanted to. It takes an incredible mind and all four of them have one. I don't feel Ringo Starr has left me with a lasting impression as the other three have, but to think of The Beatles with a different drummer would be like the Rolling Stones without Mick Jagger. It just wouldn't be the same.

If they've done anything for me, they have made me think. I see things in a different light now more than ever. They started out trying to make it as a band and ended up trying to prove that they weren't God. I think that I'm not alone when I say they're the best and I doubt that anyone will ever top them. Record sales have nothing to do with it, I'm referring to influence. My taste in music and my involvement with the recording industry has increased tremendously since my discovery of The Beatles.

I care about all of them, as if I know them on a first name basis. I cried when I read that Ringo's home in L.A. had caught fire. I laughed when I saw on the news last night that Paul was busted in Tokyo for possession of the evil weed. I didn't laugh because of the bust, but because he was stupid enough to get caught. They're only human, it's hard to keep a good perspective. I was happy for George when he remarried. And John (my favorite), he's another story. When I listen to his music, I feel all of the pain and suffering that he felt or all the joy and excitement whichever the case may be. I was first upset when Yoko got her claws into him, but I soon realized that she must be a very special person for John to go as crazy as he did over her. **"**

A.S.
Macomb, Illinois

"If they've done anything for me, they have made me think. I see things in a different light now more than ever. They started out trying to make it as a band and ended up trying to prove that they weren't God."

90

❝I am 22 years old and have been a Beatles' fan for 12 years. Both of my older sisters were fans before me. In fact, all of my family knows and likes The Beatles.

The Beatles have broadened my musical awareness and appreciation, not only of their music, but many other artists as well. Through pen-pal organizations, I have made many new friends. We share many other interests, besides The Beatles, that have brought us closer.

My first impression of The Beatles was when I was about 7 and my sisters wanted to watch their U.S. debut on Ed Sullivan. My sisters went haywire, and while I was puzzled at this behavior, I liked what I saw and heard! I continued to like it until *Hey Jude*, when I took over, myself, as the family Beatlemaniac.

I can remember thinking how nice it was of Paul to play his guitar in the other direction, so it would not hit into George. No one had ever told me that some people in this world are left handed. I remember well the high energy feeling just before the TV special about the 1965 Shea Stadium concert aired, although I remember nothing of the show itself. As I grew up, I was physically surrounded by likenesses of John, Paul, George, Ringo, Cynthia, Jane Asher (of whom I am also a proud, devoted, and loving fan), Patti, and Maureen. I must admit to not understanding about Yoko or their drug use at the time. My first self-imposed exposure was their later music. I wasn't turned off by the change as some fans I know were. When they broke up, I was saddened, but within a week of its release, I bought **McCartney**, so I quickly recovered.

The effects of The Beatles are still going on, but I have discovered that there is an entire world out there of devoted fans, who have loved, do love, and will continue to love The Fab Four. The Fab Four is the perfect name for them because apart or together they are fabulous! I shall always be a proud and devoted member in The Beatles' loving community all over the world.**❞**

"All You Need Is Love"
L.B.
Towson, Maryland

"My first impression of The Beatles was when I was about 7 . . . . I can remember thinking how nice it was of Paul to play his guitar in the other direction, so it would not hit into George. No one had ever told me that some people in this world are left handed."

66 The first time that I actually listened to The Beatles was when I listened to my brother's old record, **The Early Beatles**. I thought it was strange sounding, but a good, strange sound. For some reason I forgot all about them, and got into some other music, especially Elton John. Elton somehow phased out, and when I was 17, I started to listen to The Beatles, especially from the radio and from friends. I'm 20 years old now and I'm a full fledged Beatlemaniac. It's really weird, but every time I hear The Beatles on the radio or TV, I just freeze. I will stop whatever I'm doing. The four of them have such magnetic personalities and those personalities contribute to a somewhat synergistic effect, but they all have those distinct individual characteristics.

The Beatles are more than a favorite group, they are practically a way of life with me. I collect newspapers which mention the name Beatle or Messrs. Lennon, McCartney, Harrison and Starr. I'm a member of the Paul McCartney fan club and I subscribe to *Beatlefan* magazine, and other Beatle fanzines. I have about 50 records by The Beatles. I would have more if I had the money to spare. I have many posters and promo posters of them and I've read just about all the books about them. I influence my friends to buy Beatles albums and they're glad they have bought them.

There are a few things that intrigue me about them. They set a fashion standard by what they wore or how long their hair was. Their effect on society is immeasurable. As The Beatles changed, so did the world. Their albums were copied by other artists many times. Another thing is the quality of their albums. The Beatles changed with every album, and for the better. I like most of the ex-Beatle stuff, but I wish that John would record music more often. I can sympathize with him. He has been through Beatlemania, crowds, arrest, and I guess he just wants to raise his son correctly. I hope he is happy. Beatle Reunion? It would be the event of the year and it would get the music industry out of its doldrums. I would pay $1,000.00 to see them. I think people like Sid Bernstein put undue pressure on them to perform again. I don't think they ever will because the pressure upon them to perform well would be enormous. Paul has Wings, George and John are happy. Ringo would probably be agreeable to a reunion and it would be up to him to persuade the other three to "Come Together."

To close . . . no group today makes better bloody music than The Beatles did . . . not Fleetwood Mac, Eagles, Stones, etc. I just finished two years of college and I want to work for a record company. **99**

D.B.
West Vancouver, British Columbia, Canada

"Seeing Paul McCartney in Chicago in 1976 was one of the most important days of my life. I spent almost $200.00 to see him for all three nights he performed. Never was my money more wisely spent. What a talent, what a man! I love him and all of The Beatles. Their families as well. They have gotten me through some rough times during my life."

“Never has anyone or anything been such a part of my life for such a length of time (since 1964) as The Beatles, both as a group and now as individuals. Especially Paul McCartney, I think of him everyday. Not as a starry-eyed fan, but I wonder what he is doing, how he's doing, etc. I feel as though he is my best friend. His music influences my everyday life as The Beatles did until they broke up. I'm not a big collector, I've never had the money to buy a lot of albums, but I do own almost strictly Beatle and ex-Beatle albums. My friends all know me as a "Beatle Nut." I can talk about them for hours as if I know them personally. My house is decorated with as much Beatle memorabilia as my husband will tolerate (he's into Zappa and is sick of hearing the words "Beatles" and "McCartney"). I don't think any musician is as multitalented as McCartney. It aggravates me to death listening to the crap they play on the radio and knowing it's just a person standing in front of a mike singing a song handed to him. Not many have the talent and versatility of Paul, doing producing, writing, and arranging all by himself. I always celebrate all their birthdays, although I gave up, years ago, trying to send cards and letters because I'm sure they were never read.

Seeing Paul McCartney in Chicago in 1976 was one of the most important days of my life. I spent almost $200.00 to see him for all three nights he performed. Never was my money more wisely spent. What a talent, what a man! I love him and all of The Beatles. Their families as well. They have gotten me through some rough times during my life.”

G.M.
Carpentersville, Illinois

❝I really don't know if they changed my life, but I do know that if there had been no such group called The Beatles, a lot of my younger years wouldn't have been so much fun.

When I was about 10, my father came home and told me that one of his co-workers was upset at his children. My father's friend was British and just got back to work after he went home to England for his vacation. His daughter had gone "crazy" over a mopped-topped, Rock-and-Roll band called The Beatles. This man couldn't stand the thump-thump of the music, it gave him a headache. When he got back to the U.S., he took his daughter's singles (using the excuse they were lost on the way back to the U.S.) and gave them to my father for my brother and me.

I remember it was the most fantastic version of *My Bonnie*. It was wonderful. I played these records day and night. I knew all the words and when I was shut up in the bedroom, I sang and was a Beatle too. My parents never said anything about the volume, they liked them too. My brother really didn't care about them, he was into the Beach Boys and the Four Seasons. My girl friends felt just as I did when they heard the records.

About 6–8 months later, The Beatles premiered in the U.S. on the Ed Sullivan Show. My God, they were so young and good looking. I remember that I was in love with John Lennon. From that time on, I was a devout Beatle fan. I bought every album and single I could afford. The ones I didn't buy, my friends did. My life for the next 4 or 5 years revolved around The Beatles. Everyday my girlfriends and I would sit in one of our backyards and tell our dreams. They were dreams of us being The Beatles' girlfriends. I really was too young to be going out with boys then, but my first sexual fantasies were with John Lennon. We girls couldn't wait to get together to continue the dreams.

We even had a stage in one of our basements. We had cardboard and string guitars. "Ringo" was sitting on this huge, wooden toy box with card-

94

board drums, which had "The Beatles" written exactly like theirs. It even had "Ludwig" in small letters. The stage had a huge, old painting tarpaulin for a curtain, which opened and closed on cue by one of the girl's brothers. We would put the records on and we were great. One of us played a left-handed Paul, another was a perfect "George" with her sheepish grins. I stood with my feet apart concentrating on that curtain rod microphone as "John." And every performance was a standing ovation by one of my friend's babysitter.

Then there was the "Yellow Submarine." It was a couple of cardboard boxes, which had contained the neighbors' console stereo and television sets. We painted the outside yellow, and the inside had scores of Beatle pictures. I've always had regrets about that yellow submarine, for when it was finally destroyed by paint being poured into it, all the pictures were destroyed as well. Most of the pictures were mine and would be worth a lot to me now.

As the years went by, I got into other groups, Jimi, Janis, and Zeppelin, but I always had an eye on John, George, Paul, and Ringo. I watched for the marriages, children, and divorces. Finally, when the news of their break-up was made public, I was disappointed. However, it was due. They had made their fame and fortune and it was time they went their own ways.

The Beatles and their music will always have a special place in my heart. My love for them will never change. They have brightened my life for almost 20 years. I still have my original albums, even though they're too old and worn out to play. I have replaced them over the past few years for my listening pleasure. Even today, my life's dream is to meet John Lennon, Richard Starkey, George Harrison, and Paul McCartney personally. And still, to this day, a 4 ft. by 4 ft. poster of George Harrison graces my living room wall! **"**

P.M.
Grove City, Ohio

"The Beatles and their music will always have a special place in my heart. My love for them will never change. They have brightened my life for almost 20 years. I still have my original albums, even though they're too old and worn out to play. . . . And still, to this day, a 4 ft. by 4 ft. poster of George Harrison graces my living room wall!"

95

"On April 10, 1970, when The Beatles broke up, my father had the newspaper right near my breakfast so when I sat down to eat I'd see it. Well, let me tell you . . . when I sat down and saw that I cried. I cried so much that I got upset and my parents let me stay home from school."

"I was 8 years old when I first heard and saw The Beatles. I can distinctly remember Ed Sullivan introducing them and when they played, I went absolutely crazy even though it was on TV. As the record albums came out, I obtained each. Anybody could ask me a question about them and I could answer about 95% of them, from their birth dates to their favorite colors. My father told me that if I studied my schoolwork as I did about The Beatles, I'd be Number 1 in my class.

I've seen all The Beatles movies a number of times. Now, I am almost 25 years old and married. My apartment is literally a shrine dedicated to the Fab Four. My collection was in the New England Beatles Convention. Only part of it won. I have dolls, models, serving tray, Beatles-Flip-Your-Wig game, cards, books, magazines, wall pictures, paintings to name a few. I've been asked if I would ever sell my collection and the answer has been and always will be "NO!" I love The Beatles and I am not ashamed to say that if I ever met them, I would definitely faint . . . no doubt about it. I never saw The Beatles together as a group in person, but I did see George Harrison in 1974 at the Boston Garden. I took the day off from work to go there and my parents thought I was nuts. When I grew my hair long for the first time, it was the same way they wore it in 1966–1967. I still wear it the same way. All of my belts have Beatle belt buckles and I have at least a dozen Beatle T-shirts. Whenever something new comes out, whether it's "Beatlemania'" a convention, or a local group imitating them, I make it a point and go. I try to stay in the style The Beatles did. I hate disco and glitter. Whenever someone has a question about The Beatles, my family and friends refer them to me.

John Lennon is definitely my favorite, he is great. Even though he has not recorded much for the last several years, he's a genius. I tried to call him up on the phone, but the operator would not give me his phone number.

On April 10, 1970, when The Beatles broke up, my father had the newspaper right near my breakfast so when I sat down to eat I'd see it. Well, let me tell you . . . when I sat down and saw that I cried. I cried so much that I got upset and my parents let me stay home from school. I had been hearing reports for the past two weeks before that, but I would not believe it . . . I'm always hoping that the rumor of them getting together will come true. No matter when or where or how much, I'll definitely be there."

N.M.
Bristol, Connecticut

6

No One Could Touch Them

Music is what made The Beatles, and vice versa. It is only now, with hindsight as the great teacher, that many critics and music instructors are able to praise the music of The Beatles. When the group first appeared, most "adults" dismissed The Beatles' music as juvenile, raucous, and without any socially redeeming qualities whatsoever. But the fans knew all along that the music was great. I knew it when I heard *She Loves You* with its captivating hook of "Yeah Yeah Yeah." And with each new single and album release, the songs kept on getting better, establishing new techniques, and leaving all the other musicians' mouths open. No one could touch them.

In the beginning, the songwriting team of Lennon and McCartney imitated what they knew. They copied the styles of people like Goffin/King, who produced simple, yet cohesive songs. The lyrics were simple, boy wants girl, boy loses girl, boy has more than one girl, but wants more, etc. Sure, a lot of them appear unsophisticated when compared to today's songs, but if it weren't for The Beatles we wouldn't be past do-wops and sha-na-na's. They single-handedly stripped Rock-and-Roll, and then restructured it to suit their own needs. Everyone followed those leads. Some groups were influenced by one song, some songs have never been duplicated in technique. It is easy to forget what music was like before The Beatles. We take it for granted now, but they were the driving force in music, non-stop, from 1964 through 1970. Every change made them untouchable by other artists; all paled in comparison. They brought respect to Rock-and-Roll, a musical style that had been scoffed at by professional musicians in the 1950s. Their lyrics turned to poetry. Their studio endeavors were marvelled at, and emulated immediately by all who followed them.

This is the most difficult thing to explain to a neophyte Beatlemaniac or young person today. The music of today and its sophistication was not always around. You couldn't walk into a record shop, and find music by the likes of Pink Floyd, Yes, Kansas, Bruce Springsteen, or even Elvis Costello, in 1964. It took The Beatles to come along and reshape the sound that has progressed to the technological level we know today. In three short years, The Beatles went from the inanity of *I Wanna Be Your Man* to the brilliance of *A Day In The Life*. They could have chosen an easier route. They could have played pop stars, and simply written songs imitative of those based on earlier hit-producing qualities, relying on time-tested riffs and hooks. That would have insured them a few hits for awhile, but they weren't only pop stars, despite the media hype. All four were young men, growing up in a most bizarre environment, searching for answers not only to the problems of the world, but also to questions about their individual identities. They didn't stop and vegetate. They didn't take the easy way out. They broke precedents in music with each album, adding in oriental instruments, symphony instruments, and synthesizers. They were the first to do it. They took the chance of alienating some of the people who had originally made them popular.

The Beatles lost a lot of fans, but gained new ones with each new musical innovation. Some people who adored them for being the cute little teddy bears in the collarless suits just couldn't understand the burial scene on the cover of **Sgt. Pepper**. The Beatles had moved on. It changed so fast. It seems amazing, but during the six years The Beatles made records, the big event for the American record-buying public was to await the coming of each new Beatle album. People would line up in front of record stores everywhere on the day of a record's release. The Beatles *were* Rock-and-Roll.

The summer of 1968 was a period of transition for me. I left the secure confines of high school upon graduation that

June, and was looking upon my first semester at college in September with trepidation. August, the month of my birth, soon came, and I found myself having to do something that I wasn't sure I wanted to do at all . . . register for the draft.

I reached age 18 in August 1968, and, like any other kid in town, registered with the local Selective Service office. The actual signing up was quite painless, but memories were not. The previous night, I had stayed awake to watch one of the most gruesome horror stories ever shown to a television audience. The scenes of violence and bloodshed were still vivid as I registered . . . the war was coming home. The show had no director or producer, but it had been choreographed by Richard Daley of Chicago, Illinois. Narrated by Walter Cronkite, the street scene of the Chicago Police Riot was the most disgusting thing I had ever witnessed. It was brought live, into my home . . . my sister and I watched with horror as young people's heads were bashed in by ghouls wielding nightsticks.

Against this backdrop, I placed my name next in line to go fight a war to help protect the interests of the same people who beat up kids in Chicago. I don't know why I signed up, I guess it was out of fear of not complying with the law or maybe now, a dozen years later, I can observe that as an 18 year old, I was too scared and nervous to do anything that might get me into trouble with anyone. I remember getting into the car, and driving away from the Selective Service office filled with a feeling of numbness. Out of habit, I turned on the car radio, and the sounds emanating from it immediately got my attention.

I had already heard *Revolution*, but I had yet to hear the main side of the new Beatles' single, *Hey Jude*. I had turned on the radio after the song had started, but I instantly recognized Paul McCartney's voice, and I became carried away with the never ending chorus of "Na Na Na . . . Na Na Na Na . . . Na Na Na Na." The song took over the car, I was no longer driving, I was singing at the top of my lungs to a song which I had never heard before. I must have gone through red lights and stop signs, but I didn't give a damn . . . here were The Beatles taking me out of the pits of despair, instilling new hope for the future. It again seemed possible that things could get better.

Hey Jude ranks right up there with *She Loves You* and *A Day In The Life* as the songs by The Beatles which have most influenced me. In the next batch of contributors' correspondence, we will hear from those who consider the music of The Beatles to be the overriding reason for their importance to our society. Again, some of these letters overlap into areas emphasized in earlier chapters. It is truly amazing that so many different types of people can be touched in so many ways by a single song, yet have the effect on each one's life be so similarly profound. These letters demonstrate how the writers perceive the greatness that was and is The Beatles' musical legacy . . . .

"Without a doubt, The Beatles were the greatest group in history. I remember growing up in the 60s watching The Beatles shape and change just about everything they touched. They mentally and physically changed the entire world. I have been saving and collecting everything I can get hold of since 1968.

My favorite period of The Beatles was 1967 to 1968. Nobody has even come close to playing songs the way these guys did during that period. Everytime I hear *I Am The Walrus*, my favorite song, I instantly go back to the time when everything was mellow and just good clean living. I am quite positive that they were tripping at that time . . . which is nothing wrong in doing at all. Just listen to the lyrics. I just can't relate the way I feel for these guys. *A Day In The Life, I'll Follow The Sun, This Boy* . . . I still get chills hearing these songs.

The White Album is truly a masterpiece. I can't get over how every song they ever made is a masterpiece. Every single they ever made was a double hit. I don't recall any other group that consistently had a single where both sides became hits. Every Rock magazine mentions their names somewhere. Three years ago, I saw Wings in Cincinnati, and they drew 24,000 people, and the stadium only holds 18,000. That gives you an idea on how much drawing power even one ex-member has!!!"

S.B.
Springboro, Ohio

"The Beatles' music and constant changes to achieve excellence were the two most important effects on my life, in that they carried me with them through their music to the point of total music appreciation of poetry and universal love."

"The Beatles were the beginning of modern, contemporary Rock-and-Roll music. They were the beginning of a new era in modern living. Few people in history have had such an effect on the world as these four men. The changes they brought about through their music and lives will never be erased from the history of the world.

Their influences on my life were like most children of the 60s. My hair was allowed to grow from the usual flat-top to a longer style. I began listening to music with a greater interest than I had before, and music became a very important part of my life, as it has continued to be ever since. I began playing drums and singing in rock bands in the 60s, and I would still be playing if I could assemble the right musicians.

The Beatles' music and constant changes to achieve musical excellence were the two most important effects on my life, in that they carried me with them through their music to the point of total music apprepreciation of poetry and universal love. They still influence me by their individual lives and musical efforts today. They are also driving me mad trying to get my hands on all their albums, books about them and other memorabilia."

D.E.
Lynchburg, Virginia

101

❝I was about eleven years old when The Beatles appeared on the Ed Sullivan Show. When I saw the reaction from the audience, I just couldn't believe it. I turned to my parents and said, "That's what I wanna do! I want to be like The Beatles and have people scream for me!" So, I began buying Beatle records (no albums as I was poor) and played them over and over. I memorized all the words. Two years later, I formed my first band. Throughout the years, I wandered from one band to another, in my search for that elusive dream; to be like The Beatles. Musically, they were my idols. One band after another folded and I became the classic frustrated musician.

Years passed, until October, 1979, when I met three other guys, who had the exact same ambition. We were gonna be a Beatles copy band and also do original material only. Right now we are playing local clubs, but one in particular is our home base. We have become popular locally (in fact girls scream when we perform). We have very good original songs and we are now ready to break out nationally. All of this because of The Beatles, who so inspired my life that I don't think that I would be where I am now if not for them. They have inspired my life from age 11 to my present age, 27.❞

N.D.
Melrose Park, Illinois

❝I was only eleven years old when The Beatles were at their peak, but I still think the biggest mistake my parents ever made was underestimating my desire to see The Beatles in concert while we were vacationing in Detroit, in the summer of 1966. I had saved up the whopping sum of $6.50 for my ticket, but my parents said it was "too far" to drive and get to my cousins' farm. My cousins went without me, and sold my ticket at the door.

Disappointments aside, The Beatles were an indirect influence on my life through their effect on the music world in general. I still hear guitar riffs or snatches of old Beatles tunes in today's music. I like the album **Rubber Soul** the best and think that the song, *You Won't See Me* is excellent, well done, enjoyable, superb, etc.

My favorite musicians now are John Prine, The Band, Bonnie Raitt, and country-western music, but listening to The Beatles every once in a while makes me feel young and optimistic again.❞

C.K.
Arcata, California

❝Before The Beatles started the British invasion, everyone in my neighborhood was hooked on Elvis, Dion and The Belmonts, or Rick Nelson. There was no outside (out of U.S.A.) music listened to as far as Rock and Pop were concerned. The Beatles, Dave Clark 5, the Stones, and the Kinks changed all that.

Although I was only 10 or 11 at the time of The Beatles' arrival in February, 1964, I had heard a lot about them. In 1964, most of my friends and I bought nothing but the Motown Sound, especially the Supremes. The Beatles changed that, not that I wasn't hooked on Diana Ross and the Supremes, but I also learned to buy other groups' records. Everyone in my class loved the way The Beatles dressed, especially the girls in the class. My parents liked their singing, but they didn't care for their haircuts. Most of my friends and I became obsessed with hearing British talk. It was quaint, but classy in its own "bloody" way. We became interested in Liverpool, Tottenham, and the Mersey River.

The Beatles started the British invasion . . . the most interesting and exciting musical era in pop and rock history. The Stones, Dave Clark Five (my personal favorite group), the Kinks, the Animals, the Hollies, the Hermits (very popular with the younger kids), the Moody Blues, Gerry and the Pacemakers, the Searchers, and the Zombies . . . we kids didn't know which group to spend our allowance on. Two very popular female singers were Petula Clark and Dusty Springfield. The great Beatles started it all!

The Beatles were pioneers of Rock-and-Roll, much as Elvis was to the late 50s. The Beatles made me aware of social issues and politics. Toward the late 60s, they became a little freakier looking, but their music became greater. I think if the Dave Clark Five or Gerry and the Pacemakers had been able to change with The Beatles, they would still be around today. Lennon and McCartney also wrote songs for Peter and Gordon, and Chad and Jeremy.

The Beatles apart are not very good as far as making hits. The only one who has really made it is Paul McCartney with Wings. I do wish that they regroup one time yet, as Peter, Paul, and Mary did last summer. The Beatles will always be number 1 in my book.❞

D.K.
Orwigsburg, Pennsylvania

"The first Beatle song I ever heard . . . was *I Saw Her Standing There*. **The DJ at the time was Murray the K and the station everyone was listening to at the time was WABC—AM. Murray said one day (on this station, WINS) that he would like to play something by an English group called The Beatles. Prior to hearing the song, I remember thinking, 'Who wants to hear foreign songs?'"**

66 When The Beatles invaded our shores, in 1964, I was at the prime age to be affected by them. Although still interested in sports at the time, I was 13 years old, and quickly captivated by their catchy lyrics and upbeat, bouncy music. They stood out and grabbed the country, making people of all ages and walks of life stand up and take notice. Their music was totally different than anything going on in the country, although they had been influenced by the likes of Elvis and Buddy Holly. Their interpretation of American music gave them their unique sound.

The first Beatle song I ever heard (it wasn't the first one they had recorded) was *I Saw Her Standing There*. The DJ at the time was Murray the K and the station everyone was listening to at the time was WABC--AM. Murray said one day (on this station, WINS) that he would like to play something by an English group called The Beatles. Prior to hearing the song, I remember thinking, "Who wants to hear foreign songs?" The song just played previously was *Sally Go Round The Roses*, therefore The Beatles' song knocked me out, and I have been a fan ever since.

Peoples' lives were affected without them even knowing it. For instance, a five year old boy walking around with a Beatle haricut. The Beatles had a great influence on hair styles and dress in general. Their drug saturated lyrics, intentional or not, turned a generation onto the idea of drugs. The glasses Lennon wore became very fashionable, and I would like to know the figure for sales of Hofner and Rickenbacker bass guitars, just because Paul used them.

Lately it seems that there are groups trying to recapture The Beatles' sound with short, catchy tunes. The Knack seem the best at this and are a fast selling group. They sold over two million copies of their first album, the fastest selling album since **Meet The Beatles**.

The thing that astonishes me about The Beatles is the fact that they have not played together as a group in ten years and they are still very much alive in the minds of the people. Now that is what I call a residual effect. Thank you and I hope I've passed the audition. 99

M.S.
Bronx, New York

❝I was in the sixth grade and The Beatles were becoming the nation's rage. At the time in school, we had to do an in-depth study of our ancestral countries. Mine is England, so I deemed it fitting to put a picture of The Beatles on the cover of my report and state "England — Home of The Beatles." The teacher told me that she didn't think my cover was very appropriate and marked me down from a "B" to a "C" because of it.

Everyone's opinions, if you were young, were shot down because now we were being invaded. It was a musical revolution for America. So many people had cursed the likes of Presley, Holly, and Haley because they seemed to provoke violence which parents felt would put rebellion into their children's senses. What it was really doing was giving everyone a new opportunity to let oneself go; an opportunity to let one's spirit loose; an opportunity to rock and to roll.

My mother would buy me each new Beatles' single as it came out and all my pocket money always seemed to go for Beatles' cards, magazines, or whatever had any mention or connotation of The Beatles, I don't think my mother really thought they would last. We rode the Pennsylvania turnpike, going to my grandmother's, and we all sang *Yellow Submarine*. It had been a couple of years since The Beatles became popular and they were still with us. They would be with us as a group for a few more years, especially when we smoked a joint on the way to our high school classes and *Helter Skelter* was embedded within brain vibrations and our fast moving adrenalin.

An announcement was yet to come that The Beatles had split up. How could such a thing happen? How could a group so successful to themselves decide to break apart? We didn't understand their personal feelings then or the technicalities which were involved. We only felt that it could be the end of Rock-and-Roll; it didn't end though, and neither did the spirit or music of The Beatles. They gave me feelings of freedom and revolution. They made love seem more distinct and let me seem myself for I wasn't conforming to a musical style which my parents would have liked me to follow. They gave politics more meaning and the usage of drugs, when I felt my head needed them, the proper reasons. Though I have outgrown and taken on new habits and given up some old ones, the music of The Beatles lives on within me and will forever. They provided a fresh spirit to me as a child and an overall good feeling as a growing adult.

The music of The Beatles shall never be dead because I believe in yesterdays. It was those yesterdays which gave me good vibrations. I appreciate life a lot more than I might have otherwise. Those were my days of The Beatles.**❞**

R.H.
Ann Arbor, Michigan

66 I am 38, a businessman with a Masters degree and a resident of California with a wife and two children. I also am a pop music fan and have been an admirer of harmony since I was a teenager. The following chronological highlights stick in my mind as I think about The Beatles:

1. They entered my life during Christmas vacation of 1963. I didn't think they were anything special.

2. I became aware of their intense popularity during the summer of 1965. I still didn't know their individual names.

3. I was introduced to one of their albums during Christmas of 1966. I didn't like many of the songs immediately.

4. They were staying in a London hotel near my office in early 1968. I knew their names by then, but still couldn't link the names with the faces.

5. I began singing many of their songs in jam sessions during 1969 and 1970. I began to identify with McCartney, whose voice range is close to mine.

6. *Let It Be* was one of my favorite songs for the year of 1970. I was disappointed by their break up and expected a reunion.

7. I had an immediate interest in any song released by McCartney, Lennon, or Harrison during 1971--1974. I expected Lennon to make it, but was pulling for McCartney.

8. *Imagine* and *My Love* were two of my favorite songs of the early 1970s.

9. I realized by 1974 that McCartney was here to stay. My interest in him strengthened and I began to lose track of the others.

10. I became a true McCartney fan during 1976--1980. I bought his albums, learned the words to his songs, imitated his style and watched his TV appearances.

The Beatles influence in my life has been primarily a McCartney influence. I use popular music as a cartharsis (the music first and the words, secondary, if at all) and McCartney's music has emerged for me as the first lasting male replacement for Elvis Presley. All four Beatles appear to have brought much enjoyment both individually and collectively. **99**

K.M.
Fremont, California

"Several years ago, I wrote a cause and effect paper on The Beatles which my teacher flipped over. I was in my second semester of an English composition course. Now, I'm in the Navy, stationed at San Diego, California.

I still remember the paper and its theme. The cause was the enigmatic "number 9" and the effect was a song I composed about that particular number. I pointed out John Lennon's use of the "number 9" motif, particularly in the song which appears on the White Album called *Revolution Number 9*. Of course any moron could hear the song, but there were still remnants. In several songs such as *I Am The Walrus*, the motif is used and on *You Know My Name, Look Up The Number*, The Beatles count off numbers starting at one and ending at four, but continuing with nine. The "nine" is said intermittently throughout the song. In 1974, John Lennon came out with a post-Beatle hit titled *Number Nine Dream*. In this song are what I interpret as clues to what John Lennon remembers about his Beatle days. Also in the song, *Fame*, which John co-wrote with David Bowie, there is more mention of the "number 9" motif. Before this "number 9" revelation made itself known to me, I was totally unaware of it. There must be some reason for this."

D.M.
Gretna, Louisiana

**"The Beatles were
the greatest force in
music since Bach.
They still are."**

&&The Beatles were the greatest force in music since Bach. They still are. I first heard The Beatles when I was 10 or 11, I'm 23 now. The album was, **Yesterday and Today**. No one was home and I listened to it for 2 or 3 hours, and finally knew what everyone was raving about. I have loved them ever since.

When I'm depressed I play **Let It Be** (the album). When I'm happy I play *Dizzy Miss Lizzy*, **Abbey Road** (side 2), *Why Don't We Do It In The Road, Everybody's Got Something To Hide Except Me And My Monkey*.

I was in the 8th grade when they broke up. I still hope for a reunion. I think their total power won't be realized until they're dead.

Paul McCartney's drug bust devastated a lot of folks. It's hard to believe your hero could be so stupid, and sit in jail like anyone else.&&

T.L.
Spokane, Washington

&&I'm 20 years old. Many years ago I recall seeing The Beatles appear on the Ed Sullivan Show on my black and white TV. Initially, I was hooked on *Penny Lane* and *Strawberry Fields Forever*, now I love all their songs from early Beatles to late Beatles. I played the White Album every weekend at college. My record collection is filled with Beatles' albums and a little of everyone else. Today I appreciate their music much more because I can value the lyrics, the rhythm, and of course, all the clues that Paul is dead!

The Beatles give me a lift . . . they rule. The Beatles are a living legend, a musical revolution in Rock-and-Roll.&&

M.K.
Wantagh, New York

"P.S. The walrus was Paul."

"I was around when The Beatles first came out, but wasn't quite old enough to understand them. The Beatles didn't change the life styles of the people, the people changed themselves to copy The Beatles. Rock-and-Roll was here before they were, it's just that the older generation had to put the blame on someone, so they chose The Beatles. The Beatles wore their hair a little longer than some men. If you took the greasy kid stuff off half of the men who wore it, their hair would have been just as long.

I am glad The Beatles are who they are. Their music is the greatest, even if they don't get together for the concert for the boat people, so what? They gave us all they could before they broke up. That's the way they want, let's give them that. One of the best songs they did was *Let It Be*. That's how they want it, too bad everyone can't see it that way. This whole world is filled with fuck-ups who won't see or listen.

I am glad they made the music they did, and I will have their music around for my kids to listen to when they get to a certain understanding and appreciative stage."

W.K.
Mansfield, Ohio

"The Beatles wore their hair a little longer than some men. If you took the greasy kid stuff off half the men who wore it, their hair would have been just as long."

•LET IT BE•

EMIAJ

"There are people who once viewed them as four, long-haired pot heads, but now the people themselves, who criticized them and continue to, walk around with semi-long hair and are humming *Yesterday* or singing and whistling *Norwegian Wood*. People hear songs, instrumental versions on classical radio stations or in department stores, but if you told them it was an old Beatle song, they would hesitate to believe you."

66 Did The Beatles change my life? No, they never changed it because I was so young when they were a group, that I didn't know anything else. They broke up when I was in sixth grade.

Do they still influence me today? Yes, they have always had an influence on me and always will to a certain extent. I am a number one Beatle fan. I have a pretty complete collection of albums and singles as a group and as solo artists. I have a total of 60 albums and several singles. I always sing their songs when I'm working or driving my car. I am a worker in a photo-finishing plant, and sometimes I am lucky enough to see and actually obtain photographs of them as a group and individuals. My appearance is clean cut with medium length hair (like the early Beatles). I don't play any musical instruments, but I have an irresistable urge for their songs. I tell my friends about their songs, and things I have read about them. The Beatles are super-heroes. I realize that these guys are the only ones who are just as or more famous than Elvis Presley. I realize that Lennon and McCartney will come to be studied like Beethoven and Schubert as figures, performers or song-writers. They have done more for modern music than anyone else.

Did The Beatles change society? Yes, look at hair, look at clothing, and compare it with late 50s or early 60s. There was a change when The Beatles came along, and things have never been the same. Their music in particular. There are people who once viewed them as four, long-haired, pot heads, but now the people themselves, who criticized them and continue to, walk around with semi-long hair and are humming *Yesterday* or singing and whistling *Norwegian Wood*. People hear songs, instrumental versions on classical radio stations or in department stores, but if you told them it was an old Beatle song, they would hesitate to believe you.

If they were to reunite, I'm sure wherever they went the air would be filled with an awesome display of approval from around the world. It would be musical history all over, but in a different way. The Stones, President of the United States, or Muhammad Ali couldn't draw a crowd the size or as quickly as The Beatles could.

I like Wings, but I like The Beatles a hell of a lot better. By writing this, I am able to pay some respect to the most influential and entertaining men this generation has ever known. 99

J.M.
New England, West Virginia

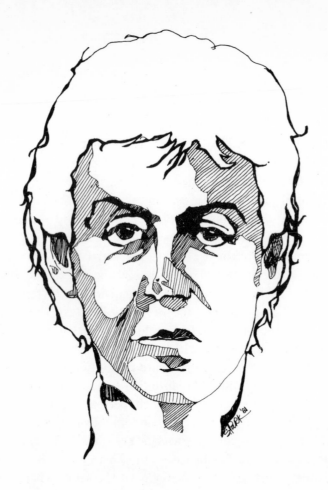

❝The Beatles brought joy and happiness to kids all over the world. I bought whatever I could get on them. They changed the whole world with their music. They came at a time when the world needed someone new. Elvis wasn't the same when he came back on the scene, and we needed someone who was young and different.

All the young girls at the time fell in love with one of them. Mine was Paul McCartney. I liked his handsome baby face. I even thought that I would meet him someday, but that was only wishful thinking. With each album, their music seemed to change, but it was all so beautiful whatever it was. Every album was a favorite song. The one I loved the best was **Revolver** and then later it was **Abbey Road**. The White Album was fantastic.

They changed my life through their music. I felt life was so beautiful, and their lyrics were so well written. My favorite song is *You Won't See Me*, but actually it's so hard to single one out of the many because they were all so great. When they broke up, it was like a tragedy. I guess they felt they wanted to do different things with their lives. I have always wanted them to get back together, but if they did, it would take them awhile to get back to where they were and also, they are much older now. They made the world a better place.❞

N.B.
Brooklyn, New York

112

" I'm 26 and I live in a nice spot in rural Mississippi. I'm not rich, but I'm happy with my existence. I took classical piano lessons from the age of 4 until the first time I heard The Beatles, and then, I wanted me a geetar. I've been playing the thing now for 15 or 16 years, and I ain't made no money at it, but it sure is nice to mellow you out. So, I thank The Beatles for making me want to do something (guitar) instead of being made to do something (piano). **"**

M.S.
Bogue Chitto, Mississippi

" I am 30 years old, and The Beatles have profoundly affected my life. I am a male and noticed the pixie posters the girls had in my junior high classes. I started singing along in 1963 and I still do.

They helped form my opinions more than any other group of musicians. My life style was altered to fit what was to me, a consciousness expansion all through the sixties and early seventies. The only band that rivaled them was the Rolling Stones. There are many great bands out nowadays, but I still pay attention when any of the four come over the radio. I've had many of their albums and intend to have more.

The first song I ever played on my guitar was *You've Got To Hide Your Love Away*. That was 13 years ago! Their music still influences my style. I've branched out in my musical interests since 1963 and there is a lot of damned good music out, but look . . . Paul is doing it again. **"**

D.D.
Anna, Illinois

❝I barely recall Beatlemania. I am 24 now, but I do remember the 60s clearly. At the time, rock music was just a fad to me. I cared for no one group over another. Today, The Beatles mean everything to me. I still can't believe the quality and quantity of their music. It is overwhelming. Their music for me is a hymn of life. I read, study, and listen to them every chance I get. Their work is immortal, truly a great human achievement. Their influence will never stop.

Life is written on the scroll of agony. Their music is timeless, it means more now to me as I've grown older, than when I first heard it. I'm uplifted and encouraged by their story. To paraphrase George Martin, they were a voice for young people all over the world. They criticized the system and life, and yet they improved and changed it. They started as just another Rock band and became one of the great social forces, a revolution of all time. I'm so sorry they broke up. They sing of the best things in life: love, girls, joy, emotion, happiness, fun, friends, and living. They also sing about the sad and unpleasant parts of life too; however when they were around, the world seemed such a happy, exciting, and great place. They seemed so innocent and beautiful; today no one could make us feel that way again.

The Beatles were such a magnificent sight in concert. No one will ever make such incredible music again. The wonder of their story is twofold. First, considering the odds and obstacles they faced, one wonders how they ever made it. Second, they made Rock respectable as a truly unique and valid art form. After them, the adult world had to listen to and respect Rock music. When people scream and roar at Rock concerts today, they are upholding a legacy left from The Beatles. We scream for what we lost and what can never be again, the phenomenal Beatles. I'm so sorry that I never got a chance to see them perform. Someday I hope their appearances become TV reruns or films.

Secretly, I harbor this ambition. Someday I'll make it big like they did. When I'm down, only this thought comforts me. I had better hurry up as I graduated from Ohio State University on 6/13/80 and the world is waiting. This is perhaps the best part of The Beatles' story; they became an incomparable success. They told and showed the world where to get off. They reached their dreams and exceeded them. I think most young people feel restless and trapped. We want to control our lives; yet for most of us this will always be just a fantasy. The system makes whores and slaves out of us. To me The Beatles represent and symbolize the ultimate in real freedom.

Sgt. Pepper is so profound. It makes me feel great everytime I hear it. The marvelous part of their history is that they improved with age. In the 'studio they did their best work as artists. I want to be as tough and genuine as they were. I'm jobless now with no prospects for the future. What can a kid with a B.A. in history do? These are my Hamburg and Cavern days, just like millions of other kids. I'm still trying and waiting to be discovered. We all want to make it so desperately. The Beatles are my single source of hope and inspiration. I use them as a model and a guiding star to find my way out of the rat race. *Tell Me What You See, A Hard Day's Night, A Little Help From My Friends, Rain, Ticket To Ride, I'm Looking Through You, Yesterday* and *Help* are the songs which help me make it from one crisis to the next. If I don't succeed, at least I hope to survive. Their music and prayer will help me to do so. No one will ever top them; only they can ease my suffering now.**"**

M.L.
Akron, Ohio

"I first heard of The Beatles through some friends at school, who told me that they would be making an appearance on the Ed Sullivan show; I think that I might have heard *I Want To Hold Your Hand* and maybe *She Loves You*, on the radio previously, but other than that I knew nil about the group. I was in sixth grade at the time, so I was probably 12 years old. When I first saw them, I thought they were pretty good, but I didn't turn into an instant Beatle fan. I did become one later on, around the time of **Rubber Soul**. I remember a girl carrying the album around all day at school, I think she played it during lunch period. It was rare after that I would miss a TV show featuring a segment on The Beatles. If I knew they were going to be on I would finagle my way into the neighbor's house to watch them; my father was not their biggest fan and this was in the days before families had three televisions in each room vertically stacked.

The effects of Beatlemania are still evident in today's world, at least the part of it which I perceive as my world. The long hair of the counterculture seems to date back to The Beatles. Maynard G. Krebs, on The Dobie Gillis Show, may have been first, but The Beatles were the first to popularize the shaggy haircuts, which weren't all that long to begin with, but just long enough to throw parents into fits when their sons came back from the barber's with hair longer than when they left for the shop.

The way The Beatles most affected me was bringing me to my love of music. I had listened to the radio when I could, but the best shows I can remember were Songs For Lovers or Songs For Lovesick People, something to that effect, a show that came out of Chicago which played heartbreak songs, *See The Funny Little Clown* or *Patches*, the one about the girl drowning in the river. Everything else I can remember from that time period were country music songs; I could only play the radio if I snuck it near the bed at night. The Beatles' music was entirely different. I can remember getting **Something New** and **Beatles '65** for Xmas one year. I played them on a portable phonograph, one of those typewriter-sized monographic players when you had to buy either mono or stereo records, and if you bought the wrong one, the needle would skip.

In 1971, I bought a beat up guitar from a neighbor. It was a classical f-hole type guitar that somebody had converted to a twelve-string; when I got it, there were six nylon strings, so I left it that way and learned to play mostly from chords printed over the music. A neighbor, a friend, taught me how to tune and got me started reading notes, but I honestly think that it wasn't until a year or so ago that I actually became good enough to really play the guitar halfway. I'm mostly a McCartney freak, now that I'm starting to slow down a bit I see Wings on TV, and I think that maybe, if I hang in there, ten years from now I'll be McCartney's age and I'll have a real honest-to-gosh band. Sometimes I think that's what kept me going the past couple of years; dreams of a Rock-and-Roll Beatlish future. Without dreams, what's to go on?

Electronic music dates back from the **Sgt. Pepper** album. I've read that when it first came out, well known bands delayed their albums until they could get back into the studio and "Pepperize" them. I don't think The Beatles' influence will ever leave us; too much of today is wrapped up in yesterday, and The Beatles are still too recent in history to be considered really nostalgic; that happening is still waiting for the future days when those of us who grew up on Beatle music are handing down the old albums to our grandchildren. **"**

K.H.
Auburn, New York

> **"I don't think The Beatles' influence will ever leave us; too much of today is wrapped up in yesterday, and The Beatles are still too recent in history to be considered really nostalgic; that happening is still waiting for the future days when those of us who grew up on Beatle music are handing down the old albums to our grandchildren."**

❝ I know for a fact that the music of The Beatles can change anyone's norms or personalities. It's changed mine and I couldn't be happier! They've changed my views of living life day by day. If ever I have a problem, I'll put The Beatles on to share my load because they really care. I look at the simpler things in life, I don't waste my time with annual societal b.s., that's for sure. They've taught me to let go and let life come as it is. *Fixing A Hole* for example.

I do think, however, that The Beatles had a heavier influence when they were around. Their music is still played, but their messages don't fit with today's society. **❞**

M.M.
North Caldwell, New Jersey

"One night, my father, an accomplished classical pianist, asked me if I would like to go with him for a drive. I was suspicious of anyone over age 30, and was not about to be tricked into anything. However, after much discussion, I agreed to go. We drove to a Katz drug store. And Dad bought me The Beatles' Second Album. I about fainted as by now I was a devoted fan."

❝ Before I was born again or became a punk; even before I found out about sex, I did find out about The Beatles. When The Beatles' first album came out, I was in the second grade. There was a girl with real curly hair cascading about her shoulders. Everyday she would wear Beatle buttons, boots, etc. The drug store sold Beatle wigs as well as boots . . . anyway, with this girl and all the fuss the adults made about the group appearing on the Ed Sullivan show, I became a big fan.

The first album I ever bought in my life was **Meet The Beatles**, the first album by England's Pop Combo (read the album's liner notes). Every spare piece of change I could get my hands on went for Beatle cards. There was a Beatle card vending machine by the exit of the super market I went to. So, I had piles of Beatle cards, and buttons as well.

One night, my father, an accomplished classical pianist, asked me if I would like to go with him on a drive. I was suspicious of anyone over age 30, and was not about to be tricked into anything. However, after much discussion, I agreed to go. We drove to a Katz drug store. And Dad bought me **The Beatles' Second Album**. I about fainted as by now I was a devoted fan. Later on I picked up on Jimi Hendrix and **Electric Lady Land**, or whatever his first album was. I was older then and lost all interest in the Fab Four, until very recently. Now, I am 23 and a couple of years ago was given the White Album, **Revolver**, and **Rubber Soul**. After hearing these albums, I again think of The Beatles as a tremendous group. They are probably the best group ever. Individually, except for Paul's bass and John's writing abilities, they leave something to be desired, but together they sound as good as any group this planet has yet to produce. **❞**

R.C.
Leawood, Kansas

"Being a Rock-and-Roll guitarist, I was influenced musically by The Beatles from the very beginning. The Beatles and the Rolling Stones are the reasons why I started playing music in the first place.

I am now 23, and was very young when they first hit, but I still remember, distinctly, the first time they appeared on Ed Sullivan. I had an older brother, so I started listening to Rock and Pop music in 1960 with people like Fats Domino, Chubby Checkers, etc., and I was ready when The Beatles appeared on the scene. Needless to say, The Beatles' music has always been gospel. I've listened to every song at least 200 times, and have seen each of their movies 10 times.

They influenced me on playing the guitar. The sound they were able to achieve is unsurpassed even in today's modern studios, by anybody. They revolutionized the music industry and wrote some of the best music ever.

It's impossible for me to put into words, but they influenced every aspect of my life."

B.B.
Kansas City, Missouri

"The fabulous Beatles have influenced my life. I find it very difficult to describe something which was a part of growing up and falling in love with Beatle music for 20 years!

It seems strange not to see The Fab Four around together, but only time will tell. Their music is some kind of wonderful experience and joy which will be affecting my course in life forever!"

K.K.
Shirley, Massachusetts

"I always can get something from the words they wrote; they are as if a textbook for all time. They could see into the future and so their music will, I hope, be ever entertaining to those who listen, even after I can hear their music no longer."

"I'm 31 years old, and I have been a Beatles fan since I was fifteen and The Beatles first appeared in New York. This group has influenced my life greatly, but in a way, in which, their music is always popular and I never seem to get tired of hearing it. I always can get something from the words they wrote; they are as if a textbook for all time. They could see into the future and so their music will, I hope, be ever entertaining to those who listen, even after I can hear their music no longer."

R.P.
Gloucester, Massachusetts

"My opinion of The Beatles and their musical and social influences can be summed up quite simply . . . "GOD" . . . well, that's a bit much, but The Beatles are the greatest Rock-and-Roll band in the history of music. There are all sorts of reasons for this, but the one I am most acutely aware of is this: unlike today's groups, The Beatles made music with feeling! Groups like Kansas, Styx, Alan Parsons, etc., play technically excellent music, but with no emotion! The Beatles sang with intensity, humor, and purpose, and that is one reason why they were the greatest.

The social influences of the group are important, but I don't pay too much attention to them. I just throw on the White Album, rev up the Pioneer, and the answers start coming to me."

K.H.
Des Moines, Iowa

"The social influences of the group are important, but I don't pay too much attention to them. I just throw on the White Album, rev up the Pioneer, and the answers start coming to me."

121

EMIAJ

Our correspondent from Des Moines represents a point of view which, no doubt, has many adherents. Many people see The Beatles as a prolific musical group, whose music will never be equaled. Indeed, some 17 years later, I fail to hear any sounds which evoke the same response as The Beatles did in 1964. Moreover, I have yet to hear any group duplicate the versatility of The Beatles. Basic Rock-and-Roll riffs, elements of the blues, classical, Eastern, and ragtime all can be heard in various Beatles' songs.

However, there is more to The Beatles and their effect on our world than their music. To many people, including myself, they were an ever changing social force. The major purpose of this publication was to seek out those who also felt that way. The response was tremendous, as we shall see in the next chapter.

We Were
Never Let Down

The Beatles as a major cultural influence . . . the notion would have brought laughter from many back in 1964 but, by 1970, far fewer people saw anything humorous in that statement. The Beatles were living testimony of the changes which occurred in the middle and late 1960s. The question which is pondered today is not whether they had an effect, but whether they caused the effect or merely acted as catalysts in social change. As stated in the introduction to this book, it is not this author's purpose to act as psychologist or sociologist on any facet of The Beatle phenomenon. My aim is to air as many different opinions as possible, and to do this by reprinting most of the letters I received on the subject. The fact that I may not personally agree with everything my correspondents have to say is irrelevant. The fact that those who answered my ads do have something to say is important, and can serve as a basis for readers to decide for themselves. However, I do have my opinions on the matter, and will add my two cents' worth.

When The Beatles first hit these shores, it was unlike anything which had happened to this country before. Their clothing, hair, and attitudes when speaking to the press caught us all off guard. It was a radical change. Fashion changes usually evolved much slower than The Beatles blitz which bombarded the United States in early 1964. People started washing the grease out of their hair, combed it down into bangs, and let it grow. This was their initial impact on our country. Their music, new and fresh, and not suffering from the tired, hackneyed, watered-down Rock of the early sixties, electrified the nation. Women screamed and fainted, overwhelmed by the whole experience. Men wanted to pick up a guitar and play, and have women scream over them.

By late 1965, The Beatles accomplished something which confused all their detractors. They remained popular, despite the fact that they were rapidly shedding their earlier huggable Beatlemania image. As their songs began to drift away from the standard lyrics of boy loves girl and vice versa, and move towards hitherto unexplored lyrics about religion, peace, and expanding one's mind, popularity remained high, but the participants changed.

This is the most confusing aspect of The Beatles to me, and perhaps a professional analyst should examine why some young people changed as The Beatles changed, and some did not. All I know is that it happened. My sister and I were friends with a girl our same age back in the mid-1960s in our hometown of Danbury, Connecticut. Our hometown still had a certain element of 1950 punk among its youth, even as late as 1966. There were people who still wore the black leather jackets, and the D.A. hairstyles, packages of cigarettes rolled up in the sleeve of a white T-shirt . . . in other words the whole "Fonzie/Greaser" image. By early 1966, there was a definite change afoot among the young people of Danbury. The greasers (we called them "hoods") were dwindling in size, and were being replaced by those who affected a more Beatlish attire. And then there were those kids with an affinity for both styles. It was an identity crisis in the making, with people choosing their allegiance between the hoods and the "rah-rahs."

The girl that my sister and I were close friends with had always had a certain liking for the hoodier elements in town, but she seemed to be able to exist in both worlds. She wasn't a total Beatlemaniac, but she definitely liked them, bought their albums, and screamed throughout "A Hard Day's Night" and "Help" in the movie theater. However, by early 1967, something changed entirely. She had been able to withstand the changing music of **Revolver**, which came out in August 1966, but after The Beatles stopped touring that summer, and went into the studio for five months, and came out

124

with *Penny Lane* and *Strawberry Fields Forever*, she became increasingly distant. In actuality, we both were becoming removed from each other. She, by her unwillingness or inability to understand the changes which The Beatles were going through, and us, by our total agreement and understanding of The New Beatles. I will never forget the icing-on-the-cake remark, which ended our relationship as close friends. It was June of 1967, and **Sgt. Pepper** had been out for a short while, but long enough to have many people going completely crazy about it. I was on the telephone with her, and we started talking about it, not on a real deep level, but just asking her if she had heard it. She replied that she had heard some cuts from it on the radio, but then she added, "Yeah and they want to change their name to Sgt. Pepper's Lonely Hearts Club Band . . . that's stupid!" I didn't know what to say as it was clear to me that we were speaking about the same thing, but on two completely different levels. She had missed the point completely about **Sgt. Pepper** and it being a concept album. She had misunderstood the symbolic burial of The Beatles on the album's cover, and had interpreted it as meaning that the band had just decided to change their name. We were never able to relate to each other again after that. Similarly, the changes which The Beatles were putting us through were also one of the underlying reasons for the break-up between my girlfriend and me, the story of which was recounted in an earlier chapter. She just couldn't deal with my views on the draft and the Vietnam War.

However, for those of us who continued to admire and dream about The Beatles, we were never let down. The Beatles served as role models. They showed that four individuals could unify to accomplish a goal. The Beatles, seen as a cohesive, unified spirit, became an image for the rest of us to live up to. They were able to work together, as a group; they did everything as a group, and it inspired other people to have their own groups. The birth of the anti-war movement occurred, and hippies and communes became a way of life. It became apparent by their songs and deeds, that an attitude of cooperation among people would yield a highly desirable effect.

The Beatles were the only religion I've known. I pursued their music and their lives with zeal and conscientious devotion. They were real to me. All those stories in the Bible were just stories, but The Beatles were real. For all I knew, the feats of men in the Bible were made up, but all I had to do was place a record album on the turntable of a phonograph, and the modern-day prophets sang to me. All of this seems a bit too much to me now, but I still harbor an almost innate belief that whatever force or being controls our lives intended that The Beatles come along, and for me to be so affected. This belief is not as strong as it once was, but it's still there, in the back of my mind.

In the summer of 1966, John Lennon got in a lot of hot water for stating that The Beatles were more popular than Jesus Christ. The statement, in itself, was harmless, but it drove people in the Bible Belt of the U.S. stark, raving mad. Beatle records were burned, reminiscent of Nazi book burnings, in Alabama and other parts of the South. It soon died down after Lennon, coaxed by manager Epstein, issued a semi-apology. I wasn't surprised or offended by the statement, as it had seemed obvious to me that he was right. I couldn't understand why all the fuss. I understood that Lennon wasn't saying that he approved of the situation, but was merely stating fact. Young people looked up to The Beatles. Organized religion, with its centuries-old dogma of restrictiveness and hypocrisy, didn't seem to have anything to do with the modern era, but The Beatles did.

I must admit that I do not really remember the anti-Vietnam war statements made by The Beatles at that time, but their songs of the time, *We Can Work It Out, Nowhere Man, Rain, The Word*, and *I'm Only Sleeping* screamed out against violence. I was influenced by their statements in song, but others were affected by both word and deed . . . .

"I lie in a drunken stupor. Thoughts ramble on like bad dreams. Work. . . boring work . . . it's power subdued by a beating. It's Ringo's drums. John is singing. Paul and George are in the background, harmonizing. *Love Me Do*. It's a Beatles Weekend on the radio . . . The Beatles, "A" to "Z." It's magic! They're just so good. Thoughts turn to high school, college, better days.

I was fourteen when The Beatles first became popular in the United States. They were strange to me. I didn't really understand. They were so different. They looked like beetles, with those haircuts! Their music was a complete revolution from the norm, still they were true, honest, refreshing, and NOW! They still are. It's difficult to describe. It was as if they played on their own level, and the Rolling Stones, Dave Clark Five, and Gerry and the Pacemakers were on another level. Still, I was not a Beatlemaniac; that would come later.

Drifting now . . . it's 1968, I'm a Humphrey Democrat. I don't understand the riots. The Beatles changed their music . . . it's *Strawberry Fields Forever* and **Sgt. Pepper** . . . what does it all mean? 1969, my hair longer, I'm against the draft. The White Album has Number 9. Number 9? A put on? 1972. Two years after the break-up. Hendrix long dead. No longer in college. Paul-is-dead controversy stimulates my interest in The Beatles once more. *Give Peace a Chance*. Years go by . . . I've bought all of George's albums, three of John's, one of Paul's, and none of Ringo's since the break-up. I recorded the Dick Cavett interviews with John and Yoko, and the one with George. I tape Beatle songs from the radio when they have a Beatles Weekend, which comes around quite often these days. My drawers are cluttered with Beatle albums and magazines about The Fab Four. I keep my hair long, over my ears. I try to write when I can. I draw silly cartoons. I try to express myself in a world crying for individual creativity and feelings. The boring seventies have passed, but I remember the sixties, man, that's what I think of when I hear them. The changes! That was it. That was the magic! I heard some religious fanatic, who screamed The Beatles were pied pipers leading our generation to ruin. Maybe it was true. That's it! They were our pied pipers. Peace, love, freedom, that's what the sixties were trying to say. Change our lifestyles, give peace a chance, for God's sake! If there is a God. My generation gave the world one statement. The Beatles were the quotation marks. I'm now a Beatlemaniac.**"**

S.L.
Willimantic, Connecticut

"I try to express myself in a world crying for individual creativity and feelings. The boring seventies have passed, but I remember the sixties, man, that's what I think of when I hear them. The changes! That was it. That was the magic! . . . . My generation gave the world one statement. The Beatles were the quotation marks."

"I grew up on The Beatles. I don't expect them to ever get together again, at least not for a public audience or a recording. They made their point in the albums that they have already released.

They seem to have been a phenomenon. They were more than just a Rock-and-Roll band, who started at the bottom, got to the top, and stayed there for ten years. They did something to me, and to us as a society. They did something with their music.

Anyone who grew up in the fifties knew how demented the world was. I, however, grew up in the sixties, and merely heard about it from others. So, in retrospect, quite a few of us have lost the sense of what really took place with The Beatles. They started with commercial pap, like the rest of them. Something was a bit different about this pop music. There was a subtle magnetism, which grew out of proportion with the advent of Beatlemania. Their musicianship was extraordinary, considering none of them know how to read a note of music. Even in '64, they were at the bottom of the musician's scale. They sang silly love songs, which didn't make much sense, but they had to work in that field because to try and record a **Sgt. Pepper** in 1964 is preposterous to think of. They were not yet mature as individuals. They hadn't yet experienced fame, fortune, and LSD to change the way they thought of the world. By the time they released **Rubber Soul**, Dylan had already gone to work on the youth of this country, and they were smoking pot, and by 1966 they were dropping acid . . . The Beatles were going through some real changes inside their heads. The world was ready for whatever they had to offer, and it just happened to turn our heads in the direction of love, peace, and all that sixties children remember about that decade. *Tomorrow Never Knows* was not early '64 or even '65 material. Timing was used, and the more I ponder it, the more I wonder if they had that up their sleeves all along. Possibly, but not probably, you say. Well, you may be right.

Harrison started playing the sitar, and Lennon and McCartney wrote songs which smacked of acid. The adults in charge were shocked, but incapable of doing anything about it. Kids started dropping out, and I for one, watched it all happen objectively. For those of us who were older and into the actual experience, it was more subjective . . . but I was fortunate to see it all from a child's eyes . . . just old enough to understand, but not old enough to drop out. But it changed me as I am a product of the sixties.

Then India and meditation happened, and unfortunately it went downhill. Epstein died, leaving The Beatles without professional help; but the music continued to expand, and that's what they were: musicians. They still are musicians, even after the split and legal hassle. The point is THEY CHANGED THE WORLD BY CHANGING PEOPLE. They turned us on to mind expansion (Timothy Leary wasn't trusted, but The Beatles were) via drugs and mysticism. They changed the direction of Rock-and-Roll. The competition became tough; you had to be a real musician to make a mark in the sixties, and you had to be willing to look in new directions.

I think this is what makes me so sad today when I turn on an AM or even an FM radio station. What Crap! Even the solo Beatles aren't as good as The Beatles. Lennon has hardly recorded. It is highly unlikely that anyone would listen to him with all the garbage, including punk and disco, dumped onto the airways today. He no longer could get his point across. If people have stopped listening to him, what makes anyone think that he could give us, as a nation, anything valuable any more?

So, long live The Beatles. May they rest in Peace.**"**

D.V.
Sebastopol, California

"The Beatles wanted
fame and fortune . . .
which made subsequent
shifts in values credible.
Instead of denying
dissatisfaction when
money failed to buy
love, or becoming
gluttons of power and
success, their energies
shifted to the attempts
to find what is true for
all our world by first
looking deeply into
themselves and try to
discover the morality
that superceded
societal rules."

❝I've been intending to write this letter for some time, but how can I say it after I have said it so many times before? These days it's time to think Beatle, rather than to think simply about The Beatles. To give the world The Beatles again, would be to give the world the Beatle ideal and the Beatle process of internal and external analyzation, an energy which is more powerful than its product of expression. It is that quality which I, personally, and we, as a culture have had the opportunity to gain from The Beatles. If we can look forward to an idealistic future which works, it will come mostly from the efforts of people who are willing to incorporate The Beatles' embodied search for vision.

The four Beatles are the only heroes I ever had, and never have they disappointed me. Mistakes, bad judgments and all by them have proved to be instrumental in gaining further insight. Our Beatles learned from experience, both adverse and good . . . and what they learned was that life is one's personal responsibility. It is by your own effort that things get better or worse. The excitement and energy created by them had direction and purpose. Unlike others (the Rolling Stones for example), the energy was constructive, providing insight for progress. While the Stones' music inspired excitement, it was not normal for it to point beyond hedonistic living or to move in a direction of new perception, as was common with The Beatles. The importance of that new perspective is not that it's handed, fully formed, to you, but that it's suggestive and therefore encourages involvement in the completion process. We all learn to do our own seeing, and we all become independent thinkers . . . ideally . . . in using our minds we could change the world.

Sounds simple . . . but it was believable apparently. Once something is believable, it can start to happen. John, Paul, George, and Ringo were not acting as directors, but instead were attractive examples of people using both good and adverse aspects of their experiences as steps to discovery. We all know how to tumble, but even to fall is O.K., we can still progress.

Another advantage over contemporaries that made The Beatles particularly attractive was that all four of them were like four parts of one person, as McCartney once said in The Beatles' authorized biography. And yet, each of them so purely represented their own part of the whole character. Four clearly defined parts . . . like having a human neatly dissected, its components clear and observable. The group was a clear and open example of harmony, achieved by the combination of diverse elements. The world, too, is made of diverse peoples, and harmony among them also is desirable.

Beatle goals adjusted as their perspective changed and vision grew. From the beginning the goals were honest . . . The Beatles wanted fame and fortune . . . which made subsequent shifts in values credible. Instead of denying dissatisfaction when money failed to buy love, or becoming gluttons of power and success, their energies shifted to the attempts to find what is true for all our world by first looking deeply into themselves and try to discover the morality that superceded societal rules. They had each other and themselves to look at, and they had drugs to take and the Mahareshi to listen to, plus a willingness to be open and naive in the gathering process, while thorough in the deep thinking analyzation stage. There were four minds to tackle each problem from a slightly different perspective. When they formed their values, they acted upon them. They spoke out with honesty about religion and politics, and on their own position, and sometimes, their ignorance. Importantly they spoke out on their ability to be wrong and to make mistakes. Illustrative events run from John and Jesus, to Paul's LSD statements, to Mahareshi, and to war. Even to George's disapproval of Haight-Ashbury hippies, and dare I say it . . . Ringo's dislike of Indian cuisine. The last example of a Beatle attempt to realize an ideal on a large scale was Apple, a very noble gesture, meant to be a very big change in bringing philosophical principles into a business realm.

I am not meaning to make The Beatles into kings and princes. The wonder of it all is that all four are so very human. Since that is so, we all have the same potential to act on our beliefs, and perhaps if we all spent the same amount of time with introspection as did The Beatles, we could have values based upon the same principles The Beatles found, sang, and talked about. *All You Need Is Love*, *Hey Jude*, *Within You Without You*, and *Blackbird* to name a few.

The Beatles, kings or not, helped us see en masse, principles which were agreeable because they are in us all as logical extensions of the values of fairness, coupled with peace . . . and for a while they flourished without the push of military and money. But just because perception becomes apparent, it does not guarantee the miracle of wholesale world transformation. People must act on their beliefs, even if it's in the way they see and treat their neighbors, dogs, or the car in the next lane. Not enough people really did that in the 60s, but we can try again in new and different ways. Here are the eighties. Thanks for, and love to The Beatles, who, in being human beings and in trying to be better, became models not bound in time and people who tried to channel energy into thought and action based on principles of fairness and obligation to belief.**"**

L.C.
Seattle, Washington

> "People must act on their beliefs, even if it's in the way they see and treat their neighbors, dogs, or the car in the next lane. Not enough people really did that in the 60s, but we can try again in new and different ways. Here are the eighties. Thanks for, and love to The Beatles, who, being human beings and trying to be better, became models not bound in time and people who tried to channel energy into thought and action based on principles of fairness and obligation to belief."

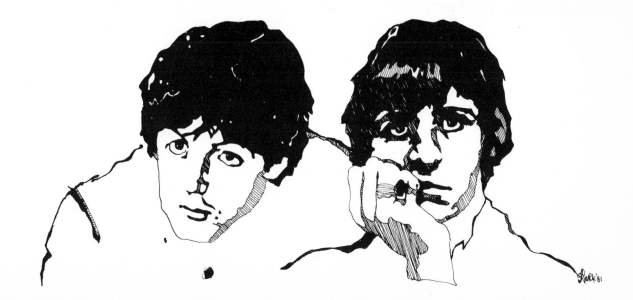

"I am a white male, 22 years old, living in the Bronx, and have recently completed four years at Fordham University, majoring in accounting. I was a mere 6½ year old on that February night in 1964. I don't remember vividly seeing their first appearance on the Sullivan show, but I do know now that everything The Beatles did touched my life most profoundly. At that tender age, one must remember that I was, like all children, most impressionable. Any kind of public hero, be it movie star, politician, or baseball star was sure to get my attention. However, it was The Beatles that won my utmost devotion, affection, and admiration . . . even up to the present time.

The Beatles were my first cognizant exposure to Rock-and-Roll. The Beatles were the first, and at the time, the only Rock-and-Rollers. I really thought that they single-handedly made their guitars, invented their amplifiers, and were the first to sing pop music. Even when I bought their second album, I couldn't figure out who "C. Berry" was, as it was almost impossible for me to fathom any other Rock stars before The Beatles. Subsequently, I also thought that later groups such as the Stones, Animals, DC5, were imitating The Beatles. At the time I referred to any kind of pop music as "Beatle Music." It wasn't long before that I was begging my father to take guitar lessons so that I could be a Beatle.

The Beatles were the catalyst for my never ending romance with Rock music. For 15 years there has not been a day where I haven't either played the radio, the stereo, or my guitar. My brother, who is three years older than I, is also really into this music scene because of The Beatles. It was The Beatles who prompted me to play guitar and thus discover one of the greater joys in my life. The Beatles dared to experiment with sophisticated recording techniques which would later yield such groups as Yes and ELO. They proved to record companies and concert promoters that there's an audience out there that is just dying to spend money on Rock-and-Roll. My present goal is to work for any record or music company that will have me, and eventually (God willing) become president of my own record label. It's funny, but a lot of my friends, who are generally disgusted with life because they lack direction, are not into music at all. I have always thought that music provided me with the impetus to face life every day. I owe all this to The Beatles.

Of course The Beatles have also affected such superficial things as the clothes I wear, and the length of my hair, but if you really think about it, even something as outward as that is bound to have some sort of influence on anybody. Subconsciously, it might have made me more vain of my appearance, always wondering if my hair was the right length or if I looked cool like The Beatles. Although some might have used long hair as a symbol of their non-conformity or rebellion against the system, to me I wore my hair in emulation of The Beatles.

At age 7, I really thought that everyone, including my parents, just had to be touched by The Beatles, but now I think a bit different. Those four lads from Liverpool, who I was totally convinced were angels from Heaven, now appear to me as a group of guys who were in the right place at the right time. Although I still revere them, I now know they put their pants on one leg at a time as I do (after all I'm older now than George Harrison was when they cut *Please Please Me*).

Culturally, The Beatles provided a soundtrack for the 60s. They were the first group to mature from a wide-eyed innocent bunch of guys singing about girlfriends and falling in love to that worldly conscious team that screamed about revolution and spreading the world with love. Because The Beatles did play genuinely good, tasteful music throughout their entire careers, they were able to maintain much of the same audience that chanted "Yeah, Yeah, Yeah" with them. The Beatles experimented with drugs as any other maturing people, and sought a deeper meaning to life through the Indian teachers as everyone, including adults, began to ask heretofore unasked questions. It's hard to say if The Beatles mirrored the ripening youth, or vice-versa, but both surely were changing.

There are many people who either can't stand, or don't understand or give a shit about The Beatles. The Beatles weren't gods, but they were an incredible phenomenon that profoundly changed my life. **"**

R.V.
Bronx, New York

"Culturally, The Beatles provided a soundtrack for the 60s. They were the first group to mature from a wide-eyed innocent bunch of guys singing about girlfriends and falling in love to that worldly conscious team that screamed about revolution and spreading the world with love."

❝I was one of the few adults who loved The Beatles from the beginning when my 14 year old daughter got their first record. My daughter (now 28 and living in London for London Weekend TV) introduced me to them. I was actually one of only two parents in our circle of friends who liked The Beatles. When The Beatles were in Chicago, I took my daughter and her younger brother, as a birthday gift, to see them. I was first of all tremendously impressed to see the thousands of young people, all beautifully dressed and clean, so admiring, so respectful (so different from the looks and behavior of concert attending audiences, in many cases, now). I was also very impressed by the showmanship, presence of The Beatles, and their respect and appreciation of the love the audience had for them.

In 1968, I considered *Within You Without You* as the most profound single piece, both musically and philosophically, although today I can't say if this would still be so. I still think the lyrics and their philosophy would be hard to beat . . . maybe added to, not dismissed. I saw The Beatles as having great empathy, not complaining, nor copping out. Even when seeing the worst in life they could be positive, they offered solutions; they were joyous . . . positive and joyous would be a good summation. Their treatment of love, besides romantic, was viewed from almost every aspect. In their comments on humanity, they dealt with a wide range . . . self-knowledge, shortness of life, death, loneliness of life, absurdity of life, and the reality of life. And it was never done negatively.

Another thing which I am sure they had a hand in was breaking down class barriers in England, and giving hope and encouragement to a lot of down-and-outers. They generally freed many areas, as mentioned above or made it possible to be less uptight. Their humor was a very important thing too. They never took themselves seriously (in public) and therefore made it easier to be taken seriously. But always, their philosophy is of prime importance to me. It's hard to recall the lyrics of any of their songs and not get a good message, such as *Help, Can't Buy Me Love, We Can Work It Out*, and *The Word*.

The Beatles' were great songs to have and share, and relate to when my two older children were growing up. We listened to the music, discussed the lyrics . . . it was GREAT! Love those Beatles. And they've grown up to be decent people.❞

M.S.
Evanston, Illinois

“When The Beatles first came to America, everyone wanted to have hair-cuts like theirs. Today, there is probably no one in the U.S. who hasn't heard of them.

I agreed with John Lennon when he was for peace. I was always against the Vietnam War. I named my new son after Paul McCartney. I think Mc-Cartney is the one with all the talent since the break-up of The Beatles. I don't think they will every get back together again, and it's too bad, because their music was the best listening music ever.”

J.M.
Phoenix, Arizona

“I am not formally or informally involved or interested in Beatlemania, but I have always loved and cherished the lyrics, scores and overall ideologies of The Beatles. The Fab Four signified a great political and spiritual elan . . . a vital driving force in the 60s and up until the time of their dissolution. The Beatles had it and said it all musically and philosophically. The Beatles were conceptually, visibly, and audibly dynamic; a vivid force for musical and social change. Long live the spirit and possible reunion of The Beatles.”

G.W.
Scranton, Pennsylvania

“The Fab Four signified a great political and spiritual elan . . . a vital driving force in the 60s and up until the time of their dissolution. The Beatles had it and said it all musically and philosophically. The Beatles were conceptually, visibly, and audibly dynamic; a vivid force for musical and social change.”

135

❝When The Beatles first invaded the American shores with their Ed Sullivan appearance, I needed parental permission to stay up because I was only 8 years old. However, I had an uncle only 9 years older than myself and I was still able to enjoy The Beatles Revolution because I obtained records from him. He would bring his records to my house on Sundays to let me listen and before he went home, I would cry until he promised me one of the records. The first record I obtained in this fashion was *I Want To Hold Your Hand*.

I distinctly remember The Beatles' first appearance in Pittsburgh, but because of my age, I was not permitted to stand along the Parkway with the rest of the neighborhood gang (who were grown-ups of 11 and 12), but after school I rushed home to sit at my desk with my radio and afterschool snack. That is where I sat, glued for the next two hours, listening to every scream from the airport, which was only a few miles from my house, and wishing I were there . . . maybe if I closed my eyes real tight . . . . A few hours later, a neighbor returned home, clutching a jelly bean that Paul had thrown out the window. No matter how much I persuaded him, he wouldn't sell it to me, not even for a month's allowance of $5.00.

I got out of The Beatle era when I went to junior high school and high school. It wasn't until approximately two years ago when once again, I became interested in The Beatles and Paul McCartney and Wings. My friends and I were sitting around the college television station, talking about music, when one of my staff members started to ask about borrowing Beatle records. Immediately I spoke up and said that I had a few, and brought them to the station. We played them constantly for the next three weeks. It was then that I realized what The Beatles had been to me . . . the beginning of a change in music for the rest of the world, but for me, it represented my growing up and identification with the past. The Beatles are even more important now that I am older and better in understanding their music and life styles. Now I respect them for what they stood for and their beliefs in music. I agree with many others when I say that The Beatles stood for individuality and nonconformity. They were often labelled as rebellious because of the way they dressed and wore their clothes, but that was probably the deciding factor for the young people of the time. Honestly, it did not make individuality in the young, who immediately copied this style, and thus made everyone the same again. And then, with **Sgt. Pepper's Lonely Hearts Club Band**, The Beatles changed their style again, and reclaimed their individuality.

Without The Beatles, it is hard to imagine what our music would be like. It is highly unlikely that The Stones, Alice Cooper, or Kiss would be where they are today had it not been for The Beatles and their innovations in every facet of the music business. Of course, what The Beatles started almost two decades ago is continuing in the sounds of today's music. Everyone, be he or she a classical musician, folk musician, rich or poor, European or American, has heard of The Fab Four.

Lately there has been more talk of a reunion, one which would probably sell movie, television, and recording rights, along with SRO audience. Some day I hope that reunion happens. After all, I feel slightly dejected that I never got to see the greatest band in music history, in person. I did get to see "Beatlemania" three times, if that's any consolation! **"**

L.B.
Carnegie, Pennsylvania

". . .'Does anyone know what a walrus is?' Well, someone took the bait, but none was prepared for his answer. In England, walrus is a term meaning 'corpse,' or what we might call a stiff. From that moment on and for the next three days, a small group of students learned things which are not prescribed for classroom discussion. We learned of the alleged death of Paul McCartney."

❝It was a cold and blustery three days in November of 1969; 7:30 A.M., and the bleary-eyed students of City College of New York entered the cafeteria at Shepherd Hall to suppress their chattering teeth and warm their numbed fingers. I had taken my seat at the current card table where we played a game called Briscola (similar to Pinochle).

After one piping hot cup of murky coffee, the other players had arrived and the cards were dealt. Another day in the pursuit of education had begun. Little did we realize that we would soon be caught up in a whirlwind of a mystery which left many doubts in at least my own mind.

One of our companions, whom I will call Blake, stopped at the table on the previous day, asked for our definition of a walrus. After a terse verbal and visual description with accompanying guffaws, he dejectedly turned away; but he returned this day with a new resolve to turn our thoughts to his dilemma. With a shaky voice and an unsettled air about him, Blake repeated his question, "Does anyone know what a walrus is?" Well, someone took the bait, and asked, but none was prepared for his answer. In England, walrus is a term meaning "corpse," or what we might call a stiff. From that moment on and for the next three days, a small group of students learned things which are not prescribed for classroom discussion. We learned of the alleged death of Paul McCartney.

Blake had a look of tired resignation in his eyes, sort of an emptiness, as he began the story, but he soon became animated, articulate, devastatingly convincing, and at times very distraught. Facts upon facts were laid on our table. Pictures . . . news clippings . . . lyrics . . . they had one thing in common . . . evidence of a death, and more. Before we rose from our seats on the third day, we had been introduced not only to death, but also to mysticism, witchcraft, kidnapping, and other more gruesome matters. We became intimate with the names of Billy Shears and Brian Epstein, with clippings from a *New York Times* dating back to 1947, and with a missing London *Times* article of the same date. We were transfixed!

The familiar sights and sounds of a large cafeteria became obliterated. Our only desire was for more information about this which hitherto had been unmentioned. It was a full week later when the first rumors of this story reached the radio stations, but we already knew the details. We were left in the midst of a triangle whose junction points were death, hoax or outrageous coincidence. I've ruled out the latter.

Shortly after all of this, I left City College and the city and moved to New Jersey. I have no idea what might have become of our little group of Briscola players, but I'll never forget the questions and doubts that were etched into my mind on a cold and blustery day in November of 1969.❞

T.S.
Oak Ridge, New Jersey

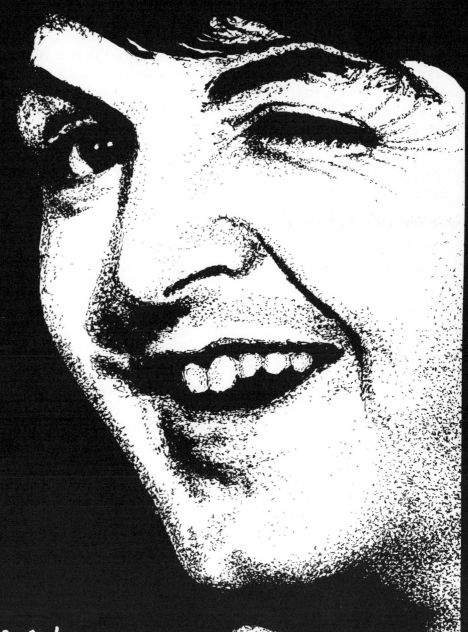

Lacey Callahan

"I was almost 17 years old when I first heard about The Beatles. I flipped when I first saw a picture of the group, especially my favorite, George Harrison. The Ed Sullivan Show was a night to remember with everyone yelling and screaming, and The Beatles looking and playing great. The music sent shivers right down my spine. The next day at high school everyone was talking about the show, even the teachers got into the discussions. After school that day, I went to Woolworth's to buy some Beatle stuff. The store was full of teenagers, mostly buying Beatle records or some collectors items.

I am one of their biggest fans. No, I didn't get to go to any of their concerts. The closest concerts were in Milwaukee or Chicago from where I lived. The tickets sold out too fast. I bought almost all their records and there are a few I don't have. I went to Europe in the summer of 1965; I loved their native country of England . . . The Beatles were touring most of our trip. We arrived in London the day the announcement came out of their being awarded the MBE award. We didn't get to go to Liverpool.

The Beatles brought on the British sound to America. The music of the 1960s is much better now than it was then. The 1960s brought a lot of social and fashion changes . . . longer hair, wilder clothes, mini skirts, fish net stockings, poor boy sweaters, the Russian look, the Shakespeare look, maxi coats, shorter heels and no pointed toes. The guys wore double-breasted suits and round collar shirts. The cultural changes . . . civil rights for Blacks, the assassination of John and Robert Kennedy, and Martin Luther King, to be able to vote and be old enough to drink at the same age, flower children and drugs, and the war in Vietnam, which everyone was against. The 1960s were a happy period, everyone was doing their own thing and trying to make the world a more peaceful place to live.

John was already married when they became famous. When Ringo Starr married Maureen Cox, everyone was sad, and the fans were surprised when George Harrison married Patti Boyd. The saddest time for most Beatle fans was when Paul McCartney became engaged to Jane Asher. When Brian Epstein died, it was very sad for the group. When Apple records started, you could see they were having trouble without a good manager and business partner.

It's too bad they broke up, but they have done well on their own: Paul with Wings, Ringo's acting, George writing more songs, and John just being John. It would be great if they would have a reunion concert, just the fun and thrill of seeing all four of them on stage again."

M.T.
Orange Park, Florida

"The first impact The Beatles had on me was to grow my hair long like theirs. Then the Beatle boots were next. I think I was in third grade at the time they made their appearance on Ed Sullivan.

The Beatles had a great impact on our society, and we also learned from them. It was a perfect two-way street, but they brought everybody back to reality by showing that perfection is short lived. They have been the most driving force in most of the young Rockers of today, but to me no one will ever quite capture the magic they achieved so well with their followers."

W.S.

Greenwich, Connecticut

"I wasn't into The Beatles very much until 1972, after I read the book, *Helter Skelter*. Shortly after that I bought the White Album and played it constantly. I was really fascinated by it, and like most of my girlfriends, fell in love with Paul McCartney. I was deeply moved by the songs, *Revolution No. 9, Helter Skelter*, and *Cry Baby Cry*, and via Charles Manson became aware of their hidden messages. I had since begun to get high, and realized that *Lucy In The Sky With Diamonds* was indeed, LSD.

So here it is, 1980, and there have been rumors of a Beatle reunion, but what the future holds for us only time will tell. If (and I think about this a lot) they do make a comeback, and if they are the four angels the Bible speaks of, and with the world full of turmoil, earthquakes, volcanoes, and famines, then it's time for a revolution. The Beatles are the ones who should tell us, and the way I see it, they have nothing to lose and everything to gain.

You probably think that I am a Manson follower, actually I am just a Beatle worshipper. The Bible, The Beatles, and Manson's beliefs parallel so well it seems so real, but I realize after much adept reading of the Bible, that one can derive any meaning one wishes to. It's all in the eyes of the beholder, and the way that the corrupted eyes of Mr. Manson saw it was only one way of interpreting their songs."

S.C.

Greensburg, Kentucky

❝ The Beatles. I feel as if I should cross myself or something. They are a part of me and of this entire generation. History will remember them with the likes of Bach and Mozart.

As a little girl, I took part in Beatlemania by carrying a Beatles lunchbox, and singing along with the radio when they played *Penny Lane*. Paul was my favorite then because he was cute. It was what a six year old could relate to. Now, at age twenty, I find that The Beatles amaze me more and more. These same guys who did catchy Top 40 tunes like *She Loves You* grew up too. Only now can I understand The White Album and **Abbey Road**. Now that I'm all grown up my favorite is John Lennon. He's brilliant. No one can match his song-writing ability. His voice can take me from the lowest low to an uncomparable high with just one verse. Even if he wasn't a song-writing genius, John would still be my personal favorite because I can identify with him. I feel as if he's real . . . as if I know him. I talked with him the last time I listened to **Walls And Bridges**. He is just like me; the me I want to be. A piece here and another there and I swear you were looking into my mind . . . not his. The things I like about John, I like about me.

John and The Beatles made me want to sing and write. They made me want to pick up a guitar and make music. John Lennon inspired me to want to write anything . . . poems, prayers, love stories . . . he made the urge in me to create greater and greater. He made me want to go beyond what was offered and create something more. He gave me something to strive for, but most important he gave me a hero . . . someone to look up to.

The feelings expressed in Beatle songs are so intense. The songs make me want to go out and experience everything . . . love, hate, excitement . . . it makes you want to be a part of the world. The Beatles' influence on music is showing up all over as the kids that were very young during Beatlemania begin to come into the picture. New Wave draws greatly from the excitement of the British Pop invasion that was created by The Beatles. They will be imitated for generations to come, but no one will ever be able to capture the initial innocence of the early days or come close to recreating all the elements which went into **Abbey Road**. They were one in a million and will live forever.

I can't help but feel sorry for young people growing up thinking that Wings is what The Beatles were all about. And is there hope for the very young who believe the Bee Gees wrote *Sgt. Pepper*? Without heroes like Lennon, why would they want to sing? **❞**

L.E.
Cuyahoga Falls, Ohio

"As a little girl, I took part in Beatlemania by carrying a Beatles lunchbox, and singing along with the radio when they played *Penny Lane*. Paul was my favorite then because he was cute. It was what a six year old could relate to. Now, at age twenty, I find that The Beatles amaze me more and more."

❝I've been a fan since January, 1964; I was 11 then, so I followed them through the important teen years. They gave me a few silly things such as I write my small "b" and the letter "s" as George Harrison wrote them. But they also influenced my tastes in music and humor (I'm hooked on British style comedy).

The Beatles had a desire for quality in their work in spite of the consequences. That willingness to experiment and to work hard has had a big effect on me, my outlook on life and my choice of occupation (I'm in art). From what I'm seeing from others in their mid-twenties, I think that they too experienced and were influenced by the same thing. The Beatles went beyond entertainers, and became models of what you should strive to be.

There is going to be a definite pattern of influence, not only in the arts but in other fields. Have you ever noticed all the young, self-made millionaires that appear on the Merv Griffin Show? There seems to be an awfully large amount of them. I wonder if they are also a product of that success striving generated by The Boys.**❞**

B.Z.
Metuchen, New Jersey

> "The Beatles had a desire for quality in their work in spite of the consequences. That willingness to experiment and to work hard has had a big effect on me, my outlook on life and my choice of occupation (I'm in art). From what I'm seeing from others in their mid-twenties, I think that they too experienced and were influenced by the same thing. The Beatles went beyond entertainers, and became models of what you should strive to be."

> ". . . I feel that The Beatles, as are all God-gifted (talented) people, are in touch with God's purpose in our lives, and have the ability to influence our destinies. I believe The Beatles were called upon to 'prepare the way' for the return of Christ. How else can He return the same as when He left?"

❝As Jesus (the Christ) ascended into the heavens, an angel appeared to the disciples and said, "Why stand ye gazing into the sky? This same man who is taken from you will return in like manner as you've seen him go."

From all our descriptions of this man, Jesus, he was a young man, between the age of 30–33, and he wore his hair long. This same Son of God was our example; however, a man called Saul (Paul) of Tarsus regulated the length of a man's hair, as well as many other things, that Christ did not (the church would have us believe this). Nevertheless, I feel that The Beatles, as are all God-gifted (talented) people, are in touch with God's purpose in our lives, and have the ability to influence our destinies. I believe The Beatles were called upon to "prepare the way" for the return of the Christ. How else can He return the same as when He left?"

W.H.
San Francisco, California

"P.S. I did a movie during the 1970–1971 holiday season with John and Yoko, called "Up Your Legs Forever," when Yoko was into her avant garde head. Have you ever seen it?**❞**

"I did a survey asking ten people if they could remember the first time they heard or became conscious of The Beatles. Eight out of ten remembered exactly where they were, who was in the room, whether it was on the radio, record, or TV, and the effect it had on them. This is markedly unusual. Was there some kind of undertone on the first Beatle record which struck the unconscious mind?"

“Consider the gap between the assassination of President John F. Kennedy, and the appearance of The Beatles in America.

JFK was assassinated on November 22, 1963 and The Beatles began their media assault on December 7, 1963. That means that the nation and the national unconscious had to go through the death and mourning of the president, followed in rapid succession by this incredibly up, joyous music which swept the country instantaneously. The Beatles did not work their way up on the charts, they blasted up in a quick sudden manner. Think about it . . . from a psychological point of view, to assimilate such a national trauma in a period of two weeks.

I did a survey asking ten people if they could remember the first time they heard or became conscious of The Beatles. Eight out of ten remembered exactly where they were, who was in the room, whether it was on the radio, record, or TV, and the effect it had on them. This is markedly unusual. Was there some kind of undertone on the first Beatle record which struck the unconscious mind?”

S.D.
Marina Del Ray, California

145

"Each new Beatles'
album produced a real
holiday spirit. You could
be assured of being willed
into swirling enticing
worlds. Until then it was
impossible to solidify and
experience unimaginable
feelings. Sounds, ideas,
and sensations were
available and somehow
secure. And even though
it was music known all
over, it was somehow
your own. It could create
personal worlds with
images and sensations
so real you could almost
taste the bitter and the
sweet; and the person
loved was never described
so eloquently and neither
was your discontent;
hearing them soothe you
to sleep and wake you
up and give you courage
to stand up for yourself."

❝I was a child of the 60s. That may be hard to believe as I am only 20 years old. I come from a midwestern family with four children, and I am the youngest. I am a child of the 60s because of my older siblings. Thanks to them, **Meet The Beatles** was welcomed into our home. Although I was only 6 years old, I was very aware of this particular album. It awakened my sense of rhythm. I danced all day to it. You could sense the magic of The Beatles in their earliest stage, but no one was to suspect their true impact.

The Beatles taught me to read, dance, be creative. They taught me that I was an individual who should be aware of how my life should be led. They led me to my career choice, and opened my mind to magic unexplainable. Practically the whole world had their shocked and unbelieving eyes on four incredible, innocent, wise men, who would change the world. Each new Beatles' album produced a real holiday spirit. You could be assured of being willed into swirling enticing worlds. Until then it was impossible to solidify and experience unimaginable feelings. Sounds, ideas, and sensations were available and somehow secure. And even though it was music known all over, it was somehow your own. It could create personal worlds with images and sensations so real you could almost taste the bitter and the sweet; and the person loved was never described so eloquently and neither was your discontent; hearing them soothe you to sleep and wake you up and give you courage to stand up for yourself.

World wide and age-wise, fully accepted now, it's hard to believe that they were initially cursed and suppressed. But it never would have worked for it was America waking up, listening to young people learning to express themselves. The world was changing its wardrobe, hairdos, lifestyles . . . everything. I don't think that we would be as individual as we are now if it weren't for John, Paul, George, and Ringo. Nothing has ever been the same. This was not an intended change, at least not on such a wide scale. Maybe they were out to change the world as we all are at some point in our lives, but did they ever imagine their impact? Did they know that the world would hang on their every word and action? I doubt it.

They have denied it . . . there lies part of their magic. They were not saviours, not gods, but real people living up to their greatest potential, changing their lives and the world. Where were you before *Love Me Do* or *She Loves You*? Can you remember the first time you heard **Rubber Soul** or **Revolver** or the feeling of awe listening to **Sgt. Pepper**? There were so many hours of amazing prolific magic from four superhumans, who created a magical decade. We can almost mark our lives by their achievements. I can remember where I was when I heard certain songs.

Looking back perhaps John, Paul, George, and Ringo would laugh at such a sentimental lifetime of memories, but it's true. Their influence on my life and the lives of others (though they may be unaware) could never be measured. No words could really do justice to their special magic. On second thought . . . perhaps only they could, but for better or worse we'll probably never see that effort. **"**

F.H.
Indianapolis, Indiana

❝I must have been around 17 years old when it all happened. High school education didn't prove to be that inspiring, and my talents and thoughts tended to drift into artwork and music. Ah, yes . . . music! In 1967, this was "The Thing." By this point, The Beach Boys had drifted away to the sea, The Stones were sniffing dandelions with honky tonk women, Barry McGuire was into "the good word," and Pink Floyd was just crawling out of the basement. Zimmerman was hiding out, after near death, with The Band, and Dennis Wilson was loaning his limo to Charlie Manson and family. There were many changes in the air, political and aesthetic, and London's Fab Four were riding the times.

"John Lennon is nothing but a queer." ruled my mother as my sister showed her the inside photo from **Sgt. Pepper**; "Look at those clothes . . . and that hair!" Luckily, Mom never found the early Zappa records stashed away, and at that time the Grateful Dead were still not that popular. Mom also ruled out Jagger as a "hopeless fag boy". Indeed.

The big mistake in the 60s generation gap was simply a matter of a certain group of people judging books by their covers. Underneath the "queer" appearances of John, Paul, George, and Ringo were four overly qualified producers and technicians, who over the years, began to master musical instruments above and beyond the call of duty. In the beginning, they were a speed freakish quartet able to hold notes and strum away, while Ringo's drums blasted out like two by fours hitting tambourines. By 1967, things were different, and I'll never forget my first earfuls of such tunes like *Lovely Rita, Within You, Without You*, and later stuff such as *I Am The Walrus*, which I consider to be the best Beatle song of them all (my all-time favorite album is still **Beatles '65**). By 1969, The Beatles would become the most technically advanced band around, with **The Beatles** (white album) as the most impressive arrangement and production of such a wide variety of music yet seen in the business, so far unsurpassed. Technically, the only group that comes close would be Pink Floyd.

Did The Beatles change my life? Well, maybe . . . or maybe I just don't see it. I've seen "Help" more times than any other film (approximately 58 times) and still find it irresistible. Their music has held up while Dylan was whining his complaints, and Jagger was stuck in premature Punkdom. The Beatles carried on . . . beautifully, I might add . . . like fresh water. Since **Abbey Road**, their last album, they have done some interesting stuff. Unfortunately, all four have met similar fates. John Lennon produced some good material for a few years and quit in the mid-70s. Ringo Starr produced some enjoyable stuff then washed out in the mid-70s. George Harrison came on like a tornado, until the mid to late 1970s. Paul McCartney sold out to commercialism after his sensational solo album. In essence all four have fallen victim to the commercial hype that built them up in 1964. Only in the 1970s, the business was different and they just could not keep up with the times. But they were a major breakthrough for music. Their improvisations during their last three albums are truly classic, bringing forth an entirely new dimension to music.**❞**

R.Y.
San Francisco, California

"Did The Beatles change my life? Well, maybe . . . or maybe I just don't see it. I've seen 'Help' more times than any other film (approximately 58 times) and still find it irresistable. Their music has held up while Dylan was whining his complaints, and Jagger was stuck in premature Punkdom. The Beatles carried on . . . beautifully, I might add . . . like fresh water."

"I was very young when The Beatles first came together as a group; I was about to start first grade when they appeared on the Ed Sullivan show. I remember vividly the first time I ever saw them on TV. They were new and different than anything I'd ever seen and I was excited and a little scared. Later, my cousin started passing her Beatle 45s on to me, and by the time I was in second or third grade, I was saving my allowance and lemonade stand money to buy their albums. As I'm sure they do with everyone else, certain of their songs have special memories to me. *I Want To Hold Your Hand* brings back a summer at the beach, and *You Know My Name (Look Up The Number)* reminds me of skating on the sidewalks around Atlanta.

I remember when The Beatles broke up. I heard it on the radio and I'm not sure I said anything for the rest of the day! The only comparable feeling I can remember is when my father told me that "Dorothy" (Judy Garland) from the "Wizard of Oz" had killed herself. The Beatles probably did not influence my life as much as they orchestrated it. It's still happening. People I know now compare current events and feelings much more often to the way a Beatles' song would present them, than the way Blondie or a New Wave group would. A funny thing about growing up is that it comes to you piece by piece, like looking at the Top 10 songs and only recognizing one. Sometimes I look back at The Beatles and wonder if we'll ever be so young again."

T.R.
Stone Mountain, Georgia

> "The Beatles probably did not influence my life as much as they orchestrated it. It's still happening. . . . A funny thing about growing up is that it comes to you piece by piece, like looking at the Top 10 songs and only recognizing one. Sometimes I look back at The Beatles and wonder if we'll ever be so young again."

"The Beatles came at a time when our generation needed someplace to escape. Their music helped us to leave reality behind. They showed us that somebody else understood what we were going through. They were a great way to rebel. My parents hated them because of their long hair and outrageous clothes.

They held us together through an exploding decade."

K.N.
Elk Grove, Illinois

> "They held us together through an exploding decade."

They did hold us together during the 1960s. I often wonder what life would have been like without them.Of course one can go on and on with "what-ifs" . . . what if the airplane hadn't been invented, what if there had been no atomic bomb, ad infinitum. However, what if there had been no Beatles?

The United States would have unleashed even more of its imperialistic aims than it did in the 1960s if there had been no Beatles around to temper the youth with notions of peace and equality. Certainly, the war in Vietnam would not have had as much opposition. I can see a never ending jungle war scenario.

Human rights would have been just something referred to in the U.N. charter. Civil rights for blacks would not have hit as many responsive white ears had it not been for The Beatles helping white culture to assimilate black music. The fight for equal rights for women would probably not have gotten off the ground if The Beatles and their new style of "masculinity" hadn't broken hitherto unbroken sexual boundary lines. The list goes on.

What about me? What would I have been like? There is no way in which I can adequately determine that. I was only 13½ years old, very impressionable, and vulnerable. Would I have been content to continue collecting baseball cards, reading comic books, and gazing at lingerie ads in the Sunday *New York Times Magazine* section? Who knows? I can only deal with "What is," or in this case, "What was." All that I know is that The Beatles had such an overwhelming effect, the likes of which I doubt will happen again.

In retrospect, one of the saddest days of my life (if not the saddest) was the day April 10, 1970 . . . when I heard the announcement by Jim Jensen (on the 6:00 News, Channel 2, WCBS--TV, New York) that Paul McCartney had decided to leave The Beatles. Some astute staff member of that TV station recognized that announcement for what it was, the end of The Beatles, and a three-minute news clip of The Beatles, shown at various stages of their career, was broadcast, musically accompanied by *Yesterday*. I watched it alone, in my room, and I tried to tape record Jensen's announcement. I played back the tape, as I was accustomed to doing after something about The Beatles had been recorded, and as Jim Jensen said, " . . . and his decision to leave that organization . . . " I shut off the machine, heard the whir of the motor die down, and I just sat there, mute for a couple of minutes. It didn't seem to matter anymore. The Beatles were over. I wasn't overly saddened at that moment because somehow, fed by a subconscious naivete that everything would work itself out, I felt that this would only be a temporary situation. Soon after I bought Paul McCartney's first solo effort, **McCartney**, and although I enjoyed songs like *Maybe I'm Amazed*, I felt that it was good he got it out of his system, as John had done with *Cold Turkey* and *Instant Karma* before him, but pretty soon they would both be working together with Harrison and Starr . . . just like always.

I recall later on that month, complete with a springtime virus, and temperature over 98.6 degrees, viewing the movie "Let It Be," and enjoying it. However, there were several times during the movie where I began to sense that something was not right, and had not been right for some time. The movie had been recorded some fifteen months earlier, and it could easily be seen that The Beatles were not acting as that unified, cohesive band which they had once been. I left the movie theater feeling distressed and uneasy about the future.

The final blow for me occurred on May 4, 1970. The Kent State murders happened on that day, and I was so outraged and horrified by it . . . that something clicked inside my brain and I realized that there weren't going to be anymore Beatles to guide the youth of this country . . . no more new Beatles songs to rally around. I was devastated. Soon Hendrix and Joplin were dead, and factionalism among the Woodstock Nation (as Abbie Hoffman referred to the sixties sub-culture) began to develop as the economy worsened and all those wonderful people, steeped in idealistic pursuits to make this planet a better place to live, were forced by the ruling class of this country to find work in order to make ends meet. Competition reared its ugly head where cooperation had once lived.

I had never experimented with drugs . . . I never felt a need to because I got high from listening to The Beatles. That was all I needed. In the summer of 1970, that same summer which followed the termination of The Beatles and the summer which found me changing into another decade, from teenager to twenty years old, I began to smoke marijuana. I must admit that I don't really recall the year of 1971. I toked up a lot that year, and I was so stoned that I wouldn't allow myself to feel anything. My heart was broken, my Beatles were gone . . . I used dope to lessen the pain. It seemed to help by making me forget ugly realities. Beatle songs had been an escape, from the false realities society forced upon me to the actual realities of life.

I do not feel any animosity towards The Beatles for the pain I felt in the early 1970s. After all, they had given me so much pleasure. I only use my disintegration upon their demise to illustrate that The Beatles were a powerful social force and cultural influence.

There are some people who don't see it that way. Some individuals felt untouched by The Beatles' phenomenon, and others openly detested The Fab Four. We'll hear their stories in the next chapter.

8

I Still Can't Understand Them At All

I have never been able to understand how someone of my generation could fail to be captivated by The Beatles. I can understand my parents' generation being less than enthralled with them, and I recognize that the vast majority of today's teenagers barely know who The Beatles were, but I find it inconceivable that anyone born between 1947 and 1957 could not be in love with The Beatles. Yet, to my dismay, there are those among my peers who don't place that much importance on The Fab Four.

I know of such people. I work and live with them. They think I'm crazy to be so involved with The Beatles; I think that there is definitely something lacking in their awareness of what surrounded them during the 1960s. To a Beatle-maniac, they are an unpleasant reality which one must learn to live with, but I still can't understand them at all. Most of these people are nice to be with and talk to, except for this particular flaw in their characters.

Not surprisingly, I received very few letters expressing lukewarm or negative feelings about The Beatles, and so, appropriately for a book of this type, this chapter is small in comparison with others. People generally respond to advertisements only if they are attracted to the theme or the article for sale, so naturally I received letters from those who basically approved of The Beatles. However, a few people did respond in a less than favorable vein on The Beatles as an influence on our world, and they deserve to be heard as well . . . so, upholding Voltaire's notion of perhaps disagreeing vehemently with the opinions about to be expressed, I do defend their right to speak their minds . . . .

"The Beatles first came to my attention as I was perusing an issue of *Life* magazine at a local teen center rec room, one weekend late in 1963. They were pictured greeting Queen Elizabeth after giving a royal performance at Albert Hall or some such place. The length and cut of their hair, facial expressions, matching attire; in essence their very appearance riveted me.

When WLS (Chicago) played *I Want To Hold Your Hand* a few weeks later, it did not impress me. The song seemed awkward. The Sullivan show appearances interest me more. The opening number, *All My Loving*, was electric in its excitement. The Beatles and their audience looked to be having a good time.

At a record store the sleeve of the Capitol 45 rpm release of *I Want To Hold Your Hand/I Saw Her Standing There* pictured the foursome closely huddled in collarless grey suits with a lit cigarette conspicuously displayed in the fingers of Paul McCartney. Their music was growing on me, but this image upset me and I wanted to dismiss them.

1970: For about one year I had been having trouble applying myself to my school work at the University of Iowa. I recall being in tears as I told someone that The Beatles were soon to split up. It seemed that they were about to lead the people of the world to a new world. In some ways I suppose they did. I've read and I believe that The Beatles are in a large part responsible for a revolution that has taken place in the recording industry, and, to a lesser degree, the revolution in changing lifestyles and values. But there is the gestalt, the figure and the background: the world was ready for The Beatles and The Beatles were ready for the world. Someone had to be a symbol.

But lately when I think of The Beatles, the cynicism returns. They were a show biz hype, an overblown diversion, more like the filmed spoof, "All You Need Is Cash." "

M.L.
Charles City, Iowa

> "At a record store the sleeve of the Capitol 45 rpm release of *I Want To Hold Your Hand/I Saw Her Standing There* pictured the foursome closely huddled in collarless grey suits with a lit cigarette conspicuously displayed in the fingers of Paul McCartney. Their music was growing on me, but this image upset me and I wanted to dismiss them."

"The beetles' influence on my life has been a rather nasty one. These ugly black creatures destroy crops and walk around on the sidewalk without any sense of humanitarian purpose. Dig? I think they have added some interesting photographs to insect textbooks.

Now The Beatles, on the other hand, are really a stroke of luck. If it hadn't been for Brian Epstein casting them down in a car to a London recording studio, they would have remained a British quartet playing as a house band in The Cavern, unheard of and unknown to the world. But since they are known to the world I would have to say that they have had a tremendous impact on record sales for Capitol. They made more prodigious, the economic influence of the recording industry.

What did they do for society? They added 20 or 30 albums, so you might say they enriched culture. They grew their hair long so you might say they changed styles, even though Washington, Hamilton and the Federalists all wore powdered wigs. On the other hand they spurred a generation gap causing waves of severe controversy between parents and children, with children dancing to beautiful C--Am--Dm chord progressions, while parents shouted to turn off that loud obnoxious Rock-and-Roll with lyrics I can't understand.

Their movies were poor excuses for their songs. What bugs me and frustrates me is why their songs are so good. So many groups emulate them in sound . . . Badfinger, Electric Light Orchestra, Raspberries, Klaatu, even Cheap Trick's *I Want You* reminds me of John Lennon belting out *I Want To Hold Your Hand*. So, in one sense you might say they were trend setters such as Jefferson with democratic principles, James Brown with soul music, and NASA with space flights.

In the end, I think as individuals they are less important than as a group. My interpretation is that they added more culture to society and offered to musicians something to look forward to in an otherwise miserable world."

C.S.
Jamaica, New York

❝The Beatles were part of an energy which made the 60s what they were. This energy influenced our thinking and actions. I don't know what it was, but things completely changed for me and everybody in 1971. It was as if the veil lifts. Whatever we were under the influence of, went away.

The Beatles went away with that 60s energy or force, as did campus riots, small town bands, and acid for the most part. A whole way of looking at things went. The Beatles are nothing but a memory of that time. They were so right for that 60s energy . . . that strange force, and that's why they may never re-form. They can't. You can feel deep in your bones that it wouldn't be the same. The good vibrations are happening now. We look back at that time and try to bring it back because we had nothing to replace that 60s energy with when it went away. We were left in an Elton John void and he burned out trying to fill that gap. Something else will undoubtedly come along sometime soon. Rock will progress and move on to something else. The Beatles and their fans are not sick, like the Elvis fans are.

The Beatles do not influence my present life. Their music was interesting. It was not physical like Elvis' music. It let you enjoy it while you went ahead with your own life. It enhanced life in the 60s, but it wasn't the 60s and that's why it can't really come back now.

The Beatles' music was basically false and unreal, hopeful and idealistic. The Fab Four realized this and that's why they no longer make that kind of music. They don't have the 60s energy to drive them, tickle them, or stimulate them. We will never hear an idea like *Strawberry Fields Forever* again. You can't and don't look back. It's scary really . . . ever wonder what the fuck happened to the music of John, Paul, George, and Ringo? In the 70s it was like the 60s never happened. They can't find the groove. They don't ever talk much to each other. They know what held them together is utterly gone. They probably try not to think about it, and so do I.**❞**

L.R.
Green Bay, Wisconsin

"The Beatles' music was basically false and unreal, hopeful and idealistic. The Fab Four realized this and that's why they no longer make that kind of music. They don't have the 60s energy to drive them, tickle them, or stimulate them."

"It hardly seems possible that it was 15 years ago or so that as a 10th grader I rushed home one night to turn on my parents' old black-and-white television set, like so many others of my generation, to tune in and watch old Ed Sullivan introduce the new English rock group: The Beatles.

In the week or two prior to that show, which supposedly hit new highs in the ratings for old Ed, it seemed as though every other song on the favorite high school set, Flint area, radio station had been a Beatle song. Obviously, a well-coordinated publicity effort. The next day, in our English class discussion, one smug little girl announced that "their success wouldn't last."

In superficial terms, I think that The Beatles were the first group of any kind that I know of during that period (male) who let their hair grow long; and then before you knew it, nearly everybody in creative circles and others, had grown their hair. In 1966 for example, when I first went to college, virtually all of the young men had bushcuts and "Princetons" and wore white socks. Their influence in dress was eventually felt.

As so far as the influence The Beatles have on society; I could personally point out dozens of little horror stories about persons whom I know of, who formed groups, and perhaps unconsciously followed The Beatles into drug experimentation . . . even pushing . . . and eventually winding up in jails, mental hospitals . . . that sort of thing and even worse.

When I was a student at Ann Arbor, about 1970, they had a huge wall sized poster that you buy in head shops. A picture of John and Yoko standing spreadeagled, full front nude; and later on that year, John Lennon himself came to the campus, not to perform, but just to wander around and take in the sights. He had his head almost shaved at that time, and looked like a strange looking person . . . the big past obviously behind him. He attracted medium-sized crowds just walking around.

In retrospect, having lived through that period, The Beatles just seemed to hit the American market just as the economy was coming out of a slight recession, and just happened to roll along for about six fat years. At times they seemed so close to the forefront of "movement" directions, it was hard to tell if they really had some kind of pervasive influence during their times . . . I kinda doubt that."

G.S.
Burton, Michigan

"I am 26 years old now, but back in 1971, when I was in college, I got into the hippie scene. It was fading at the time, but that's when I got into it . . . the long hair, the feeling of love and understanding, the drugs, seeking one's inner self. These things weren't really happening before The Beatles. The Beatles allowed me to go into a type of world, a counter-culture so to speak, a world where I could stop dressing up to go to class . . . where a pair of jeans and a T-shirt were O.K. They were a big factor in my life, listening to their albums and for hidden messages in their songs.

As I look back on them, The Beatles were an attempt by the Devil to turn people away from God. Sounds weird, I know, but you have to think about it. So many people looked up to these non-Christians. These were our heroes. What they did and thought about is what a lot of us wanted to do and think. Consciousness-raising groups have risen up since The Beatles. I practiced on intense meditation for five and a half years. The Beatles drew a lot of people away from God with promises of freedom. There is no salvation without accepting Jesus Christ. You can't get to Heaven meditating, at least not the Heaven described in the Bible. One can look at Christianity as a type of meditation or consciousness movement that goes further than any man-made trip. The Beatles gave rise to so many other ways of getting there. The Devil is busy and very clever.

The Beatles took me through an era of my life that I loved and wouldn't have changed for the world. It was great! "The Life" as I have called it so many times. Kids grow up. I hope the individual members of The Beatles are touched by God. Pray that the individual members will be touched by God. If it is His plan it will happen. New heroes with a different value system to inspire the millions that they inspired in the 60s and 70s. Amen.**"**

G.J.
Maplewood, Missouri

"As I look back on them, The Beatles were an attempt by the Devil to turn people away from God. Sounds weird, I know, but you have to think about it . . . . There is no salvation without accepting Jesus Christ . . . . The Devil is busy and very clever."

159

9

A Discovery
After The Fact

There is no doubt that the next three chapters include the letters which shocked and amazed me the most. Just as it had always been a mystery to me that anyone born between 1947 and 1957 could not be a Beatle fan, it had also never occurred to me that anyone born in the early 1960s and after could relate to The Beatles at all. However, after initiating my search for correspondents in June 1979, I became aware that for every letter received from an original Beatlemaniac, there were two letters from people who I had always considered too young to be influenced by The Beatles. Present-day teenagers as Beatle fans . . . people who were only two or three years old when The Beatles first appeared on the "Ed Sullivan Show," and in some instances, kids who were born after Beatlemania began! How could this happen, I wondered? In some cases, it was simply an inherited interest from an older sibling, but in many instances it was an acquired taste. Somehow these post-Beatlemania teenagers had discovered them. This discovery process was totally different from that described in letters of prior chapters; it was a discovery after the fact.

I was skeptical at first, but the sheer volume of letters from teenage Beatle fans has convinced me otherwise. I now know that they are among the most loyal Beatle fans. Most are unaware that there are other people their age who are into The Beatles, but as indicated by the hometown addresses, this phenomenon is not isolated to one geographic location, but is widespread across the United States.

It was difficult to divide these letters into chapters, but again, for reasons of convenience, I have arranged them thematically. The first group focuses on those teenagers who wished that they had been old enough to experience The Beatles as The Fab Four evolved . . . .

"I am fifteen years old and was born at roughly the same time The Beatles first came to America. I was four years old when **Sgt. Pepper** came out and only in the first grade when they broke up. Nevertheless, The Beatles had a tremendous effect on my life, even though I was too young during the time they were together to really understand what was going on. I missed out on Beatlemania firsthand, but in those years when they were at the top (and even later), they literally changed the world, including me.

As a child, I liked them. I liked songs such as *Penny Lane, Lady Madonna*, and *Lucy In The Sky With Diamonds* without realizing any of the social implications . . . on the strength of the music itself. It was only later that I rediscovered them, the hidden meanings, oblique, charming poetry, and the subtleties hidden beneath. I believe that their sheer music itself is a lasting strength; the timeless melodies which I loved as a child came from childhood itself, with the sharp observations of their Liverpool youth. The amazing, true-to-life characters like Eleanor Rigby were depicted in a pure, clear, unbiased way . . . brutally honest, and yet, innocent like childhood. They were people that your mother should know, and probably did, even if the lines were not scanned for hidden nuances, the simple stories in The Beatles' music could stand alone.

The Beatles were like divine messengers in a way. They showed the youth of America, who were at a desperate point, that there was another way of life besides that of their parents, thus bringing on the birth of the counterculture. As they changed from the loveable, cheeky moptops of Beatlemania into everybody's favorite gurus, America and the world changed behind them. The Beatles were spokesmen for the young, a symbol of the timeless rebellion of young people against authority. And now, nine years later, it's all over . . . The Beatles have gone their separate ways and the dream has dispersed.

I'm sorry I wasn't a part of their generation, but I still idolize The Beatles in the face of all that has happened since then. Why should I ignore the music of today, and retreat to the past? After all, isn't today's music my birthright, like the music of Janis Joplin, the Stones, Hendrix, and The Beatles were the birthright of those who came of age in the sixties?

The music of The Beatles is indeed timeless, as well as magical. It must have been magic which drew those four young Englishmen together out of the Liverpool slums to rise to immortality . . . to legend. They shook the foundations of society; they wiped clean and drew again the face of popular music, and they wrote songs which are destined to become classic, if they aren't already. The freedom and individuality that John, Paul, George, and Ringo brought to the world have reshaped my life over a distance of ten years, as well as the lives of countless others. If their magic works for me, a person who is only listening to their songs second-hand, think of what it must have done to the people who lived during their heyday!

I love The Beatles, and will always love them, even though they no longer exist. I grew up on them, and the enchantment, the sheer joy of their music will last long after everything else has faded away."

D.T.
Grenada, Mississippi

"I believe that their sheer music itself is a lasting strength; the timeless melodies which I loved as a child came from childhood itself, with the sharp observations of their Liverpool youth. The amazing, true-to-life characters like Eleanor Rigby were depicted in a pure, clear, unbiased way . . . brutally honest, and yet, innocent like childhood."

"Throughout my three years of reading books on The Beatles, I often have wondered whether or not the information written was true. I wanted someone who had lived through the 60s and The Beatles to tell me what really went on. Yet, finding that person seemed to be out of my limits. I compared information from different books and then formed my own ideas."

❝I'm only sixteen years old, so it's ironic that The Beatles and their music have even touched upon me. I can remember when I was in 7th grade, I had a friend two years older, who was really into The Beatles. He kept trying to get me to listen to them, and I barely knew who they were. Then, my brother, also two years older, began listening to them and I think that's how I got started. First it was all the early tunes, you know, the Red Album (Beatles greatest hits 1962--1966), and then slowly, but surely I progressed through every phase The Beatles went through. It was twice as difficult for me because I could only imagine what things would have been like during the sixties (as I was born in 1964). Through books I realized what an impact The Beatles had on the world. It's incredible. I've seen every Beatle movie, read every Beatle book, listened to every album, and still my mind is blown from the tremendous part that they played in shaping music, society, and the world. I can't imagine what the sixties or music would have been like without The Beatles. I still feel they are one of the greatest bands of all time.

People (mainly my parents) thought I was crazy for getting so wrapped up in things that happened before I was old enough to understand them. The Beatles helped me to learn about other things that went on in the sixties like Vietnam and dope and flower power and all those other good things. I've gained so much knowledge . . . it's phenomenal! Throughout my three years of reading books on The Beatles, I often have wondered whether or not the information written was true. I wanted someone who had lived through the 60s and The Beatles to tell me what really went on. Yet, finding that person seemed to be out of my limits. I compared information from different books and then formed my own ideas. The real highlight of my studies of The Beatles came on January 13, 1980, when I saw a performance of "Beatlemania." That has got to be the most incredible experience of my life. It sounded like the fellas, kind of looked like them, but didn't quite make it. Then I realized that this was the closest that I was ever going to come to seeing a real Beatle concert. It made a pretty close second. The slides which showed all aspects of the sixties were so enlightening and the light show was fantastic. As the group traced the different eras The Beatles went through, I think people imagined what they themselves were doing at that time. When the tripping songs were played (*Lucy In The Sky With Diamonds, Strawberry Fields Forever*, etc.) the smell of pot drifted towards my seat and it was so moving. Hell, I figured, those four guys up on the stage pretending to be The Beatles were enough to put me on a high I'll never come down from. I'm just glad I discovered The Beatles when I did; otherwise I would have been missing out on something pretty big. Maybe some day they will re-unite, but if they don't, it wouldn't really matter because they've already made a contribution great enough.❞

S.S.

Macungie, Pennsylvania

164

❝The Beatles first influenced me with their White Album. I never knew they existed until my brother brought that album home one day. It wasn't until 1974 that I became interested in them. I got hooked from that album.

I wanted to know more about the group and I needed to hear all of their songs. I listened to the White Album constantly and my family didn't really like me to; however most of the time I'd listen to it when I was by myself; whenever I got lonely or depressed I would play that album and it somehow had the power to keep me from feeling lonely and depressed. I still like to put it in whenever I feel that nobody cares anymore. I especially listen to the second side; I could listen to those songs all day.

The second album my older brother bought was the Blue Album (Greatest hits 1967--1970). He stopped buying Beatle albums so I took over from there. I bought the Red Album, and then bought all of the originals. It took me less than two years to buy complete collections (not counting bootlegs) and many of the solo albums after they broke up. I bought every new or different album I could find. I went to conventions, watched their movies, and taped the movies "A Hard Day's Night" and "Yellow Submarine" on my portable cassette player. The only movie I have yet to see is "Help"; one of these days I would like to see it. I wrote to each of The Beatles' recording studios asking for information. All of them wrote me back and sent me things.

The Beatles had a great impact on society. The Beatles were growing and living through the same kind of problems and situations their fans were going through at the time of their success. Their influence can be seen by John Lennon's statement that The Beatles were more popular than Jesus (the critics always neglected to include the end of that statement . . . "and that's too bad") being taken so seriously. The Beatles were constantly in the spotlight and everybody wanted to know their opinions on everything from what kind of clothes to wear to who should become the next president. Many people took whatever one of the four said as "gospel" and would pattern their lives after them. Some people may still do so.

Even though they are no longer a group, they are still influencing society. They represent "Angels of Mercy" to some who want them to give benefits for the good of many less fortunate people. Even today, some people think that if The Beatles get back together, everything will be all right. I don't think they could fulfill all the hopes and expectations we place on them.

I am 19 years old and most people think that I am too old to be freaking out on The Beatles. Fortunately, I do not pay much attention to them. I wish I were older now, so that I could have had the privilege of growing up with them. I have the desire to meet Paul and/or George; to talk to them for a few minutes.

Not only have The Beatles influenced the people of the 60s, they are still influencing people through their music which will live on forever even if they become a distant memory.**❞**

E.P.
Alexandria, Virginia

> **"I listened to the White Album constantly and my family didn't really like me to; however most of the time I'd listen to it when I was by myself; whenever I got lonely or depressed I would play that album and it somehow had the power to keep me from feeling lonely and depressed. I still like to put it on whenever I feel that nobody cares anymore."**

"The love each Beatle held for the other was so strong that I still feel it whenever I see Beatle films. That kind of friendship is something I have been looking for my whole life and have yet to find . . . . They never tried to change the other; each person was their own self and they didn't try to change."

❝ I never had the opportunity to experience The Beatles while they were still together as a group, but they still had an impact on me and changed my life. I am a second generation Beatle fan, and I just became interested in them after a friend of mine started liking them and never stopped talking of their views and music. We really started liking them after hearing how good their music was. Today, there are very few groups who are seriously worth listening to, so we looked back and realized The Beatles have been the best group to ever come along.

Their views and attitudes on life have influenced me also. I greatly admire and intensely respect and love John Lennon because he has always stood up for what he believed in, and he didn't let other people influence him. Learning about his life and the pain he experienced made me realize that I should be the person I want to be and not let others influence me. I always look to Lennon when I feel down and alone. I see that he spent his whole life by himself, yet he still stood on his own two feet. He never conformed to the rules of society like his counterpart, McCartney, did, and that also is my attitude on life. Lennon showed society that everyone should be themselves and learn to love one another. The Beatles showed the world that love is all you need. They had their differences and fights, but they stood together and led the way for many maturing adolescents.

Each Beatle stood for different aspects of a personality. McCartney was the conformist, hardworking Beatle who wanted things to center around him. Lennon was the opposite; he was the non-conformist, the one who stuck his neck out for what he believed without thinking of the consequences. He was the one who never seemed to care and took everything in stride. Ringo was the loner; the pitiful one who everyone loved; the clown who gave the world a smile. Harrison was the quiet one; the one who was inside of himself and the mystical one. Each fan identifies themselves with the Beatle(s) who is most like them.

The Beatles changed my life. It probably seems ridiculous to a non-Beatle fan that four men who I'll probably never know personally could influence and change me. It is not a deep physical attraction; I am attracted intellectually and emotionally as well by their bond of friendship. The love each Beatle held for the other was so strong that I still feel it whenever I see Beatle films. That kind of friendship is something I have been looking for my whole life and have yet to find. I am jealous of them and I always wish that I could have friends like them. Their type of friendship is so rare because they are four totally different men who cared and loved each other and helped each other out. They never tried to change the other; each person was their own self and they didn't try to change.

The Beatles had a lot to say and they said it beautifully. The whole deep message was that everyone should love each other. And what they say is not idealistic nonsense; it is the truth. If everyone loved each other, everyone would be happy and problems could be solved. True Beatles' fans have a certain love for each other that no one else can share in. It is a love that can't be explained in words, but it is there. I witnessed the breakup of The Beatles and we all cried together when it happened. I didn't cry in 1970 when it happened, but I cried in 1976 when I fully understood all they stood for. We probably wept harder than they did. We laugh with them at their press conferences and films and we all got excited and happy when each of their children were born. We share in their lives even though they don't know we exist.

I attended the Beatlefest in New York City last year, I could feel the presence of The Beatles in the room, and I felt their love. The Beatles are a symbol. They are four different people who went through hell to give the world a smile. Maybe they didn't affect everyone and some people might think The Beatles are nothing more than a headache, but I know that for myself I feel love whenever I think of them. I have a worldwide family to share my feelings with. People who aren't in this family can't and won't ever understand. People laugh at me all the time because of my intense feelings for The Beatles and I say go ahead, let them laugh, it doesn't bother me because they will never know what they are missing.

I wasn't there in the 60s; I wasn't there, but I was. I lived through the same things fans did during the 60s, but I wasn't actually there. I relived everything through their films, books, and talking with other fans. Most people who talk to me wouldn't be able to tell if I actually witnessed them or not because in a way I did experience their impact. It is very hard being a second generation Beatle fan because we have no personal memories of The Beatles. It is really sad for me when I realize everything I missed because there were thousands of people to share your feelings with and The Beatles were actually real. I missed all that love and excitement, but that doesn't mean I didn't experience it. I experienced everything everyone else did, but I could only share it with 3 or 4 other people. When I watch The Beatles at Shea Stadium, I can't say I have any personal memories of it, but I feel the same feelings those people in the audience did.

Time is an irrelevant factor with The Beatles. Their attitudes and views are still heard and seen through films. Try to imagine the feelings of third and fourth generation Beatle fans. They might not even have one of the ex-Beatles to see, but I am sure that there will still be Beatle fans for many years to come. The Beatles stood for many, many things, but their one dominant view is universal and will go on indefinitely; That is love.**"**

D.H.
Newark, Delaware

"It is very hard being a second generation Beatle fan because we have no personal memories of The Beatles. It is really sad for me when I realize everything I missed because there were thousands of people to share your feelings with and The Beatles were actually real."

"When I was 4, I felt the excitement they radiated. Now at 16, I can still feel it . . . I just hope I don't outgrow it."

66Although I am only 16 years old, The Beatles are a major part of my life. When I was about 4 or 5, I remember watching them on The Smothers Brothers Show. I could feel some sort of energy, but I couldn't understand what it was all about. I got the same feeling when I watched "A Hard Day's Night," "Help" and "Yellow Submarine." Now, at age 16, I get the same sort of feeling when I see those films. I still don't fully understand why I should feel this way about a group that I can barely remember, except that the four of them together had a magic that just knocks me off of my feet.

My favorite part of the year is attending the Beatlefest. It's really fantastic to share the Beatle fever with hundreds of other Beatle freaks. Nearly all of my money goes towards Beatle records, books, magazines, posters, etc. With all the Beatle shops there are, my money disappears very quickly. If I had a million dollars, I could easily spend it in one day, entirely on The Beatles.

I have many Beatlefan penpals and friends. I've found that many people have a general knowledge of The Beatles and if not, they're always willing to listen and learn a bit about them. I think the two main reasons I began collecting Beatle material two years ago is that I wanted to find out more about the excitement which I missed during the 60s and my very favorite performer, Ringo Starr.

When I was 4, I felt the excitement they radiated. Now at 16, I can still feel it . . . I just hope I don't outgrow it.99

S.N.
Sunland, California

" The Beatles are (sorry . . . "were") the best! To me, in a special sense, they still exist. One of my deepest regrets in life is that I was born in 1966 (that's right, I'm only 13 years old). I never actually saw The Beatles; I have to live in their memory, but WOW . . . what a memory! I am so grateful that John, Paul, George, and Ringo left me movies, posters and records. With these things, The Beatles will live forever.

I grew up listening to The Beatles. They have shaped my life. They started my interest in music. I love to play their songs on piano and guitar; I also love to sing. It is virtually impossible to have a favorite Beatle song. They had so many and every one of them was fantastic. Almost everyone has a favorite Beatle; I love them all, but Paul McCartney is special. I don't know what it is about him, but to me he's the greatest. I particularly like early Beatle songs. The tunes are not too involved, but they are fun to listen to. Sometimes I could sit for hours listening to their later music and find out what they were really trying to tell me. If you listen really hard, you can find the key to all your problems.

I wake up to The Beatles in the morning, I eat with them, wash to them, and dress to them. I have been late to school many times for staying to hear "just one more song." When I get home from school, it's back to The Beatles. I listen to about two albums a day, two times each. Then and only then, do I turn on a radio to keep up with the latest music.

I try to keep up with what they are doing now. I was shocked and kind of hurt when Ringo Starr recently said that he did not want to be known as a drummer anymore. I know that it is his life, but come on! . . . never again! He also said that The Beatles would never get together again. I know they probably won't and that it would never be the same again, but I think every Beatle fan adds that little petition to their prayers at night. It's just a silly dream all of us will carry for the rest of our lives. **"**

C.M.
Long Beach, New York

> "I wake up to The Beatles in the morning, I eat with them, wash to them, and dress to them . . . . When I get home from school, it's back to The Beatles. I listen to about two albums a day, two times each."

❝I was born in 1962 and was a child during Beatlemania, but somehow The Beatles greatly affected me. I call myself a Beatle Baby. The music of The Beatles has always been with me. As a child I heard my oldest brother playing The Beatles. Something about their music and the feeling of the time struck deep inside me and stayed there. To this day, I long for the 60s, and for some strange reason I wish that I was a teenager then instead of now. I feel as if I missed something, and yet, I must have caught something.

In the past year I have come to realize my desire to have been a part of that time. I have become so involved with my feeling that I am confused. I become deeply depressed when I read about the four Beatles now, and realize that what was will never be again. I wish to experience the excitement of the 60s as it happened, not as a child unsure of what was going on. Now, I can only reminisce. I don't understand my feelings. Are there others like me? Who genuinely feel affected even though they are kids now?

I have come to understand the real influence The Beatles have had on me. I am really into their music, lives, and the 60s. Writing this letter has helped me try to find someone who might understand. For me, a Beatle Baby, they were even more god-like than they appeared to be in the 60s. I guess it is because they were so intangible. Beatle fans of the 60s are still around, but they have grown up and moved on in life. Of course they do not forget The Beatles; it just isn't the most important part of their lives. However, I haven't had my fill yet. My mind is still heavily preoccupied by The Beatles. I find that there are not so many my age who share my enthusiasm for The Beatles . . . they are not aware of them.**❞**

K.L.
Marietta, Georgia

"I am a 14 year old girl, so naturally I was not around when The Beatles came to our shores in 1964. But even so, The Beatles, in my mind, will always be the greatest group in the history of the world. My only regret is that I was never around (or I was too young) to feel the power of Beatlemania, to really know what pandemonium it was, to wait with curiosity for their new albums to be released, and to know them as The Beatles, not as the ex-Beatles.

The Beatles have made me more of an independent person because I'm not at all like my friends in their musical tastes. They like people like the Bee Gees, Village People, etc. So I feel really independent and proud to say, "I like The Beatles" when most of my friends haven't heard of them or call them old.

It's strange how my love for them has grown. About two years ago I was in New York City, and I saw "A Hard Day's Night," "Help," "Let It Be" and the Broadway play, "Beatlemania." I enjoyed them of course, but if I saw them now, I think I'd faint. The Beatles have made my life more happy and enjoyable. Whenever I feel blue or sad, I think about them and start singing their songs. It cheers me up a lot.

I've never thought of them as gods because I know they took LSD and other drugs and had premarital sex (all of which I think is wrong), but they've always been great people to me. Paul is my favorite and of course it is because he is a living doll! Also I'm into Wings. I think they're a fantastic group, but I don't think they're as good as The Beatles, of course. I think I'd do almost anything to meet Paul! Someday, maybe I will meet him. Some day I wish!

My brother loves The Beatles as much as I do. He is 21, and does remember seeing The Beatles on the Ed Sullivan Show. I think that he must have been the one who got me interested in them because I remember him playing their music, and gradually I came along. I don't think it would be very good if The Beatles got back together . . . maybe for one concert or show, but not as a working group. They've grown apart from each other and I'm totally satisfied to see them as good friends."

E.F.
Austin, Texas

"My only regret is that I was never around (or I was too young) to feel the power of Beatlemania, to really know what pandemonium it was, to wait with curiosity for their new albums to be released, and to know them as The Beatles, not as the ex-Beatles."

171

" Even though I am 16 years old, and The Beatles have gone their separate ways, I still continue to buy their records whenever I get the chance. They have always been and will always be my favorite group. I love them when they sing their love songs as much as I love them when they sing songs of suicide.

When I'm feeling unhappy, all I have to do is put on *Hey Jude* and everything goes away. I guess you could say that they are like a drug to me . . . the more I hear, the more I need. When I'm down I listen to them to get me feeling good. I only wish that I had been born about 3 decades earlier so that I could have been old enough to appreciate them while they were together.

My friends (also big fans of The Beatles) and I have promised each other that we will meet at least one of the ex-Beatles in our lifetimes. We don't care if they are eighty years old. We still love them as much. **"**

N.F.

Bala Cynwyd, Pennsylvania

" I am 14 years old and crazy about The Beatles. When I was ten years old, one of my friends gave me an old Beatles album. I started listening and getting interested in them. Now, I have 11 albums, 2 tapes, posters and pictures all over my walls, magazines, books, and a scrapbook full of Beatle pictures. I have written to Paul McCartney four times, but have never received a reply. He's my favorite Beatle.

I got just about everyone in my school interested in them. We have a Beatles fan club and I am the president. We have 72 people as members. I wish that I had been about 16 years old when The Beatles were at their height. I love them so much. My only dream is for them to get back together and to meet them.

They have changed my life. I saw a film clip of them on TV and started crying. My favorite album is **Abbey Road**, but I also like the White Album, and the Red and Blue Albums. My father has promised to take me to Paul McCartney's concert when he comes to Houston. **"**

K.C.

College Station, Texas

❝I will be 15 years old in August and have been a Beatle fan for two years. I think it all began once I heard McCartney's mellow voice singing *Yesterday* over the radio. It changed me and give me a different kind of feeling. Since then I have learned more about The Beatles.

The first album I got was the **Love Songs** double LP set. I would play it for hours everyday, adoring their music and the picture printed inside the album jacket. Soon after, I joined a Beatle fan club located in Boston. This fan club had a lot of Beatle items for sale. After seeing and reading about all these items, I decided to collect memorabilia as a memorial to The Beatles. My small allowance never went far enough to buy the things I wanted to buy. Finally, I got a paper route about a year ago earning $20.00 a week. I spent almost 95% of all my earnings on Beatle records, mostly the expensive ones.

I read a lot about The Beatles and probably know as much as any old Beatlemaniac does. Their views and attitudes on matters became mine. I'm learning to be myself and to like myself for what I am. I think some of their songs are pure philosophy and I try to live by it. I don't like the establishment for what it is. This caused me to miss a lot of school in eighth and ninth grades; I missed an awful lot of school and could have cared less, but I got worried when they called up my home.

I am writing songs. I've already written close to 20 songs. One of them is in honor of The Beatles, called, *Yesterday And Today*. I want to be in a rock band when I'm old enough. That's why I'm writing songs. I want to be prepared. I know there is a lot to learn about it and I'm naive now. My parents bought me a bass guitar last March, and I've been learning to play it. If it wasn't for The Beatles, I would not be the same person I am now. I know that I would never have thought of getting into the music business if I wasn't a Beatle fan. I have a friend, who is a lot like me. We're thinking of forming a band after school is over for sure, but she is all fucked up when it comes to The Beatles. As she says, "I have no opinion of them." So, I don't know if I'll be in a band with her.

I think about The Beatles a lot through the day. I go to bed thinking of them and I wake up thinking about them. Sometimes when I think about them, I feel a deep resentment inside because I wasn't old enough when it all happened. I wish I had grown up in the 60s more than anything else.❞

V.F.

New Castle, Pennsylvania

"I was born right around the time The Beatles became popular, but I still love them even though I wasn't a teenager at that time. They have affected my life in many ways. Their songs had so much meaning, and they had a song for everyone. For example, if I had a problem, I could associate it with one of their songs; or if I was happy about something, one of their songs would fit the situation. The Beatles will be remembered forever.

The Beatles affected many lives, especially during the Vietnam War. They had songs that helped many people. I only regret having been too young to be able to see them in 1964."

C.K.
Deer Park, New York

"I am a big fan of The Beatles and collect all their records. I am 16 now, so when The Beatles came out in 1963, I didn't know what was going on. I have two older brothers who liked The Beatles then, but they weren't devoted fans. It was only three years ago that I actually took a poignant interest in The Beatles and discovered how much I really had missed in the 60s. So I feel as if I have some catching up to do.

I still like other groups of today, but no other group will ever capture the sound and imagination that The Beatles did. I have spent about $200.00 on them by collecting their albums, and I plan on purchasing some other material concerning them. I want to recapture what I missed in the 60s and The Beatles seem to fit into my life perfectly. They will always have an effect on me.

The greatest thrill of my life would be to see them get back together on stage to an unexpecting audience, but it's unlikely that something that spectacular will ever happen. If it did I'm sure the music world would sit up and take notice."

S.W.
Emmett, Idaho

❝I first heard The Beatles on a TV show about 7 years ago, and I rushed out and bought **Meet The Beatles** as a result. They just knocked me out and ever since then I have been a Beatle fanatic about their songs, personalities, films, and even the instruments they played. I am currently the proud owner of a Rickenbacker guitar, just like John's. The Beatles turned me on to music like nothing else could have. I would never have known how much I love to play the guitar, if not for The Beatles and their music. The members of my band feel the same way about The Beatles as I do. We are all aware of the happiness and joy their music has brought to us over the years. Even though I am too young to remember the 60s, I still love to talk to people from that era. It's a delightful experience to meet someone who appreciates the real contribution The Beatles made to the arts as much as I do.**❞**

R.W.
San Francisco, California

"The Beatles are a very big part of my life. I first heard of them through my brother. He came home one day and told a make-believe story about *Maxwell's Silver Hammer*. He started buying albums and playing them really loud when my mother was at work. I liked what I heard. Then I saw "A Hard Day's Night." It's now my favorite. After seeing it, I fell in love with the personalities of these guys. I loved John Lennon's fast one-liners. After seeing "Help" and listening to their music, I wanted to know more about them, how they started and where, their childhood, etc. I wanted to know everything.

One day I got up early one Sunday to help my brother with his papers, and he told me everything he knew about them. I don't know where he got his info, but it was pretty accurate. After some research on my own, I knew all I wanted to know about John Lennon, Paul McCartney, George Harrison, and Ringo Starr, and what they had done with their lives before, after and during their years as The Beatles. I think they, themselves, must know the joy they brought to many people just by doing what they liked to do.

I still love The Beatles, but in a generation like mine (I'm 14 years old), it's very hard. Everyone says to me, "We'll be going to live concerts of the groups we like, but I'd like to see you try to go see a Beatle concert." I do like many new groups, but I have a special feeling for The Beatles. I think there are too many phony Beatle fans today. You can't like The Beatles for a month or two like some people do. Once a Beatle fan, always a Beatle fan.

I know they have touched the lives of many. They have certainly affected mine in many ways. I am a true Beatle fan because I stick up for them when Beatle-haters criticize them. I have one regret in life . . . that I was born after the Beatle era."

M.D.
Long Beach, New York

> "I do like many new groups, but I have a special feeling for The Beatles. I think there are too many phony Beatle fans today. You can't like The Beatles for a month or two like some people do. Once a Beatle fan, always a Beatle fan."

I never desired to be born at any other time than the one I arrived in. The Beatles were largely responsible for that. I sometimes wish I had been old enough to remember The Marx Brothers when all of them were young and making movies. And although I was alive at the time, I really don't remember Lenny Bruce, but, like many of today's teenage Beatle fans, I researched Mr. Bruce, laying my hands on all his records and any book about him. Still, I have no regrets about having been 13½ years old in February 1964, when The Beatles came to the U.S. I can't imagine what life as a teenager in the 1960s would have been like if I hadn't had those four guys to guide me along. However, I can understand the feeling of regret that pervaded the last chapter's worth of letters.

It must be very strange to have the whole Beatles' repertoire to choose from, as today's young Beatlemaniacs do. I grew with The Beatles, from *I Want To Hold Your Hand* to *I Want You (She's So Heavy)*. Imagine how very weird it must be to a neophyte Beatlemaniac, who could conceivably begin his/her awareness of The Beatles with *A Day In The Life* and discover, much later, a song such as *Things We Said Today*, only to realize afterward that the former came second, and the latter first, with many moons of development in between.

In the next two chapters we will hear from more present-day teenage Beatle fans. Some will tell us how they view The Beatles' affect on society, and others will prove to be more loyal and fanatic than some original Beatlemaniacs.

10

Just As Full Of Spirit

I received a plethora of letters from present-day, young Beatle fans. Unlike older Beatlemaniacs, who grew up with The Fab Four, have had career choices determined, and developed an adult philosophy from the music itself, these younger people are just starting out. Nevertheless, teenage Beatle fans of the 1980s are just as full of spirit regarding the boys from Liverpool as my generation. My difficulty lay in trying to divide the rest of these letters into chapters with common themes. Due to the fact that these younger correspondents did not have a lengthy past to draw upon, and their discoveries were not in the normal chronological order experienced by their older counterparts, their letters often did not reflect one central point. Those in this chapter, however, were filled with enthusiasm, and overflowed with a potpourri of Beatle lore, love, and hopes. And so, rather than describing them any further, let's let these modern-day Beatle fans speak for themselves . . . .

"I was only four years old when The Beatles first became popular in the U.S., but I was mesmerized by them nonetheless. I knew the words to their songs by heart, made my parents take me to see each of their movies, and even managed to perfect their Liverpudlian accent. It was a crush, I was in love with all four, especially Paul. After 1967, I lost interest in them due to their obsession with drugs and longer hair, and did not regain it until 1973 when I accidentally saw an old film clip of them on the Ed Sullivan Show. Something in my memory bank snapped and suddenly I was in love again.

Today I am a collector who loves their music, personalities, etc. Their influence on me has been such that even the men I date resemble them in their clothing and looks. My personality has changed; I have learned that one must be himself, no matter how different from others that may be. I do not feel that The Beatles caused any trends directly, but possibly acted as a catalyst to many. Pot and LSD were already being consumed when they announced that they took it; however their announcement did not stop Beatle followers from experimenting with drugs. The Beatles went along with whatever was happening at the time; they dove in head-first whenever they noticed a new trend (e.g., Transcendental Meditation) and thus aided in convincing their fans to take up the same.

Their music is a different matter. If it weren't for them, we would never have been so far advanced in music as we are today with deeper lyrics and sound experimentation (disco is not included). They practically invented a whole new type of music. How awful it would be to still have to listen to "shoo–lang, shoo lang" and other such meaningful lyrics which were popular right before The Beatles became popular. *A Hard Day's Night* may not sound so great today, but compare it to other tunes that were out that year. It sounds almost alien."

B.M.
Amite, Louisiana

> "After 1967, I lost interest in them due to their obsession with drugs and longer hair, and did not regain it until 1973 when I accidentally saw an old film clip of them on the Ed Sullivan Show. Something in my memory bank snapped and suddenly I was in love again."

"I've often sat and thought about how much The Beatles have changed my life. In 1976, when I was about 15, I bought a Beatle album. It had all of their old songs. I would listen to it and it made me feel really good. It was so fresh and seemed so innocent. I really didn't think that much about them then. I really don't know how I became a fanatic. There just seemed to be a Beatle song when I needed one. Every time I was down, *Hey Jude* seemed to make life worthwhile; every feeling of loneliness and being heartbroken, The Beatles sang about it the way I wished I could.

Without The Beatles and their music, I would be pretty lost. Everyone needs something to idolize. Thank God for The Beatles!"

J.A.
Chicago, Illinois

"Every time I was down, *Hey Jude* seemed to make life worthwhile; every feeling of loneliness and being heartbroken, The Beatles sang about it the way I wished I could."

"The Beatles were more than just a terrific Rock group, they were geniuses. Anyone with musical taste knows that. A lot of people seem to feel that The Beatles had a tremendous effect on the younger generation. Now, it's true that in the beginning they did. They changed the whole style of music, but from then on they just went along with what was already happening. Dylan and Baez were already protesting Vietnam and some kids knew that there was more to life than doing it like the Establishment told them. People also think that The Beatles influenced teenagers to use drugs. However, this cannot be true. If you didn't already know about drugs, you wouldn't understand what "to turn on" meant. The link I see to The Beatles and drugs is that if you use drugs and know about them, you can understand a lot more of what Beatle songs really mean.

The Beatles are a very big part of my life. They've given me more happiness than anything. It's really a bummer that they're not together now, but they've proved that they can be successful separately. Just listen to Paul McCartney, and you'll know what I mean. If everyone listened to and thought like The Beatles this would be a better world."

J.Y.
Baltimore, Maryland

181

❝ Born in 1960, I endured the life of an orphan until I was adopted at the age of seven. My early childhood was very unpleasant with many painful memories of uncaring foster parents, orphanages, child abuse, constant moving, anemia, the works. I never spoke unless I was spoken to. I kept everything bottled up inside of me. No emotion was ever displayed. During this period I thought I had only three friends, Petula Clark, the Three Stooges, and The Beatles. The song, *Downtown*, with so much force put into it, just captivated me and another orphan buddy, who was stuck at the same foster home. For hours we sat outdoors and sing the few words we knew to it. When I got older I was certain that I would marry this girl with the pretty voice. Every morning, the Three Stooges entertained me with their slapstick comedy. Once in a while they could make an otherwise somber little boy crack a smile or even laugh.

I can't remember when I first heard of The Beatles, but the song, *I Want To Hold Your Hand* sticks firmly in my childhood memories. In the mornings I'd watch a cartoon of The Fab Four running away from a throng of screaming women in hot pursuit. *Help* would accompany the incident. It was all rather amusing to me. I'd go outside, convert my broomstick horse into a guitar, and be John or Paul. Two girls would chase me around the yard while I strummed the horse's head and yelled "Help." In 1967, I gradually broke out of my shell with a new and permanent home, a new life so to speak. I could make friends without worrying if I was moving the next day. I still was very timid and took a lot of crap from people. By the time I was in high school, I turned into a rebel. I was called a radical by friends and foes alike. Everybody in the late 70s was so apathetic and I was just the opposite. "All you have to do is protest in number and you'll get your way," I always said, but everybody was lazy and didn't give a damn about anything except going out and getting stoned.

I always looked at the 60s with the greatest of envy. People didn't take shit from the system back then. They did their own thing. Take The Beatles for example. They wore their hair and dressed the way they wanted, not the way others wanted. Even The Beatles were somewhat weary of protests, but later changed their minds as can be heard in the background of *Revolution 1*, on their White Album. While in high school, I ran the newspaper and refused to tolerate any form of censorship. Interest in the school paper soared because of my sensationalism and yellow journalism tactics. Some friends told me they looked forward to seeing me someday write a book, so the song *Paperback Writer* has a personal joy.

When I hear The Beatles, and I think about the lively 60s, I realize that no one was apathetic then. I welcome the 80s with open arms after the dismal 70s. Hopefully a new era of awareness will come forth. I'll be there to contribute my part and The Beatles will always be singing tunes in the back of my mind.**"**

R.C.
Mitchellville, Maryland

"When I hear The Beatles, and I think about the lively 60s, I realize that no one was apathetic then. I welcome the 80s with open arms after the dismal 70s. Hopefully a new era of awareness will come forth. I'll be there to contribute my part and The Beatles will always be singing tunes in the back of my mind."

> **"I go kind of weird if I don't hear music all the time . . . .The Beatles, in a broad sense, changed the direction of my life. I was heading toward being a bookworm . . . they saved me in the nick of time."**

❝The Beatles let me know how naive I was regarding Rock music. I was sitting in a locker room in 3rd grade, listening to some girls talk about a TV show they had seen the night before. One girl said to the other, " . . . and she couldn't even sing *Let It Be* . . . . " I'd never even heard of the song at the time. From that day forward, I gradually turned into a full-fledged Rocker. I started with the radio, and then worked my way up to record companies and concerts. I've actually become addicted to it. I go kind of weird if I don't hear music all the time.

The Beatles, in a broad sense, changed the direction of my life. I was heading toward being a bookworm . . . they saved me in the nick of time. Thank you John, Paul, George, and Ringo.❞

G.Y.
Buffalo, New York

❝I'm 17 years old, and have been listening to The Beatles for about 4 years. I got interested in them when I was going through our attic and found some albums that my sister had bought. Since then I have bought seven of their best records. I really love their music. I listen to The Beatles when I come home from school and during any spare time I have.

My mother thinks I'm out of my head because I like The Beatles so much. I keep old magazines like *Teen Scoop* and *16*. I also have books on facts of The Beatles, pictures, and a button. Their early music is faster and more direct than their later years such as in the White Album. I find George's music more religious and relaxing, but there's nothing like a Lennon/McCartney tune to make you smile or think of wild and fun Spring nights.

I know many Beatle-freaks would like to see them get back together, but from the many articles I've read, maybe things would be better left the way they are. In any event, for many ages to come, the Beatle memory will grow.❞

A.T.
New Rochelle, New York

❝I am only 15, but I have feeling of what it was like to experience the 60s. My older brother brought home The Beatles hits from 1962–1966. He played *Help* quite often. Then I got hooked on it and decided to play the whole album. I swear that I had heard every song on the album before, but I did not know it was The Beatles. Then I discovered their greatest hits from 1967–1970. One night I watched TV and the show I was watching (Tony Orlando and Dawn) announced that they were going to sing *All You Need Is Love*. I didn't know it was a Beatles song. So, I discovered The Beatles when I was 9 in 1973. So, I would play *All You Need Is Love* and *Strawberry Fields Forever*. I bought more albums.

The Beatles were ahead of their time and *Got To Get You Into My Life* proved that when it was released as a single in 1976. My music teacher said there would be no such thing as Rock if it weren't for The Beatles. Then she played some Beatle songs and I guessed everyone she played. She looked shocked that a 9 year old could pick out their songs. Then she put on **Sgt. Pepper** and played *When I'm 64*, I had never heard it up to that time. I went home and described the **Sgt. Pepper** album cover to my parents and they bought it for me.

I eventually got my friend hooked on The Beatles, and have continued to do so with other friends. I would like to meet The Beatles. I have so many questions I'd like to ask them. I think they still have a grip on society today. However, there are very few people my age who know what The Beatles did. Today we have more sophisticated groups, but in the 60s everyone went crazy over The Beatles. There never will be another group like them. I get so mad at people like Elton John and the Bee Gees because they give Wings competition on the *Billboard* charts. What if The Beatles did get together and they didn't play too well . . . what then? . . . no more great stories and "how clever" stories would come out. But you have to admit they did leave people on their toes.**❞**

M.T.
San Antonio, Texas

"I'm 14 years old. If it weren't for The Beatles, the music industry would be completely different. They have been my favorite group since I was about 4 or so. I listen to them all the time after school (right now I'm listening to **Abbey Road**). They affected me in a lot of ways. Back in the 60s there were hippies, my friend and I think we're hippies. I won't do my homework unless I listen to music.

The Beatles didn't really care what others thought of them, so the kids had that attitude too. They did things that meant a lot of good, such as John's bed-in for peace. It didn't do any real good, but it helped."

E.T.
Pico Rivera, California

"The first time that I heard The Beatles was when I was 5 years old. At the time, I didn't think much about it. The first time I really heard and understood the music and the words of the songs, I was hooked. However, the songs nowadays really don't mean anything; they are just a bunch of words.

The Beatles were the first at just about everything. If not for them, music would be a lot different today. They had a certain philosophy to their songs. I can't really put all of my feelings into words. I guess you could say that The Beatles leave me speechless.

I still think they are the best group that there has ever been."

L.S.
Amelia, Ohio

"I began my interest in The Beatles at age 5; my sisters, avid Beatle fans taught me the words to several of The Beatles' early hits. When we moved from Mississippi to Tennessee in 1964, I could sing *I Saw Her Standing There* verbatim. Whenever my sisters weren't home, I would sneak out their old Beatle albums and play them incessantly. I listened to them all the time until just after they broke up.

The Beatles prompted me to play the guitar. I learned to play all of The Beatles' hits and still find myself plucking away at *Mother Nature's Son*, *Her Majesty*, *Rocky Raccoon*, *Back In The U.S.S.R.* and others when I should be practicing. The Beatles gave me respect for music. Their records also taught me how to sing, harmonize, and write music. Their records kept my parents awake at night and still do though my tastes have expanded incredibly. The White Album got me interested in several types of music. Now I will listen to Willie Nelson one minute, Frank Zappa the next, and later on dig out my old Carole King, Jimi Hendrix, and Eric Clapton records. I love classical and jazz too. I'm only 18, but a successful and respected musician and songwriter. If it weren't for The Beatles, I might be bussing tables."

T.S.
Knoxville, Tennessee

"Their records also taught me how to sing, harmonize, and write music . . . . I'm only 18, but a successful and respected musician and songwriter. If it weren't for The Beatles, I might be bussing tables."

"The Beatles have made me aware of things. In the song, *We Can Work It Out*, they tell us that our lives only last a short period of time and we shouldn't fight, but to get along and make the best of it. They tell us that money can't solve everything. They tell us that love is more than holding hands, but something that is deeper. They tell us that it must be shared by two people. They tell me that yesterday things were much simpler and today, to survive, we must help each other. They tell me in *Here Comes The Sun*, that when things look the darkest, something will brighten your day."

M.S.
Piqua, Ohio

"I'm 17 years old and started to buy Beatles' music about 2½ years ago. So far, I have bought 13 albums. I'm a member of Paul McCartney's "Club Sandwich." I tape all Beatle programs on the radio (I have 15 hours on an 8-track tape of Beatle interviews). As far as posters go — well you gotta see it to believe it.

Before I was interested in The Beatles, I didn't buy records. Now, most of my money goes into buying music. I have centered my taste of music around certain rock groups. I can't get enough of the Knack. Paul McCartney once said, "The Beatles are like a dead person, and it's weird spending all your time trying to revive a corpse." Well, for me they've never died. When I first started listening, it was all new to me. It became my music. It should have been my folks' music, but they never outgrew Elvis Presley. So, The Beatles were a new experience for me.

I'm from Iowa and a typical day for me is 1) work, 2) school, 3) music. That's the way my life is centered, and music is at the top of my list. The Beatles are the ones that made it that way."

K.S.
Charles City, Iowa

"I'm from Iowa and a typical day for me is 1) work, 2) school, 3) music. That's the way my life is centered, and music is at the top of my list. The Beatles are the ones that made it that way."

"My Mom said to me, 'What's the matter, do you have wet pants?' I said, 'No! I don't! It's just that their music does something to me.' "

"I was only three years old when The Beatles first came to the United States. The other night, on the ABC–TV show 20/20, they did a special on Paul McCartney. In that interview they showed some film clips of The Beatles at Shea Stadium, on the Ed Sullivan Show, and one where they were singing *Revolution*. I got so excited that I thought I was going to have a heart attack. My Mom said to me, "What's the matter, do you have wet pants?" I said, "No! I don't! It's just that their music does something to me."

The Beatles gave people something to look forward to. It would be the greatest thing in my life to see The Beatles perform again together, just like they did on the Ed Sullivan Show. I have three older sisters who know of them, particularly the middle two, who are in their late twenties. They tell me that I don't know anything about them, but they're wrong. I know them in a way they don't. You see, people make them out to be some kind of gods. That's where the mistake is made. They're just ordinary people, that's what makes them so special. They started from nothing and got everything. They never forgot where they started from.

I think that The Beatles are very good looking. Maybe someday I'll get to meet them. I especially like John Lennon. When he was growing up people told him that he was different because he was going to be something someday."

L.P.
Reading, Pennsylvania

188

"I am 17 years old, and all my friends think The Beatles music is just cute . . . I could never explain to them the supreme depth in all their compositions. I have been self contained, quietly sitting in my room and letting the whole street know the glory which is "Beatle."

My favorite masterpiece is *Revolution*. To me this broke all barriers. I can't relate to the destruction that Manson found in this song. I finally figured out what *Strawberry Fields Forever* was all about. I try to tell people at school this. I'll tell you one thing, when at 107 years of age, my great great great grandson asks me what Ringo Starr's mother's middle name is, I'll disown him for his ignorance."

P.R.
Great Mills, Maryland

"I'll tell you one thing, when at 107 years of age, my great great great grandson asks me what Ringo Starr's mother's middle name is, I'll disown him for his ignorance."

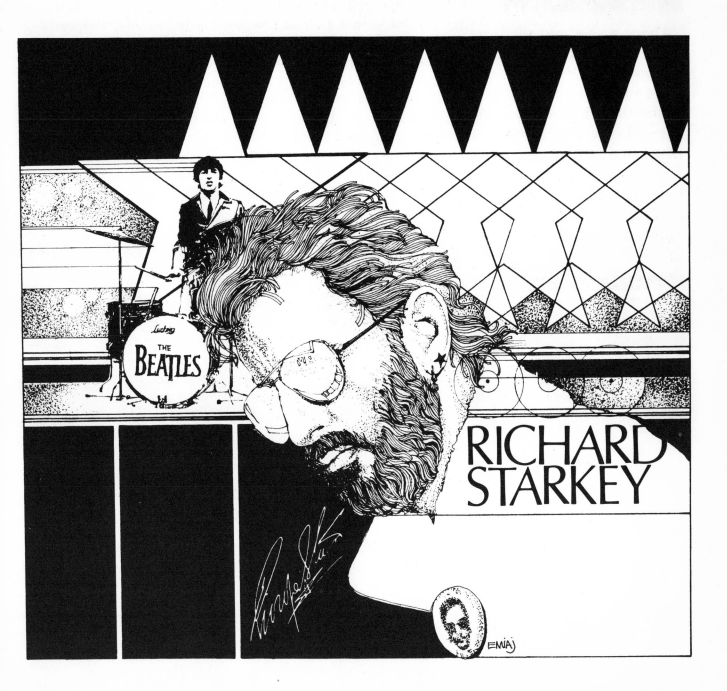

RICHARD STARKEY

> **"About a year and a half ago, I came across an old album of my Mom's. It had four guys on it, who, at the time, all looked alike. Little did I know that I had just opened a whole new world with four guys who would become the most important part of my life."**

"About a year and a half ago, I came across an old album of my Mom's. It had four guys on it, who, at the time, all looked alike. Little did I know that I had just opened a whole new world with four guys who would become the most important part of my life.

I began to memorize the words to the songs, and I found that each song had a special message to give in its own way. When I knew every song on **A Hard Day's Night** by heart, I went to the record store and bought **The Beatles** [a.k.a. the White Album]. Well, this blew my mind, so I told my 3rd grade teacher about it and he turned out to be a Beatle fan too. None of my friends were into music. Now all they like is disco. So, I soon found that I was alone with my obsession. I would call local radio stations to request songs and soon built the reputation as "the world's only 12-year-old Beatle fan."

I wanted to get on a more personal level with The Beatles, so I went out and bought a complete biography on all four of them. When I finished the book, I knew all about their childhoods. John's is my favorite. I love the story of him growing up in Woolton, Liverpool and all the wonderful things he and Pete Shoton did together. It just breaks me up.

The boys (as I call them) are the most important thing in my life. When I meet someone for the first time, I find myself asking the following questions: "Hi, what's your name?" "Do you like The Beatles?" I not only like The Beatles, but I also like the people surrounding them such as Brian Epstein, Derek Taylor, Mal Evans, and all the wives and children.

I've learned to keep to myself as far as my musical interests go. Some classmates think Abbie Hoffman is a girl and Jimi Hendrix was the head janitor at our school.

C.P.
Kenilworth, Illinois

"I am a seventeen year old female, living in a small Wisconsin town. I am a senior in high school, planning on going to college next fall for business administration. I am also absolutely crazy about The Beatles. They're excellent!!

Their music is never the same; all their songs are different. I first became interested in them after reading the book, *Helter Skelter* in 1977. It was bizarre. The Beatles had such an influence on the Manson family. Charlie would give sermons on Beatle songs, and named a follower Sadie, after the *Sexy Sadie* song. They wrote "Helter Skelter" on the walls in blood of two homes. I can't believe the impact.

Paul McCartney is so incredible. His songs are beautiful. All of The Beatles were so warm and friendly, I enjoyed their songs. This may sound weird, but I also liked the pants they wore. They looked so cute in those pants. They had super hard Rock songs like *Come Together, Revolution*, and *Helter Skelter*; high pitched songs like *I Want To Hold Your Hand, Help* and *She Loves You*. I enjoyed both types. I am a fan of the 60s. I would have given anything to have seen Woodstock or a Beatles concert."

M.O.
Kewaunee, Wisconsin

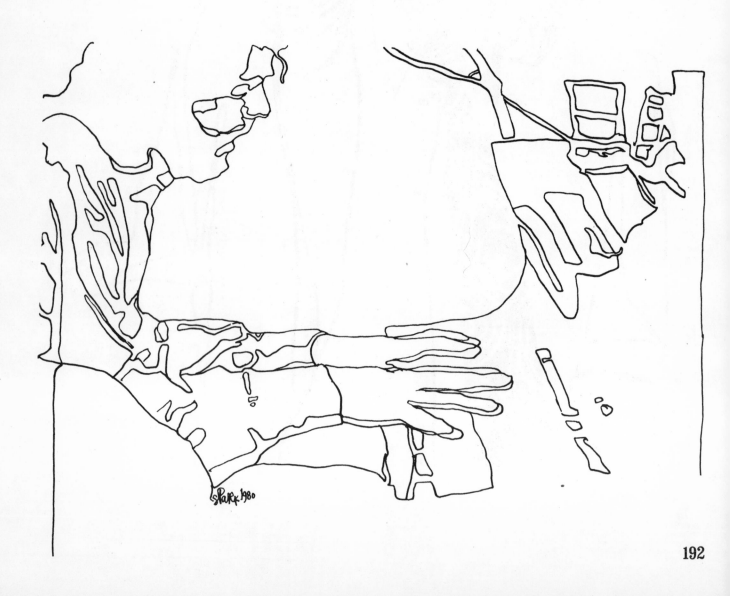

"When I hear one of The Beatles' songs played on the radio, it gives me an exceptional feeling, and I could play the same song on my record player and it wouldn't feel anywhere near the same. I suppose I'm glad that other people love them besides me, but when I hear all these reunion rumors, I get mad because people are pressuring them to do a concert. I realize that it wouldn't be the same, even though I never knew how it was. All the original Beatlemaniacs would not be satisfied with it.

The Beatles have done many things for society such as bringing long hair, giving us great music, great memories, and most definitely getting a reaction from all of the people all of the time."

D.M.
Tulsa, Oklahoma

"The 60s were a time of change. Everyday something would be a new headline and there was restlessness in everyone; everyone searching for something new. The Beatles remained through this decade, giving something for everyone and anyone to hold on to . . . the young and old alike. They brought their music and a new way of life. Many older people associated only the bad with The Beatles. They were far from bad. The young people wanted to attach themselves to something different.

These four men inspire me. I was really messed up once, but when I learned about The Beatles' story and their music, I was helped through a pretty rough time. I'm not saying it was because of them that I was helped, but they and their music did help me an awful lot. Just to listen to the words and music of those great musicians was help enough.

Their music will live on forever. There could never be another group like them. All of them gave up a part of their lives for us and now they're on their own, giving us another part. If I ever met them, I would thank them for that part of their lives. They're the best!"

L.K.
Nanticoke, Pennsylvania

"The 60s were a time of change. Everyday something would be a new headline and there was restlessness in everyone; everyone searching for something new. The Beatles remained through this decade, giving something for everyone and anyone to hold on to . . . the young and old alike."

193

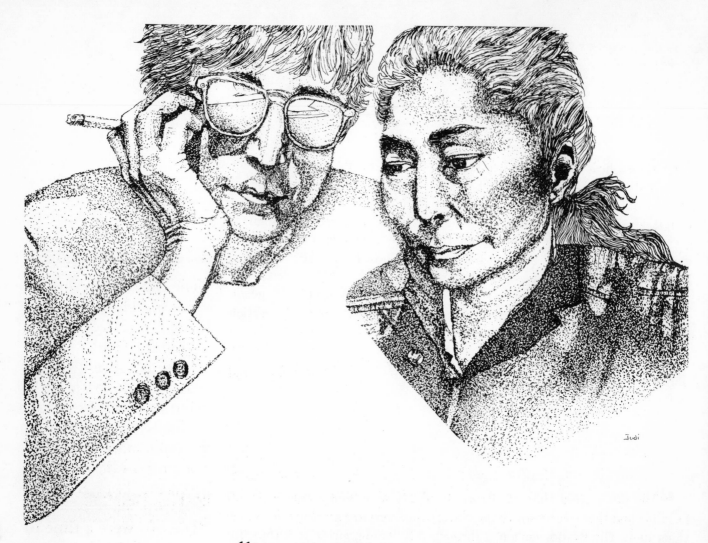

&&I am a high school senior and I'm involved in a social group named after a very renowned Beatle. John Lennon University was started by my friends and me in the school year of 1978. My friends made applications to J.L.U. as a joke and placed them in a teacher's class room. People quickly started asking questions about J.L.U. and a small cult started calling themselves the John Lennon University Fighting Walruses. By this time a new school year had begun and I personally became involved in J.L.U. We ordered purple and white football jerseys and started wearing them to sporting events. Apparently, the other students in the school saw this as a challenge and we were challenged by numerous other "Universities" to football games. We played such teams as Paul McCartney State. Our football team won 6--3. Eventually we absorbed the other universities, and in June, 1979 we had a John Lennon University banquet for members and certain friends.

We eventually put out a newsletter, application forms, acceptance notices, and a list of curricula, and we have made a movie based on the song *Two Of Us*.&&

D.M.
Lebanon, Ohio

"I'm seventeen, rather a teeny-bopper as they say, but not quite. I am, of course, only a second-wave Beatlemaniac, but I've been a fan for about four years now, since **Wings At The Speed of Sound** and 33 1/3 came out the same year, and I found out that Paul and George used to be in the same group once. So, I took a listen to The Beatles, and I've had the mania ever since. I don't know what first attracted me to them. They're just exciting, and my life's basically boring. Maybe it's just because I'm at that rebellious age. I'm quite sure now that it's their music. There is something to it, it's magic . . . hard to explain.

They did change my life completely around. I can't remember any hobbies before them, but now I play the piano and guitar. I'm also into other arts. My dream is to be a paperback writer, whether through their influence, I don't know, but they do encourage it. One of my songs won a songwriting contest at school. They are an inspiration. They're also a crutch, an escape. When I'm depressed The Beatles come to me and make me feel better. Sometimes when I'm lying there with them in my ear, I think that I really don't need anyone or anything else, or that I don't care about anyone or anything else. It's the most amazing feeling, that only Beatlemaniacs can understand, I suppose.

The Beatles have sent me into this whole Rock-and-Roll trip; now I like the Stones and Who among others. The White Album is one of my favorites; I find it very alienating, hateful, angry, depressing, but I love it. I find that their moods rub off on me too. Attitudes. I don't know about the rest of this generation, but I don't think I'd be so tolerant of drugs and sex without The Beatles. Drugs are all right, I don't have to do them to think they're all right. Acid seems fascinating, and if I ever do drugs that would be the one I would try. And sex? Well, it's peoples' private business, people should have their own morals, and I don't care how high or base they are. Who cares about society? It's up to the individual, and besides . . . what's fun is fun. John and Yoko's relationship in the early days was maybe disgusting in 1968, and is maybe disgusting now, but it is not to me. And I think it is only funny that George married Olivia after she had his child . . . hey, that's O.K.

I've made many friends through The Beatles, and in a way, I've lost many friends too, because not everyone can understand it, and they think I'm crazy. I think they're idiots. The Beatles give me a sense of belonging, of being associated with something great. I have a cause because of them. When I'm down, after I listen to them, I can take on the world. Who cares if I fail a math test if I can go right home and listen to **Abbey Road**? They made Rock-and-Roll more respectable and influential. The Beatles weren't the only social force, but they led it . . . they were the loudest voice. Maybe society was headed for a change anyway, and The Beatles just inspired it . . . it's hard to figure out."

H.G.
Ottawa, Ontario, Canada

"The Beatles give me a sense of belonging, of being associated with something great. I have a cause because of them. When I'm down, after I listen to them, I can take on the world. Who cares if I fail a math test if I can go right home and listen to Abbey Road?"

195

" I've been listening to The Beatles constantly since I was 8 years old. I'm 12 now and my life has been totally changed by them. I look at life with a different aspect now. I used to think it was a joke, but now I'm taking advantage of it.

The clothes I wear are different. I really don't care what the latest style is anymore . . . if I like it, I wear it. My musical tastes are different than before. Prior to my discovery of The Beatles, I listened to Top 40, disco stuff. That's all boring to me now. I like album-oriented, Rock radio stations better than AM stations. I think differently. My conversations reflect this. My whole life is different and I quite like it!**"**

A.B.
Richmond, Kentucky

"Not having been around when The Fab Four came, I did not know them as mop tops. I discovered them after it was all over, but still the music and message exist. I can see what happened to them, unlike the original Beatle fans, who didn't know what it would turn out like."

" Why did The Beatles appeal to original Beatle fans? They were looking for people to put their feelings and thoughts out in the open. They needed someone to say what they could not say themselves: The Beatles. Well, people nowadays are still looking for people like that. Still to me the answer is The Beatles. I am 15 years old.

To me, the sound and the music is important, but so is the message (e.g., *All You Need Is Love*). Not having been around when The Fab Four came, I did not know them as mop tops. I discovered them after it was all over, but still the music and message exist. I can see what happened to them, unlike the original Beatle fans, who didn't know what it would turn out like.

I like John Lennon the best. He wasn't going to put on a fake act, he let himself come through. Most of the time he was put down because of this (e.g., "We're more popular than Jesus"). The people refused to see the truth. I like his ideas and pattern mine after his. I seem to have some things in common with him, but then if he stood up for something I didn't believe in, I would not follow him. My friend and I can talk for hours about John, George, Paul, and Ringo, but the thing is that our friendship would still be there without them. We choose to fill our minds with Beatle facts.

They are the main forces in my life. When I was younger, I really looked up to John Wayne, now it is John Lennon. These four people have so influenced so many people that it is hard to believe one could call them a band.**"**

W.E.
Anchorage, Alaska

❝I'm fifteen, but I still love The Beatles. The Beatles were the greatest thing to happen to Rock-and-Roll. Every time I hear one of their songs it cheers me up. My hairstyle is like Ringo's because I'm part British. My favorite songs are *All You Need Is Love, Help, All Together Now, I Am The Walrus*, and *Yellow Submarine*. My favorite Beatle is Ringo, followed by Paul, John, and George in that order. I'm glad there is a Beatle Convention so Beatle fans can see their films again.

I have seen "Yellow Submarine" about 11 times, and I've been drawing scenes from the film. The Beatles have made me happy for the years they were together.**❞**

K.D.
Chicago, Illinois

❝I didn't realize how much I liked The Beatles until they were already broken up. I am fully into them now. I just went to Knott's Berry Farm when there was a "Beatlefest" there. They played Beatle music all day, showed over two dozen films of The Beatles, and had many booths selling Beatle memorabilia. Murray the "K" was the host of a show with a live band. The band dressed like the early Beatles and they sang an hour full of songs. I felt I was at a real concert. The show was so good I had to come back the next day with a camera to show my friends the remarkable resemblances of this band to The Beatles. All four resembled certain characteristics of The Beatles they were portraying.

After developing the pictures, I was outraged. I had one print with about 24 pictures of the group all in one. The film teeth must have broken or something. Now I have no pictures and only thoughts of the event. I guess I'll have to wait for the next "Beatlefest." I have decided to start playing guitar again. I am learning Lennon's chords. I'm going to buy a book of them pretty soon, after I learn how to play again.**❞**

R.G.
Westminster, California

"I've been into The Beatles' music since January, 1979. I think they are great. They've changed my life in so many ways. After I first heard them I wondered how it had been that I had never heard of them sooner. I never used to listen to Pop music or Rock-and-Roll or the radio, now I'm into all of these things. When I feel down and depressed, their music makes me feel so much better. They possess some magical attractiveness that makes you want to hear more and get to know them.

I've read a biography about them and found it to be very informative. Even though The Beatles disbanded in 1970, I still refer to each one as a Beatle. Paul has always been my favorite because he is still around with Wings. I like his voice and baby-face. I've started to write songs and have styled them after The Beatles' style. Two of the six songs are about The Beatles. The third song I wrote when I was mad at a friend. It was spontaneous writing, whatever I thought I wrote down. Someone saw it and said that they thought it was written by John Lennon. I told them I did it, and they didn't believe me.

The Beatles changed the music world. Other people tried to duplicate their work and style. I hate it when other artists do Beatle songs. They mess them up royally, like the Bee Gees did with *Sgt. Pepper*. I feel as if I know The Beatles personally, and they know me as we're good friends. I wish I could meet them, any of them. The drug scene, I don't approve of, but the bit with drugs was bound to happen sooner or later. I think The Beatles are the greatest!**"**

V.F.
Hornbrook, California

> **"I've started to write songs and have styled them after The Beatles' style. Two of the six songs are about The Beatles. The third song I wrote when I was mad at a friend. It was spontaneous writing, whatever I thought I wrote down."**

66 I am a 17-year-old female, middle class and white. I was born in 1961 so I never really felt the initial impact of The Beatles. My mother says that I saw them on Ed Sullivan, but I couldn't remember that if my life depended on it.

My first experience with The Beatles was when my friend let me listen to her brother's **Magical Mystery Tour** album. It was magic! Their music was so different from any other. It's almost as if their music is charmed and that is why it is so different. I scream at old Beatle film clips, and I'm near hysteria when I watch "Help" or "A Hard Day's Night." I'm physically and mentally addicted to The Beatles. Every time their names are mentioned or I see them in print, I tingle all over and my stomach gets queasy. I know everything there is to know about The Beatles. Why? Because they're something untouchable, yet touchable; something you can build fantastic fantasies around and yet still relate to them realistically. And of course, they are talented. **99**

T.D.
Niles, Michigan

> "I'm physically and mentally addicted to The Beatles. Every time their names are mentioned or I see them in print, I tingle all over and my stomach gets queasy."

66 I have only liked The Beatles for about 8 months, but I know as much as any Beatle freak (almost). If it wasn't for my friend I'd never know them. She lends me her Beatle albums, books, etc. And I'm starting my own collection of Apple labels. So far I have **Yellow Submarine**.

The Beatles changed me, but as for society . . . what has that got to do with it? Oh well, I was too young to know, but I'm knowing now. *Getting Better* helped me. *Act Naturally* proved to me that anyone can make it. *Fixing A Hole* showed that we are all flighty and shouldn't let silly people in our door. And *She Loves You* is an up song. It makes you feel like you've taken pep pills. **99**

C.C.
Montebello, California

> "*Getting Better* helped me. *Act Naturally* proved to me that anyone can make it. *Fixing A Hole* showed that we are all flighty and shouldn't let silly people in our door. And *She Loves You* is an up song. It makes you feel like you've taken pep pills."

"The first Beatles' song I ever heard was *All My Loving*, and I was about five years old. I'm now 17 and through the years I have bought The Beatles' Red, White, and Blue albums, and memorized every sound on each. When I first heard their music, I had a keen perception for it. I remember playing the song over and over. It wasn't until I was a freshman in high school, though, until I really understood what The Beatles were trying to say to me. After listening to the Red album, which I had just bought, I knew nothing could ever be the same. I felt that I looked at everything in a different way. I felt like crying. I think I had matured . . . I was changed. No more could I be the happy kid, who saw the world as it was. Everything I saw had new meaning. That may sound silly and trite, but when applied to the legend of John, Paul, George, and Ringo, it is surprisingly possible. Everything I saw and knew and did was in accordance with what The Beatles had to say in their songs. The defiance and revolution of the Blue album hit me like a tidal wave. It made me aware of the generation gap, of the rebellion locked inside of me, the rebellion caused by youth. Finally the White album brought me The Beatles as a more mature, drugged-out group who had seen and done everything and who had decided to tell me about it. It rounded out my vision of a legendary group who were before my time, but when captured in myself, filled every vein and capillary of my body. I am and always will be a part of The Beatles; for they are responsible for the shaping of my ideals, of everything I believe in, and of everything I stand for. I love them forever.**"**

R.C.
Silver Spring, Maryland

"I'm only 15, so I wasn't old enough to be into The Beatles when they were popular. I was really shy and never had any close friends and never knew what to talk about when I was with other people, so I read books all day and spent lots of time at the library. My life had no meaning till one day in 1974, I was at the library and I went to the record department because my Dad was into music a little bit, and I wanted to see if there were any records I could get him. I noticed **The Early Beatles**. That night I played that record for my Mom and Dad and I fell in love with it and the four cute guys on the cover.

I would go to school and dream about The Beatles and try to get "A's" on my spelling tests so I could get a quarter from my Dad to put in the box marked "money for Beatle records" and when I got enough money to buy **Meet The Beatles**, I had every song memorized. I had a boyfriend then and he knew much more about The Beatles than I did. When they showed "A Hard Day's Night" on TV, he told me who was who and the title of the songs. Now, I know a lot about The Beatles and music. In fact, I want to be a rock 'n' roll singer so I can make the world happy as The Beatles did.

Now when I'm with people, I know what to talk about; The Beatles. No more shy, little girl. I have a pen pal who shares interest on The Beatles (and Wings). I am also interested in politics, thanks to John Lennon; travelling from McCartney; meditation from George; and my love for music from The Beatles as a whole.

They gave me a reason for living."

T.G.
Lakewood, Ohio

"I'm only 15, so I wasn't old enough to be into The Beatles when they were popular. I was really shy and never had any close friends . . . . Now when I'm with people, I know what to talk about; The Beatles. No more shy, little girl . . . . They gave me a reason for living."

My prejudice is showing. Although I honestly believe that all the teenage correspondents are fervent Beatle fans, and am convinced that the feelings they have for The Beatles match my own, there is still a world of difference between experiencing an established art form and living through its creative stages. Nevertheless, The Beatles, now over ten years gone from the recording world, still have that incredible influence . . . that magic (a word that cropped up in more than one teenage correspondent's letter) to play a major role in peoples' lives . . . lives that hadn't even begun until The Beatles were already a reality.

11

An Age Which Has Passed

Young Beatles fans of the 1980s can see the 1960s from a different perspective than their counterparts of that earlier decade, but they also view the decade in which they came of age, the 1970s, in a different light than do we original Beatlemaniacs of 1964 vintage.

This last grouping of letters from present-day teenage fans expresses a remarkably worldly outlook on the past two decades. The correspondents look at personal and societal changes which The Beatles caused in much the same manner as those who contributed letters in Chapter Seven, but these younger fans view the group as historians might, looking at an age which has passed, rather than at an era they find themselves engulfed in.

It's a viewpoint that I cannot personally identify with, so let the tellers tell their tales . . . .

“ The Beatles have changed my life more than any world leader, individual, or lifestyle. In other words, The Beatles have changed my life completely.

On the musical aspect, The Beatles' influence shows up every time I turn on the radio. Before I discovered John, Paul, George and Ringo, I was influenced by the crowd and accepted anything I heard. If my friends liked it, no matter what type of trash it was, so did I. After discovering The Beatles, I went crazy; becoming an incurable Beatlemaniac and now I am constantly saying in reference to other music, "How can anyone listen to that?" When I listen to records or occasionally hear a Beatles' single on the radio, it is easy to see what impact they had on me. I wonder what I would do without The Beatles, or everyone else would do for that matter. Thinking of a world without The Beatles, I see a generation of crewcutted boys still listening to The Four Seasons. Thank God for The Beatles.

The fact that The Beatles broke up is a terrible let down for me. I've read more than I needed to about the breakup. I know all the reasons, yet I feel that if I hadn't, my life would still be different. John Lennon and George Harrison are the most influential Beatles. John Lennon and Yoko Ono have fascinated me for quite a long time. John was definitely the most outspoken of The Beatles. I have always felt partial to him because I am also the loudmouth who finds that I have put my foot in my mouth again; and the one who people secretly think is crazy.

As an aspiring poet, I had reached a dry spell for about seven months. The only poems I composed belonged with a Beatles creation like *Polythene Pam*. I read in a magazine about John Lennon's two books of poetry, yet my local library doesn't have them. So, in excerpts, I found parts of poems in several Beatles books I had at home. I proceeded to write about 20 poems, with John Lennon's nonsense style prevailing throughout. Now, I am finishing my second book, which I call *Strawberry Fields*, dedicated to John Lennon. George Harrison has influenced me as well, but in a different way. He began his career with The Beatles as the quiet, gawky one, yet in the end emerged as the greatest talent. I became fascinated with meditation and the Indian philosophy (e.g. if I cut you, I bleed, because we are all part of that wonderful organism called the universe) which Harrison so seriously believed in. Unknown to my parents, I turned on the stereo and meditated to The Beatles when no one was home. Those strange chants of Hare Krishna were mysterious and unknown to me. After reading about Krishna, I went on to write what I consider the best poem I have ever written, "Ode to the Mahareshi."

I am mostly non-sentimental. I never cried watching a movie or reading a book, or listening to songs, but The Beatles changed that. Songs like

"Thinking of a world without The Beatles, I see a generation of crewcutted boys still listening to The Four Seasons. Thank God for The Beatles."

Here, There, And Everywhere and *For No One* leave me with a lump in my throat every time I hear them. I studied to The Beatles, wrote poetry to The Beatles, meditated with them as well as fell asleep with their music on. The horrors of going away for the summer and not having a phonograph, for two whole months, on which to play The Beatles almost made me run away. Then my Dad agreed to bring it along. I have no idea how I could have survived this far without The Beatles.

Their influence on society is apparent, even 15 years after their arrival in New York City. Their novel haircuts, speech, clothing, beliefs, contrasting personalities, and of course, music were the voices of at least one generation of the turbulent ever-changing, rebellious sixties. Their total impact is virtually impossible to estimate. Their music built a bridge between slow, sentimental ballads, and hard core Rock tunes. They present a problem of classification, and are identified as both Rock and Pop. John, Paul, George, and Ringo were always first. Their music and album covers are immediately recognized as unique and creative, but other underlying elements, indirectly related to their music, changed us all. They were among the first to, without fear, let their hair grow long and wear mod, colorful clothes. On the cover of their first American album release, their hair doesn't even cover their ears, but to the conservative Americans, their hair was worse than blasphemy. Their hair grew longer nonetheless and by 1965 covered their ears entirely. By **Abbey Road** Harrison's and Lennon's hair was longer than many girls. Although most discovered The Beatles in snappy, smart, tailored Pierre Cardin suits, not many expected the psychedelia and beards of 1967. They were the first to use drugs and publicly admit it. Their sound, language, and attitudes were so different and unique that when they began their rise to fame, they took us all along. Without Lennon, McCartney, Harrison, and Starr, Rock-and-Roll, and music in general, would be about as appealing as liver.

Imagine how it would be without them. It pains me to think of it. Music would have no content, no innovation, just some so-called musicians drumming out simple, dull tunes. There would be no meaning, no art; in other words, music would be a solid rock with no uniqueness or sentimentality. In fact, who knows if music, itself, would have survived without The Beatles to push it along. Men might still be afraid to wear colorful, outspoken clothes, long hair or shaggy beards, were it not for The Beatles. Marijuana, LSD, and such wonderful things as transcendental meditation, the sitar, and mantras might be virtually unknown were it not for them. The outspokenness and eccentricities of John Lennon wound up making the world a lot less dull. At the time of his anti-religion statement, the world was in an uproar. However, without someone openly discussing it, people who still share this feeling might be afraid to admit it. Those opposed to Vietnam might have been afraid to air their views for fear of being scoffed, but with such people as John Lennon and Muhammad Ali with them, the burden was made a little easier. The words in Lennon's songs paved the way for others. His open love affair with Yoko, if happening now, would be dis-

> **"Imagine how it would be without them. It pains me to think of it. Music would have no content, no innovation, just some so-called musicians drumming out simple, dull tunes. There would be no meaning, no art; in other words, music would be a solid rock with no uniqueness or sentimentality. In fact, who knows if music, itself, would have survived without The Beatles to push it along. Men might still be afraid to wear colorful, outspoken clothes, long hair or shaggy beards, were it not for The Beatles."**

missed as nothing, in this age of unwed mothers and living together, while in 1968 it was considered distasteful.

John's personality was contrasted by the suave, more straight, Paul McCartney, who, although much more quiet about his affair with Linda Eastman, and his drug use, also paved the way for others. His simple ballads and Rock tunes gave aspiring Pop singers like Barry Manilow, the assurance he needed, proving that Rock could be sentimental as well. John was a bit crazy for some so the majority of female Beatlemaniacs found Paul to be their ultimate fantasy . . . finding a place in their dreams at night.

George was stereotyped as the quiet, gawky one, but actually he was far from that. His instrumental talents were the best of the four, and virtually all of his compositions gained critical acclaim. He was the one who introduced Indian Mysticism and meditation to The Beatles. His influence on youth, no doubt, had them lugging sitars to meet a Maharishi or guru to learn the secret of inner peace.

Ringo was the least noticed, but influential nonetheless. *Octopus' Garden*, one of his rare solos is still sung as a children's song by Kermit the Frog on Sesame Street. His rings and nose had many young girls swooning. The melancholy disposition and effective drumming he promoted inspired thousands.

The Beatles, as a whole, although not recognized until much later could be identified as the blending of the world's elements: Fire (Lennon), Air (McCartney), Water (Harrison), and Earth (Starr). The Beatles' musical influence is felt wherever you go. Although some of it has vanished, they gave Rock a certain respectability. They set the precedent that still lasts today . . . that composers can sing and singers can compose. New terms came about to describe their music. If the only music ever written was that of The Beatles, it would be enough. There are so many songs that one person could not possibly explain each one's impact without writing an essay approximately the size of *War and Peace*. Their music made us laugh, cry, be shocked and be chagrined. They had some duds such as *Everybody's Got Something To Hide Except For Me And My Monkey* and *Happiness Is A Warm Gun*, but one line from *A Hard Day's Night* or a chorus of *The Long And Winding Road* makes up for every mistake.

The music of The Beatles will always be in our hearts and minds. They changed society more than most people care to realize. Their impact will always be felt. "

A.V.
Larchmont, New York

> "Ringo was the least noticed, but influential nonetheless. *Octopus' Garden*, one of his rare solos is still sung as a children's song by Kermit the Frog on Sesame Street. His rings and nose had many young girls swooning."

> "I'm just like a Beatlemaniac from the 60s except that I don't dream about marrying them or silly things like that .... They are very good friends of mine, nothing more, nothing less. I love all four because they're people, they have feelings and opinions just like me, and they're kids at heart."

❝I am age 15, and I first heard of The Beatles when I was seven (I was born in the year of The Beatles — 1964). At the time, I was staying at a close friend's house. Her mother happened to be a big Beatle fan, so one day, out of boredom, my friend decided to play some of her mother's records for me. I remember that day quite well because we had a fight over who was the cutest Beatle. She chose Paul McCartney, and I chose George Harrison (an opinion I hold to this day).

I never really thought much about them because I only heard The Beatles' music when I went to my friend's home. Then, on one hot summer night in 1976, I heard *Silly Love Songs* on the radio. When the D.J. announced, "that was Paul McCartney and Wings . . . " a wave of recognition swept over me. As I sat down on the bed, wondering where I had heard that name before, I recalled that little argument of long ago, and soon after that I became a Beatles fan. Now, a day doesn't go by without my hearing a song by The Beatles or Wings. I'm often upset around my house (most teenage girls are) and I always listen to my records to calm my nerves. I know exactly 143 Beatle songs by heart, except perhaps one or two words in a song which I can't understand because of their accents. I get excited when I see them on TV or the announcer says something about them on American Top Forty radio show.

I'm just like a Beatlemaniac from the 60s except that I don't dream about marrying them or silly things like that. I feel as though I've known John, Paul, George, and Ringo all my life. I'll read an article about what The Beatles thought about a controversial subject (e.g., dope, sex, religion) and I'll say to myself, "Hey! I feel that way about it too!" They are very good friends of mine, nothing more, nothing less. I love all four because they're people, they have feelings and opinions just like me, and they're kids at heart. I also like them because I like to be different from everyone else and so did they. Everyone is into disco; I sit back and enjoy listening and sometimes dancing to it. I'm not crazy over disco at all! The Beatles are a very personal thing to me because I'm the only Beatlemaniac in my school. My friends are fans of The Beatles now (thanks to me), but they don't keep up with current happenings, they just enjoy the music. It seems that *Yellow Submarine* and its lead vocalist, Ringo Starr, are the best known song and singer in my school. I am the main supplier of Beatle facts; sometimes I can give out more information than people who actually saw The Beatles.

The mark on society, left by The Beatles when they split in 1970 was only temporary. "Do your own thing, be your own self." That stayed around for awhile until the disco craze. I like disco, I think everyone likes disco, but kids are all trying to be like everyone else. They try to be "mature," I am still a goof-off. I like to play jokes on people. People were sort of like that in the 60s, but after awhile everything The Beatles did, everyone else did, so I really shouldn't complain, should I?

In the beginning of their career, the music that John and Paul wrote didn't seem personal at all. They were just cranking out "Yeah, Yeah, Yeah" to earn a few bucks, but after the LSD trips they decided to get more

"Dylanish" (furthermore they met the great Dylan himself). From 1966 on is the music I like the best. Of course, I like early Rock too. I especially think John Lennon was very imaginative and creative. I love *I Am The Walrus*, but my favorite song of all is *Hey Jude*, because everybody sings all together at the end. My next favorite is *Mull Of Kintyre* by Wings because my ancestry is Scot, and everyone sings together at the end. It reminds me of people getting together and just being plain folks, singing together.

John Lennon: My favorite Beatle. His words come through to me like no one I've ever heard. He's honest, open, intelligent, and himself. I feel so close to him, like we're best friends. I wish that John was my older brother, and Yoko, my sister. I like them both so much, and he is the funniest man in the world.

Paul McCartney: Practically rid of the Beatle name. He's not considered a Beatle anymore, which I think is fine. While the others stay in seclusion and rest on their millions, Paul and Linda get out and enjoy themselves. He's one of the best Rockers in the world; by far the most talented, and he's got a great sense of humor. I like him because he is more social and outgoing than the others.

George Harrison: Very contemplative, a real thinker. I admire him for trying so hard with his religion. He is second only to Eric Clapton in his guitar work. George also has a good sense of humor, and he's the best looking. I like the way he talks as well.

Ringo Starr: The least satisfied with the split. He was close to his three friends and he acted as an arbitrator during the arguments in the last few years of the group. He's a fine actor, but he seems to always fall into the wrong hands. He is probably the easiest to get to know, and his eyes, those lovely eyes. He makes girls, including me, like him even more. Ringo seems so sentimental and soulful, and an all-around, cool guy.

I would love to see them get together for a charity concert, but I would never want them to become a group again. That would destroy the myth. I've never seen a Wings concert, John hasn't toured in years, George hasn't toured since I was ten, and Ringo has never toured alone in his life, but I like them better now than as Beatles because I've grown up with them that way. **"**

M.L.
Mansfield, Missouri

✲If a Rock group ever influenced, controlled, and mesmerized America, it was The Beatles. In the early years, 1964--1965, The Beatles had America's youth in the palm of their hand because The Beatles did and said things that kids had wanted to do and hear for so long. The Beatles went against the rules; they had shockingly long hair and they mocked and made fun of the older generation.

Musically, they were geniuses. They were original and refreshing from what Rock sounded like before. They were four stars. Groups had always had one lead singer and an anonymous back-up band . . . John, Paul, George, and Ringo were all important in their own right . . . a character in each of them. The Beatles grew up with their audience and fans. In 1966, they withdrew from the pop sound, and became more sophisticated in their music. With the emergence of **Rubber Soul**, drugs also came into the picture. They sang about life, sex, drugs and lived it. They had such a hold on the youth at that time, anything The Beatles did, they did. I have heard people of that time call **Sgt. Pepper** the bible of 1967. The Beatles put so much of themselves into their music. One can feel their confusion, and sometimes, anger. There will never be anything like them again.✳

D.M.
Lansing, Illinois

"As I am only a college freshman it is impossible for me to remember The Beatles' arrival in America in 1964 or even the events which led to their breakup in 1970 because all of these things happened in my childhood. Nevertheless, The Beatles have shaped my life and have always been part of my life since childhood. I'm up to the point now where Beatle memorabilia is becoming an obsession.

The Beatles mean an era in which I lived, but was too young to experience. The Beatles were products of the sixties just as much as the sixties were products of The Beatles. Through the development of their music, I can see a decade developing within. From the early 60s when life was as simple as *I Want To Hold Your Hand* to a time when young people found themselves and shunned the establishment with *Revolution* and *All You Need Is Love*. The Beatles were there to speak the minds of the young people, but also appealing to the older set as well. They represented the youth, vigor, and vitality of the new generation, and remain as figureheads to another decade (the 70s) which has lost all its drive, and sense of ambitions compared to the 60s. My generation has no real music heroes to look up to. All the people I really admire are from the sixties, such as Dylan, the Doors, Baez, Mitchell, and of course, The Beatles. In our apathetic ways of today, we people of the 70s look back in retrospect at The Beatles almost hoping they could come back again, but realizing that they never could. They meant the 60s and not any decade afterwards.

However, I'm still into The Beatles. If one were to turn on the radio at any given moment, he/she could hear a Beatles' tune on some local station in just a short time. Movies such as "Help" and "A Hard Day's Night" are shown regularly in the Boston area, and finding a not-too-rare Beatles' disc is an easy task. Society still accepts The Beatles and holds on to them, unwilling to give up such a good thing. Their songs have a special meaning to me; they are so varied that in any mood there are ample songs to fit that mood. When I am feeling happy, songs like *Octopus' Garden, Ob-la-di Ob-la-da* fit the bill. Whenever I think of my girlfriend, *If I Needed Someone, I've Just Seen A Face, And I Love Her*, and *Something* enhance my feelings for her. Their songs are like a close friend who will listen to you when you are blue or unhappy. How many people can relate to *For No One* when they break up with their girlfriends? The Beatles go much further into your surface; they go into your hearts, not willing to let go once inside.

Their music, lifestyles, and just them, as people, go further than a group/fan relationship. I feel that they are close friends always. The Beatles music will probably outlast any new fad (disco, electro-computer crap out now) and they will always be known as the four young men who changed the whole world."

E.C.
Manchester, New Hampshire

"The Beatles mean an era in which I lived, but was too young to experience. The Beatles were products of the sixties just as much as the sixties were products of The Beatles. Through the development of their music, I can see a decade developing within. From the early 60s when life was as simple as *I Want To Hold Your Hand* to a time when young people found themselves and shunned the establishment with *Revolution* and *All You Need Is Love*."

211

"My brother wakes me up and tells me, "Hey wanna wake up? There's a new group out now and they're called The Beatles!" He said it like it was the greatest thing in the world. I immediately jumped out of bed in all my four year old inquisitiveness and ran to find my sister and a friend of hers laughing and listening to a song about a girl whose boyfriend got a Beatle haircut, so she got one too. After that, I constantly asked my mother if I could get a Beatle haircut. It was one thing I wanted the most, aside from wanting to marry Ringo Starr. I saw John as a wise father, Paul was sweet and bland, and George was very mystical. I never got to marry Ringo and was distraught when he married Maureen. I would flip through articles in my father's *Life* and *Look* magazines and see the pictures of them, and feel sadly happy for them. I never got to have a Beatle haircut either, but I got a Beatle wig. I think I won it as a prize in an amusement park. I also had a little Ringo doll, and ended up cutting its hair off. Saturday mornings brought me Beatles cartoons. I always made sure to sing along with the song of the week. My favorite one is when the deep sea diving Beatles are held hostage by an angry octopus and they try soothing the savage beast with *I Want To Hold Your Hand*. There was Beatle wallpaper on the walls of my room which I shared with my sister. There was a black-and-white picture of George that was very eerie looking. It was by my pillow and I had trouble getting to sleep at night with it there. It was like he was singing *Do You Want To Know A Secret*. I compared his sharp pointy features to Margaret Hamilton's wicked witch in the "Wizard of Oz."

My brother, sister, mother, and I sat through "A Hard Day's Night" twice in a Bronx movie house on Fordham Rd. It still cracks me up to see John sink down a drain in a bathtub, much to his manager's dismay, and then immediately reappear in full dress telling him to hurry or they'll be late for the show. I saw "Help" with my brother and his friends when I was about six. We sat up front and there they were, The Beatles on this huge screen, and in color yet. The girls never stopped screaming. Being so young, I dug it but couldn't understand the hysteria and ecstasy on their faces. The Ed Sullivan Show. Deadpan, stonefaced, Ed announcing The Fab Four and the girls shrieked. Sometimes The Beatles would joke with Ed. Lennon would bounce up and down by bending his knees. My brother used to imitate them in the mirror before his band's rehearsal. Their drummer looked like Ringo. My brother's Beatle boots made him a man. It happened when he had a fight with my father (who hit my brother a lot). At 17, my brother was sick of this. He removed his beloved Beatle boot and raised it over my father as if to hit him with it, although he didn't. Dad still picked on him a lot, but he never hit him again.

The Beatles made my childhood fun. I was at a vulnerable enough age to enjoy all the hype. It made everybody have something in common. Everybody had an opinion about them whether they had their latest album or they thought their son's new hair length made him look like a girl. When The Beatles found themselves in India, their filmed performance showed them in a totally new light. They had become very groovy and did their thing. Paul covered his sweet face with a beard and lost many female fans. I was about 8 or 9 when I sat in my sister's dark blue room with a different colored lightbulb in every available socket and incense covering a pungent and then unrecognizable thick smell, listening to *Hey Jude*. Mom liked the way Yoko Ono sang. She liked George until one day she saw a very unflattering picture of him in the paper, informing the world about his drug bust. She pointed to it and said, "See what happens when you take drugs?" In sixth grade we were taught drug education and our teacher interpreted *Hey Jude* as a pro drug song. There was a line about letting something get under your skin, and she considered it to be about shooting a needle under one's skin . . . I had always thought it was about love. What did they ever teach you in school anyway?

I remember that sad night, when The Beatles split up and they showed people upset with music playing over the film. The Beatles had split up, but they lived on. I had a classmate in high school who knew all the words to *Sun King* and *Revolution 9*, special effects and all. He was great to get stoned with. I didn't get into the post-hype hype, except that I sold Beatles T-shirts which I had hand painted, in front of the Winter Garden during its "Beatlemania" run, and the manager got pissed off at me. I hope that they get together to help the boat people. It would be a nice thing for The Beatles to do.**"**

F.D.
Bronx, New York

"In sixth grade we were taught drug education and our teacher interpreted *Hey Jude* as a pro drug song. There was a line about letting something get under your skin, and she considered it to be about shooting a needle under one's skin . . . I had always thought it was about love."

Marie Heerkens 1981

213

"The Beatles are very personal, you can feel very close to them at times, even though they, as people, are quite unaware of your existence, but when they are together as The Fab Four, the magic is released. The magic that no one has yet been able to quite pinpoint. It's beyond explanation and will be there forever."

❝I am not a child of the sixties, but am having my youth in the seventies. By the time I began to realize music, The Beatles had grown apart and no longer existed as a group. Yet, somehow I am drawn to them and would eagerly trade one of their songs for any ten of the abundantly meaningless songs which fill the airwaves today. With The Beatles, Rock-and-Roll began. As The Beatles grew with their music, so did the new generation of the sixties. The Beatles represented a new way of approaching life. To quote a familiar phrase, "All You Need Is Love," and thus sprang forth the carefree values of the flower children, etc. Ideals changed; many believed that a peaceful existence and doing your own thing was far more worthy than going off to war. I think they had a point.

Unfortunately, much of this counterculture disappeared with the sixties, and so here we are with sweaty discos and Punk Rock. Yet, The Beatles remain favorites. Maybe one reason The Beatles are still popular is they represent the things many grew up with and still believe in. Now, perhaps, their music is an escape back in time to when music reflected the youthful turbulence of the times. People are just now beginning to realize that the 60s were very important.

The Beatles are my life, and when life gets tough, I can crawl into my little world of Beatle things and find it heals all wounds. The Beatles are very personal, you can feel very close to them at times, even though they, as people, are quite unaware of your existence, but when they are together as The Fab Four, the magic is released. The magic that no one has yet been able to quite pinpoint. It's beyond explanation and will be there forever. Some people (such as good ol' Dad) will never understand. It's something very special that only Beatle People can share, but if one wishes to know what this special feeling is, all one needs to do is listen to the music . . . nature will take its course.

The Beatles no longer exist as a group, yet I choose them above all others. From the happy and whimsical songs in the beginning (*Love Me Do* and *She Loves You*) to the seriously heavy songs at their ending, showing the disintegration of a legend as the White Album does, The Beatles tell it all. For people, such as I, who were never there, The Beatles' magical description makes us wish we had been there.❞

H.B.
Santa Ana, California

"I was born in the year The Beatles made their impact on the U.S. . . . 1964. Even though I am so young, I am still a devoted fan and own 22 of their albums and singles. I have obtained many of these from older people who, supposedly, no longer have any use for them because of their newly caught disco fever. I think it is a shame that people have forgotten the greatest group of all times to a new craze which without The Beatles may never have been created.

My life has been changed because of them. Once I discovered that Paul McCartney was a Beatle (after receiving a Wings' album for my ninth birthday), I have been in love with Beatle music. Even though my first individual knowledge of The Beatles was through Wings, I can still realize the power of The Beatles music as compared to the music of Wings. In school I am known as "that Beatle freak"; my room is plastered with Beatle posters, I do own almost all of their albums and I play Beatle songs on my guitar which I have been playing for three years. I own six books about The Beatles, and a large collection of clippings and pictures. I have even converted many of my friends into becoming Beatles fans. This is not just a phase I'm going through, The Beatles caught a lot of people up in their web, and even though they may still not be together, their music lives on. I think that I am an example of someone who can still be influenced by their songs. Their music has helped me get along in life with some of the hard times which I thought I could never get through. All I had to do was put on a Beatle record and I would be able to make it. They have also helped me to decide what I want to do in life. I want to get into the music field in either recording engineering or a radio technician. They have also made me appreciate classical and swing music.**"**

J.H.
Dallas, Texas

215

66 I am a fifteen year old girl, who has been a Beatle fan since I was five years old upon hearing *The Two Of Us* from the **Let It Be** album. While most of my friends were playing with dolls, I was listening to The Beatles and gathering info on them. Instead of being 15 when they first came to America, I grew up with four big brothers. Paul McCartney is my favorite. Listening to one of Paul's songs can have me in tears because I love him so much.

The Beatles were more than just a group. When I'm having problems, I can go into my room and put a Beatles' album on the turntable and just relax. They make me feel much better. When I'm mad, they make me cool down. They are my friends. They are something of my own. When someone compliments them, I say "Thank You." They give me a feeling of friendship and security. They make me feel special. Every song they sing for me. They gave my life direction. One day, as I was listening to a Beatles album, I said to myself, "I want to be just like them," so I started taking guitar lessons, and I found that I have a talent. I can sing also and plan on majoring in music at college. If I can make people feel even a fraction as good as The Beatles make them feel, then I'll know I'm making peoples' lives a lot brighter.

I watch, buy, and collect everything on The Beatles. I cringe at the mere mention of John Lennon, Paul McCartney, George Harrison or Ringo Starr. There is just a certain kind of magic that was in the air when The Beatles were together. The Beatles gave and give people a purpose in life. They weren't a dirty Rock group who supposedly encouraged young kids to revolt, but rather they gave meaning, helped us with problems, and gave people a brighter outlook on life. Physically, they are gone, but spiritually they will be with us forever. They express in their songs what people would say to each other if they were able to. When I hear people say that The Beatles stink, I get mad, but even more I am saddened because I know that person may never come to understand that magic.

I hate the crap that is on the radio now. No, never will those Bee Gees or the Stones or anyone else ever take the place of The Beatles. I grew up on The Beatles and I got spoiled. So when I listen to something else, it doesn't always meet my standards. There are technically better musicians than The Beatles, but no one can play lead guitar like George or drum like Ringo Starr. Some people say that it is bad to idolize people, but I don't give a damn what anyone says, I wouldn't have it any other way. After a long, hard day at school, what a pleasure it is to put on a Beatles' album and float downstream. Some people don't have any brains in their heads and are narrow minded enough (as well as insecure) to take drugs just because people they love and admire do, then they deserve everything they get. The Beatles did grow up and they did try drugs, but none of them are druggies. Everyone does things when they grow up. The Beatles did much more good than harm.

For those people who like other groups better, and do not know The Beatles, they just don't realize that without The Beatles they wouldn't have their favorite group. Almost everyone was inspired by them. The Beatles did make money, but they made music for the sake of making music, they

> "When I'm having problems . . . . They make me feel much better. When I'm mad, they make me cool down. They are my friends. They are something of my own. When someone compliments them, I say 'Thank You.' They give me a feeling of friendship and security. They make me feel special. Every song they sing for me. They gave my life direction."

weren't totally commercial like other groups. Disco is crud. All disco is a song with a syncopation of one note (combine one-eighth notes, ¼ notes and dotted rests and sing "Ring my bell" to the note B-flat).

Whatever happens to me in my life, The Beatles will always be with me, helping me and cheering me on. I'm glad that I love The Beatles the best. They are truly the best. No matter what anyone says, they can't take that title away from them. Pick up one of those wonderful, beautiful, magical, irreplaceable Beatles' albums and listen to the MAGIC!"

Z.G.
Littleton, Massachusetts

"Pick up one of those wonderful, beautiful, magical, irreplaceable Beatles' albums and listen to the MAGIC!"

217

"I was visiting some relatives in Florida and decided I wanted to do some shopping. My cousin and I went to a mall, and somehow landed in a record store. I was really into the Bee Gees at the time, like everyone else. I really wanted to buy **Sgt. Pepper** by the Bee Gees, and while I was looking for that record my cousin mentioned something about having The Beatles Hits, 1967–1970. My answer was, "Oh, maybe we can listen to it later." It was no big deal. Well, we did listen to the record later and it did become a big deal. No one could get me away from the stereo the rest of the vacation. I ended up buying the record.

Around the time I discovered The Beatles, I was pretty snobby. All I cared about was money and school. That changed after I became a Beatles fan. Before I wanted to be a rich and famous movie star, live in a mansion in California, and marry a rich husband. I was all for women's liberation, and wanted to go to college. Now, I would be happy with a small apartment or house. I don't care how rich my husband will be as long as I love him. I have also started playing guitar and have no real intentions of going to college. I'm not totally for women's lib anymore. I don't know why these changes happened once I started listening to The Beatles, but they did happen.

Since that time in Florida, I've read 15 book on The Beatles, have posters all over my walls, and go to Beatlefest every year."

M.F.
Lincolnwood, Illinois

"I feel that The Beatles were the best group ever. If you can name a better one, say so, but I will still think they're the best."

T.F.
Lincolnwood, Illinois

"I think it was inevitable that I should become a Beatle fan. I was born in 1963, just about the same time The Beatles were attaining prominence throughout the world. As I grew older, The Beatles attained maturity as a group. They became more popular, controversial, and influential. It never ceases to amaze me that while all this was going on, I could be totally oblivious to it. I was never aware of them (except that I hated them) until 1970 when *Let It Be* was a hit and even then they didn't make too much of an impression on me. It is probably because I'm an only child and never had the influence of an older brother or sister. As I got older, I became more aware of them. I began to encounter Beatle fans everywhere. There were people at school, summer camp, and especially at Star Trek conventions I attended. I've found that many, many Star Trek fans are also Beatle fans.

It was about the time I started to attend Trekcons (1977) that The Beatles started to become an influence in my life. My junior high school music class taught a unit on The Beatles and their music, and I started seeing a guy who was a Beatle fan. Then, in 1978, I met my (now) best friend in a play we were in. She asked me if I liked The Beatles and I told her I did. She invited me to see "Let It Be" and "A Hard Day's Night" with her at a local movie theater. That was the beginning of it all; from then on I have been an absolute freak about The Beatles. Through my fanaticism I have met almost all of my close friends and many people from different cities. All told, I correspond with and have close friendships with 25 Beatle fans, including my boyfriend, who I have been seeing for two years. I have become more aware of other Rock music, and in addition to The Beatles, I am into the Stones, Knack, Kinks, Doors, Who, Blondie, and many new wave groups.

The Beatles are responsible for the development of my budding literary talent. My friends and I publish a struggling new fanzine called *Get Back*. The Fab Four have changed my life in other, smaller ways. I absolutely freak out when The Beatles are played on the radio or by a band or juke in a bar. I travel a lot more now because of all the Beatle fans I know in different states and all the Beatlefests I go to. All my extra money goes for posters and memorabilia. Most importantly, The Beatles have filled a void in my life by becoming my very best friends. They are always there whenever I need them. If I'm happy, they are too. If I'm sad, so are they. If I've had an unhappy romantic experience, they understand. I can always rely on them to be there when no one else will. That is the greatest way they have changed my life."

J.E.
Elmont, New York

"Most importantly, The Beatles have filled a void in my life by becoming my very best friends. They are always there whenever I need them. If I'm happy, they are too. If I'm sad, so are they. If I've had an unhappy romantic experience, they understand. I can always rely on them to be there when no one else will. That is the greatest way they have changed my life."

"It happened four years ago when I got **The Beatles, 1962–1966** as a present. I was not that wild for them, but I didn't dislike them. One day, late in December of my 8th grade year, I was hanging around, feeling bored, so I put the album on, sat down, and for the first time, instead of doing something while a record was on, I really listened to it. Then, *She Loves You* went on, and I totally freaked. I had never heard a sound like theirs, or lyrics, and even the feeling was different. I listened carefully to the rest of the album, and frankly, I got more and more excited with each song. After that, I bought every Beatle album, book or souvenir I could find and became a total Beatles freak. I learned the words to all the songs, plus millions of facts about them. When I reached the end of 10th grade, I became more serious and began playing guitar and learned some of their songs.

As for their effect on society . . . it's obvious . . . we loved them. My favorite is John Lennon, my favorite song is *I Am The Walrus*, and my favorite albums are **Sgt. Pepper** and the White Album."

C.D.
Whippany, New Jersey

❝I am now in the 12th grade, my senior year of high school, and first became interested in The Beatles when I was in the 7th grade. They have guided me through friendships, at least one boyfriend, and affected my taste in guys. I like long, lean guys who play guitars, are in bands and who also enjoy The Beatles. The Beatles have also helped me through some difficult periods in my life. They have given me values, the idea of reaching your dream or goals was their message. Heroes like Superman, Batman, or Peter Pan wear off as years progress from childhood, but for any fan of The Beatles, the devotion just grows and grows. The Beatles were from a working class background and they had their dreams and aspiration, and came to realize many of them. I am also from a working class neighborhood where it would be easy to fall back with a crowd and not concentrate too much on getting out, but here The Beatles have influenced me too. I've set high goals and I'll attain them.

Beatle fans are all cool; there's a common camaraderie when you meet other Beatle people. The Beatles have also influenced me in my choice of smoking marijuana. I first became curious about smoking it when I was in sixth grade, and heard *I'm Fixing A Hole*, but I never tried it until I was in the ninth grade. Up until now, I have never been high at any Beatles function, movie, or convention. I don't need to. I have a good time screaming and singing. The Beatles are a good way to get a natural high because they've got so much energy. Whether or not you've smoked, snorted or drunk anything, The Beatles, alone can be good for your head.

John Lennon has been my favorite Beatle because of his concern for other people. I feel that he was one of the first Rock/politics heroes, and that in the future politics can only benefit from having closer associations to Rock because as a form of expression, Rock is honesty. John Lennon is also beautiful because of the optimism he always expressed for so long in his music. No matter how heavy one of his songs may be emotionally, it is never so heavy that the listener feels burdened by it. The listener hears that John is burdened by it and loves John even more because he's so sensitive. John Lennon is beautiful.**❞**

L.C.
Los Angeles, California

"Heroes like Superman, Batman, or Peter Pan wear off as years progress from childhood, but for any fan of The Beatles, the devotion just grows and grows."

❝I will be fifteen in September, 1980 (5 days after Zak Starkey), so I really don't remember when The Beatles were together, but I knew who they were and thought their music was O.K. By 10:00 on April 26, 1978, that "O.K." turned into "the best." On that Wednesday night from 9 to 10, I had seen Ringo Starr's TV special and turned into a Beatlemaniac. Not the kind who would go to a concert to hear herself scream, but the kind who had to get Beatle and solo albums, as well as books about The Fab Four so I could learn what I missed. So, the first changes that The Beatles caused in my life were to increase my library and record collection slowly, but surely, and decrease the amount of money in my wallet quickly.

Music became the most important thing in my life, and I listen to the radio and records more often than I watch TV. I would love to be a Rock star, but since I can't play an instrument or sing well enough, I'll stick to what I'm good at . . . creative writing. My first book will be dedicated to John, Paul, George, and Ringo. The Beatles taught me that I don't have to be a conformist, and they gave this quiet kid an identity. Practically everyone at school knows that I love The Beatles. The Beatles also changed my relationship with my sister, 2½ years my junior, but also a Beatlemaniac. Our similar interest has drawn us together. Instead of being two little snots who hate each other's guts, like most siblings, we are best friends. I'm sure this change would have happened anyway, but The Beatles helped bring it about faster.**❞**

S.B.
Cedarhurst, New York

"I am a total Beatlemaniac, born in the year The Beatles first became popular in England, 1962. I have all of their American releases, a few British imports, and some bootlegs. I'm an artist and I spend a great deal of time drawing them.

My interest in The Beatles started with my sisters, who were teenagers in the 60s. Because of them I have a lot of valuable Beatle items. They changed my life. I'll buy anything with their names on it. I'm also into ex-Beatle albums. I spend most of my money for certain Beatle-related items that I wish to buy; items that I find advertised in magazines.

The Beatles changed the lifestyle of young Americans in the 60s by showing them how to wear their hair decently and showed them different styles in clothing. I heard it compared once to "The Wizard Of Oz," you know, when Dorothy lands in Oz everything went from black and white to color; The Beatles changed Rock music from *Hound Dog* to *Eleanor Rigby*. They deserve the title of "The Kings of Rock and Roll." "

L.C.
Stuart, Florida

"I am only 17 years old and a male. So, I actually only caught the tail end of Beatlemania when it was going on, but have relived the whole period through films, video tapes, and best of all, their music. I now own all their U.S.-released albums and recently spent over $100.00 on the collection of all their U.K. albums.

The Beatles were four distinct personalities that were instantly appreciated, if not for their fab music, but for their likeable good humor. They did it all; they introduced the Mersey Beat to the rest of the world and eventually changed the face of popular music. There will never be another Beatles. There are so many people today who just can't get enough of heavy metal and Ted Nugent, and anything thought of as good music is put down without even listening to it . . . well, surprise, surprise . . . if it weren't for The Beatles, that type of music would never exist.

I had the pleasure of meeting John Lennon, very briefly, three years ago. John, to me, had always been the magic Beatle, the leader of the group, the most outspoken, and perhaps, the most talented. That's why meeting him stands out as one of the most if not THE MOST important experience in my life, and made me feel even more a part of the greatest rock and roll band in history.

John was very polite to me, and very quiet, not at all like I had pictured him. I told him how much I enjoyed his music, and kept the conversation mostly towards his solo work. He loosened up a little and told me how much he enjoyed his life "now that things had calmed down a bit." Before I left, he signed the cover of a magazine I had, and shook my hand.

In my opinion, I've shaken hands with one of the four most important and influential people on Earth."

L.R.
Amsterdam, New York

Epilogue

I am a creature of habit. When I write an article, a short story, or even a letter to the editor, everything must be in sequence. Although I like to think of myself as being someone who doesn't watch the clock, or dwell upon how long it takes to get from point "A" to point "B," or remember what happened and when, I am a most chronologically-oriented person. I wish I weren't and that I didn't think about time slipping by, or my getting older, but I've accepted myself for what I am, a person who needs order.

On Sunday, December 7, 1980, I was putting the finishing touches on Chapter Seven of this book. I was in a pretty good mood because I had just transcribed letters from people approximately my own age, who were describing how they felt The Beatles changed our society. The whole impetus of this work was to discover if others felt as strongly as I did about The Beatles affecting our entire societal structure and here were these people, reinforcing my beliefs. This is great stuff, I thought. I finished the chapter, and once more sat back and listened to side one of **Double Fantasy**. I had been engrossed in the playing of that album since its purchase on November 19, 1980. Except for a short Thanksgiving holiday interruption, I had listened to the album every day for the previous weeks. The message of the album fit in so beautifully with the contents of an article I had written for *Bedroom Magazine* in October 1980, in anticipation of the re-emergence of John and Yoko into the limelight once again. I was looking forward to seeing that article in print within the next few days. I turned off the switch on my electric typewriter. It was Sunday night, and I had to go to my "day" job bright and early Monday morning.

Monday morning was hectic; the rest of the day quite forgettable. Monday night was uneventful. I probably watched "MASH," the only show on TV worth watching nowadays, and began to make preparations for turning in early and getting a good night's sleep. My wife and I went to sleep around 10:15 p.m. I sometimes have difficulty in falling asleep, and remember seeing the digital clock flash 10:53 on that evening, the 8th of December, before I finally drifted off. I awoke at one point during the middle of the night, and turned over to see what time it was. The clock flashed 12:43. I thought to myself, how odd it was that I felt so thoroughly rested, even though my sleep had been less than two hours. I felt at ease, and very comfortable, snug in my bed, when the telephone rang. Ordinarily, if the phone rings in the middle of the night, I am awoken out of a deep sleep and can barely get my wits together to answer it, let alone speak intelligently to the person interrupting my slumber. I had never really fallen back to sleep, though, and in the fraction of a second from the time the phone began to ring until I reacted (by asking my wife, who was instantly awoken by the sound, to answer it because she was closer to the phone), I glanced again at the digital clock. It said 12:49. Late night phone calls usually terrify me but, although I was curious as to who was calling me at that hour, I wasn't alarmed. I was feeling very restful.

As my wife went to answer the phone, I got out of bed to turn on the bedroom light. She spoke very briefly to the party on the line, and I distinctly remember her saying, "Oh no," and handing the phone to me. She mumbled something that my ears heard, but my brain could not comprehend. I heard the words, I knew what she said, but I thought that, suddenly startled into wakefulness, she had become confused and didn't know what she was talking about. She handed the phone to me, and told me that it was one of our very close friends, a close Beatle fan friend of mine from Arizona. I hesitated for a second or two, and then said hello into the mouthpiece. I don't remember the beginning of what he started to say to me, but I could tell that he had heard my wife tell me the news because he said: "Yeah . . . some guy just walked up to him and shot him . . . killed him . . . ." I managed to say "When?" and he answered "about 11:00 p.m. your time." I felt as if someone had just hit me over the head with a sledge hammer, and ripped my stomach out at the same time. As I had been drifting off to sleep that night, John Lennon bled to death.

I told my friend that I couldn't talk to him. I hung up. I still couldn't believe it. It had to be a bad dream, but I knew that I was awake. My wife tells me I was a borderline hysteric, talking to myself and not really to her, as I ran to the room which houses my stereo. I turned on the FM receiver, and that's when I knew it was true. Without even hearing one DJ's voice say the words, I knew because each station was playing a Beatle song. I turned to my favorite station, and heard *A Day In The Life*. John Lennon was dead. No, he wasn't just dead . . . he had been killed . . . deliberately murdered. In that instant of recognition, I was overwhelmed with the knowledge of how the last seventeen years of my life had been affected by John. His death had suddenly made me realize that part of my life was gone, too. The one man who had held me together was gone. The man I loved and respected most in the whole world was gone, and suddenly nothing seemed to matter anymore. I looked at the posters of The Beatles I have on my walls . . . it all seemed a mockery, an incongruous situation . . . John Lennon and death, the words were antonyms.

I turned off the radio. For the first time in my life, I could not listen to a Beatle song. I cried. I cried like I have never done before and hope never to have to do again. I couldn't stop crying. My wife stayed in bed . . . what could she possibly have said that would have consoled me? So she didn't try. Everything in my life seemed meaningless, My first thoughts were of Yoko and Sean. I had been so involved with **Double Fantasy**, its message of the importance of the family, the implication that John and Yoko still had more music to come out, and that they might go on tour. I would have flown to New York City, Boston, or Hartford to have seen them in concert. I thought of Yoko, all that she and John had been through, and then of Sean . . . that poor little boy, raised fron infancy by his father, and, in an instant, his father is cruelly taken away. I remember wondering what kind of person Sean would grow up to be. Then I thought of

John himself; the night seemed so unreal to me that I couldn't grasp that he was really gone. It all seemed so unfair. The worse thing was this raging impotence inside of me . . . unable to do anything about it, yet feeling as if I had to do something. There was nothing I could do.

I thought of this book. I decided to forget it; there was no sense in finishing it. How could I bring myself to finish it? Then I thought of the article I had submitted to that magazine on John and Yoko, and how it would be out in a few days. I vowed to call the editor, and tell him not to print it. He could have the money back that he had paid me. John Lennon was gone and that's all that mattered to me.

It was too early in the morning for any TV coverage to be on. So, I again switched on the radio, and heard the details. The police had just identified the alleged assassin. I turned off the radio as the telephone rang again. It was another friend, a woman whose letter appears in this book, who I have never met; but she cared enough to call. There were many more calls that night. I called back my friend in Arizona. It was something similar to a sixties happening, except we weren't grouping to protest the war or wait for The Beatles to land at JFK airport, we were talking about the death of a Beatle. How could a Beatle be dead?

I tried to get some sleep, but the whole thing was such a nightmare that I never did fall asleep again that night. I was confused and I was grief-stricken, but on top of that there was something else which was bothering me. I couldn't quite get it into focus; then all of a sudden it hit me. The last name of the murderer was the same as someone who had contributed a letter to this book. I jumped out of bed, scared to death that I might have in my possession a letter from the man who had killed the best friend I ever had. I tore through all the letters, and discovered the one I was looking for. Same last name, but thankfully not the same person. If there was any way in which I could feel relieved, I did feel a slight bit better knowing that a letter to have been included in this book was not by the assassin.

Finally, the light of the rising sun filtered its way through my sleepless night, and I began to watch TV. I watched ABC's "Good Morning America," with a somber David Hartman announcing the news to many people who had not heard it up to that point. I was numb. I was absorbed by the image of all those people outside The Dakota, standing around, not knowing what else to do, except that they had to do something. I thought back to my own memories of The Dakota.

During the 1960s, my aunt and uncle lived on West 72nd Street, just a couple of buildings away from The Dakota. Even then it was a landmark known for its famous residents. I can recall staring at the gargoyles on the metal fencing which framed the building. I remember walking by there one day in the late sixties, seeing the gate where the cars drove in, and the uniformed doorman. At the time, I wanted to try to get in because "Rosemary's Baby" had been filmed there. In 1972, I showed my future wife the building on our way to walking through Central Park to the bandshell. John and Yoko were living in the Village then, so I never got to wait outside the building and try to catch a glimpse of them. The fact that I was familiar with the location, though, made it all a bit more real to me. What finally brought it all back home for me was seeing the news film of the ambulance leaving Roosevelt Hospital, the men wheeling the stretcher containing a body bag, and the realization that inside that bag was John Lennon . . . my John Lennon.

As the morning of the 9th of December progressed, my grief overwhelmed me and I became angry. I was angrier than I had ever been before . . . uncontrollable anger. There is a large portion of that day which I don't recall. I vaguely remember driving to a large shopping mall near my home, and wandering around it. I ate something while I was there, but I don't recall what. I must have appeared dazed, as I do recall passersby giving me wary looks. My eyes must have looked like hell, after a sleepless night accompanied by long periods of crying. I think I asked a young woman working behind a counter, "Why would anyone want to kill John Lennon?" I knew I had to get away, and go back home. When I arrived, I made a tape on my reel-to-reel about what I was feeling, and somehow I got it into my head that I should take down every Beatle poster which adorned my stereo room. I remember methodically, almost ritually, prying loose the tacks, and rolling the pictures up, including the large poster my sister gave me on my 21st birthday. It shows the four of them as they appear in the photo on the back cover of **The Beatles Again — Hey Jude** album . . . a poster which had been placed in no fewer than seven different abodes of mine over the past nine years. I couldn't stand it. Nothing seemed to matter, this book included. For the past year and a half, I had been working on a manuscript by transcribing letters from people explaining how The Beatles changed their lives . . .

231

and suddenly I felt it didn't matter anymore. I decided that I would not finish the book. It made no sense to do it.

The last chapter of this book was to be a rather lengthy treatise on why The Beatles should *not* get back together. It would have been a smart, smug, and pseudo-intellectual rationalization, with me revealing a schizoid personality: one part of me wanting more than anything to see The Beatles get back together; the other, a more logical one, arguing that The Beatles owed no one anything else, they had all changed. It would be like asking each one of us to go back to high school and pick up on all our friendships and activities as youths, to ask The Beatles to go back to things they had out-grown. John's death made me realize that I was full of shit; I had been lying to myself all these years. There weren't two sides to the issue. I had pretended to believe that I thought they shouldn't get back together. I still realized that for them it was best that they had parted company, but under-neath it all I was a greedy bastard. I wanted my Beatles back. Nothing made that more apparent than when I sat in my room, no pictures to look at, no music on the stereo, and realized that this was *really* the end of The Beatles. Scratch the surface of any Beatlemaniac, and no matter how they may protest that they are glad because The Beatles found happiness as four individuals and were now no longer living in a forced extension of adolescence, you'll find that they still want to see the group on stage just one more time for that one last concert. John Lennon's demise ended forever and rendered moot all speculation about reunion possibilities. It wasn't April 10, 1970 when The Beatles died; they died with John Lennon. Don McLean's *American Pie* notwith-standing, December 8, 1980 was the day the music died.

As the week went on, my grief turned to anger, then to bitterness. All of a sudden, the news media discovered The Beatles, proclaiming them as saviors. Where had they been for the last 17 years? Now, in the hour of his death, commenta-tors were proclaiming John Lennon a saint; just where were the voices of Walter Cronkite, John Chancellor, and Frank Reynolds when the press portrayed John and Yoko as freaks and misfits? Where was the media when Lennon was being wiretapped by the Nixon Administration? They had a lot of gall calling John one of their own. They never did anything for him while he was alive. I was bitter. My bitterness sub-sided only when I saw all those beautiful people gathered in different cities all over the world for the ten-minute silent vigil on Sunday, December 14, 1980. The question which had motivated my book was answered for me: there were other people out there like me.

But the other question still remained: where had the members of the counterculture been all this time? Some could be seen, but many of them had surrendered to acquiescence. The ruling elite of this country had made it so difficult to be a hippie and survive in the late sixties and early seventies. The notion that people could be so unstructured, yet so happy . . . so tolerant of others, instead of viewing others as the constant enemy . . . snapped the corporate minds. They had to do something. A little inflation here, an energy crisis there . . . make it impossible for anyone to survive unless they had money, the desire for power, and the three-piece Wall Street suit. The Blue Meanies had won. They forced us all to become part of the establishment. We were worse than our parents; they at least hadn't known any better. We knew that there was an alternative, but we let ourselves be bought out, and found all sorts of rationalizations to justify it. A lot of people, who had deliberately put those days behind them, came out of the woodwork when they realized that one of the few honest, sincere, incorruptible influences of their time was dead. Many cried for their own failings as much as for the death of John Lennon.

I spent that bitter cold Sunday afternoon completely alone. I must admit that I felt something within me become a little more peaceful during those ten minutes, although my silent vigil was marked by uncontrollable sobbing. I played the rare version of *Imagine*, taped from the One-to-One Concert of August 1972, where John had changed the lyrics to say "a brotherhood and sisterhood of man." Soon after, I resolved that the only thing I could do to honor him was to finish this book. I'm sure now that if I hadn't gone full speed ahead to complete the book, I would have had too much time on my hands and continued to wallow in grief.

As I write this, just six weeks after the assassination, John Lennon's killer awaits trial. Most peoples' first reaction must have been a wish for revenge. Revenge, however, is as bad as the act which precipitates it. Revenge makes the person seeking vengeance sink down to the same low level as the original perpetrator. Being so emotionally involved, I at first found it quite difficult to sympathize or feel sorry for the accused assassin, but then I remembered that if there was anything that John Lennon stood for, it was Peace and Love. There were no exceptions to his rule. He sincerely believed that peace bred peace. It would be a dishonor to the memory of John Lennon to submit to the baser emotion of revenge. It has no place in the world he envisioned. Most people can't grasp such a magnanimous gesture . . . the idea of trying to understand one's detractors and enemies . . . the idea that a person who performs such a terrible act is sick and needs help. I have had troubles dealing with it myself, but I have tried, and it now makes sense to me.

Clarence Darrow, the famous defense lawyer and thinker of the late 19th and early 20th centuries, had a similar theory concerning individuals who performed such antisocial acts. He felt that one could not place blame or punishment on a human being anymore than one could blame or punish a piece of machinery which breaks down. There had to be a cause for the breakdown and, as with a broken piece of equipment, one should try to repair the human being so that he or she can become useful and productive again. You wouldn't destroy a defective piece of machinery because it had failed to perform properly; you would seek to find a reason for its failure, not punish it. Darrow believed that there had to be a reason for every antisocial act, and that once a cause could be ascertained, it could be removed or eliminated entirely, so that the person could be made well again. He felt that it was unduly cruel to further punish a person who was obviously ill, and that modern medicine and science should be used to offer the finest treatment possible, as one would to a person who had a physical malady.

John Lennon would have agreed with most of that philosophy. He honestly believed that love could conquer all. I feel a need to go over his accomplishments, but all have been fully documented. To go over each one would be an understatement, as I wouldn't know where to begin or end. I can only add my personal remembrances. I saw the man on three different occasions, twice with The Beatles, once with Yoko . . . all three times in concert. Though I never spoke to him, I felt as if he did know me; he knew there were people like me and he reached out to me, whether through his stage presence or singing voice. I remember a John Lennon who wore a leather cap in "A Hard Day's Night," and mocked Victor Spinetti in his role as the TV director in that film; a John Lennon who gripped his guitar as if his life depended on it during the opening credits of "Help"; a John

Lennon who began to wear wire-rimmed glasses and wrote of his search for identity in songs like *Rain* and *Strawberry Fields Forever*; a John Lennon who met a Japanese artist, and who thereafter redirected his unchanneled talents into a perpetual search for truth, peace and love; a John Lennon who, just like the rest of us, had a rough time going it alone in the early 1970s; and, ultimately, a John Lennon who found inner peace by being himself and centering his life around his wife and son. John Lennon was a modern-day Jesus; not in the orthodox religious sense, but a Jesus-like figure who benefited by having major communication devices at his disposal. Lennon was delivering a message of peace, love, brother- and sisterhood to a modern "Roman" society which would not listen. Unlike Jesus, we were able to witness the frailties of the man through the same media which brought his message, and for that reason he gave us confidence because we knew he was one of us. We knew he put his pants on one leg at a time because we saw him with his pants off. He admitted his errors but, more importantly, he stood up for what he believed in and did it proudly, even in the face of adversity and criticism. Unlike Jesus, he was not a martyr. He wanted to live . . . his message was to keep on living, learning, and surviving. He didn't believe that anything was worth killing or dying for. Of course, there will be many who will seek to add some greater religious significance to his life and death. I read somewhere in recent weeks that a writer said that "Jesus died for our sins, John Lennon died for our dreams." I don't believe that, even though his death shattered many dreams.

John Lennon wasn't supposed to die this way. He was supposed to be found dead, by natural causes, in his bed, with a smile on his face, in the year 2020. But it didn't happen that way. I saw him three times. I remember the dates well: Sunday, August 15, 1965; Tuesday, August 23, 1966; and Wednesday, August 30, 1972. In 1966, at Shea Stadium, he stood on stage with his three friends and sang his heart out. I had field glasses, and from my seat on the Field Level of the stadium, I could see his face quite clearly. For once I could see him without some camera man deciding what scene or angle I should look at. I watched him for the longest time . . . at one point, in between songs, he smiled . . . a big bright, wonderful smile that illuminated his entire face, and he was staring at something just over my head. I gazed in back of me to see what he was looking at . . . it was a banner which read, "We Love You John."

John, I always wanted to meet you, to thank you for being you, and for influencing every facet of my life in such a positive way. I guess I may have fantasized that because of this book I could have met you, and we could have spoken to one another. If there is a God, if there is an after life (and the circumstances of your brutal departure make the agnostic in me come to the forefront), we shall meet someday. As long as my ears can hear, my eyes see, and my heart feel, you'll be part of me, and many others.

Like many writers, I keep a ledger to jot down ideas for articles. I use mine as a diary at times. I have just looked at what I wrote in the midst of my grief on the day after that terrible night in December:

"Tuesday, December 9, 1980, 11:49 a.m.

The real King is dead. No words can adequately express how I feel today . . . . He said, "don't believe in yesterdays," well Johnny, without you I don't really look forward to tomorrows.

God damn it John, I really loved you."

M.A.C.